The New Shape of Pastoral Theology

The New Shape of Pastoral Theology

Essays in Honor of SEWARD HILTNER

edited by
William B. Oglesby, Jr.

Abingdon Press
Nashville and New York

THE NEW SHAPE OF PASTORAL THEOLOGY

Standard Book Number: 687-27879-1
Library of Congress Catalog Card Number: 72-84721

SET UP, PRINTED, AND BOUND BY THE PARTHENON PRESS, AT NASHVILLE, TENNESSEE, UNITED STATES OF AMERICA

foreword

Seward Hiltner is not an ordinary person. Through the nearly twenty years of our association in connection with *Pastoral Psychology* this fact has borne in upon me again and again. The breadth of his understanding, the keenness of his perception, the range of his interest continue to fascinate me after all this time. It is fair to say that he, more than any other person, has molded and directed the course of this journal; and the support which it has received from writers, consultants, and readers is due in large measure to his influence. In this brief foreword my purpose is to indicate three factors which have been of utmost importance to me as editor and which, I believe, are illustrative of Hiltner's basic concern in shaping the direction of the emerging emphasis on the minister as pastor.

In the first place, he has maintained a profound conviction that the ministry must always be seen as a whole and never diluted or "specialized-out" by undue emphasis on this or that aspect, however important. This may strike some as odd since it is certain that Hiltner has pioneered in bringing new depth and breadth to the ministry through his contribution to such areas as pastoral theology, pastoral psychology, clinical pastoral education, and the like. However, through all this tremendous enrichment there was always the urgent note that in no sense must any function or aspect become an area of specialization at the expense of ministry as a whole.

This leads directly to Hiltner's second emphasis, which has been a guiding principle in the editorial policy of *Pastoral Psychology*, namely a concern lest ministers become, or try to become, psychotherapists as a result of the materials in clinical psychology and psychiatry made readily available today. While always stressing the importance of the minister's need to be aware of and to understand as fully as possible the contributions of the behavioral sciences, he never lost sight of the fact that it would be tragic if as a result of this newly acquired knowledge the minister ceased to be a minister and became instead an amateur psychologist, psychiatrist, or social worker.

The third basic emphasis Hiltner has continued to stress through the years is the insistence that *Pastoral Psychology* be kept on an intellectual level totally accessible to the average parish minister. Despite repeated demands by many persons that articles of a more scientific or "scholarly" nature be printed, it was his conviction that such an approach would defeat the primary purpose of the publication and run counter to the concern already noted above—that the central focus of the clergyman is ministry, not some sort of specialization. For Hiltner this in no sense represented a lack of appreciation for basic theory and scholarly investigation; it did signify his insistence on the necessity to make the results of sound research accessible to the minister whose training did not include a knowledge of research techniques.

It is always risky to single out two or three emphases held to be important by another person, and that is particularly true with someone whose work covers as wide a scope as Hiltner's. Nevertheless, in reviewing these two decades, I am convinced that it is these guidelines that have kept *Pastoral Psychology* from being a directionless conglomeration of articles with no real central goal and purpose. This is one reason why I am happy to have the opportunity to express my deep appreciation to Seward Hiltner on the occasion of this publication. I do this not only as an editor who has continually benefitted by the wisdom of his counsel, but more particularly as a person whose life has been enriched by a friendship which I cherish with warm and genuine affection.

Simon Doniger

contents

Introduction

William B. Oglesby, Jr.

The idea which has brought this book into being emerged from two sources. In the first place there was the desire to pay tribute to Seward Hiltner for his tremendous contribution to the life of the church through his work in pastoral theology. We could think of no more fitting fashion than the preparation of a *Festschrift* since Hiltner's driving passion throughout the years has been to set forth in written form the developments in pastoral care and to encourage his colleagues to do the same in order that all of us may benefit from the insights and discoveries of our fellow ministers.

The second concern which gave rise to this volume was a desire to explore the various aspects and factors in pastoral theology which have been set in motion or enhanced by Hiltner's own experiences and publications. Every essay is written by a person who has had a close relationship with Hiltner, either as a student at the graduate level or as a colleague in research and teaching.

In this introduction my purpose is to sketch in brief fashion something of the scope of Hiltner's contribution to the field of pastoral theology, looking specifically at his writings as an index of his life and work. Following that, I propose to comment on the essays themselves, indicating the structure and movement of the book as a kind of guide or "road map" for the reader.

I

The work of the pastor in caring for the people is inherent in the structure of the Hebraic-Christian tradition and, in some sense, can be said to be a distinctive characteristic of this tradition. The bearing of "one another's burdens" may be the unique manner for fulfilling "the law of Christ" (Gal. 6:2). It is in this sense that pastoral care is the thread that runs through the entire fabric of the church from the beginning to the present. "Where is . . . your brother?" is a question that is as relevant today as it was when first addressed to Cain (Gen. 4:9).

Even so, the answer to the question has not always been unambiguously consistent. Setting aside the fact that in many instances there has been some sort of disavowal of responsibility as was true for Cain and for the elder brother in the story of the prodigal son, there is a curious lack of consensus throughout the history of the church regarding just what concern and caring for one's brother actually mean. This discrepancy has been documented many times,[1] and there is no need to rehearse it here. Suffice it to say that the practice of pastoral care has run the gamut from scourging to permissiveness and back again with a kind of swing from pole to pole in pendulum fashion. It could be argued that the motivation of those exercising pastoral care at any given time was open to question; indeed, it is likely that mixed motivation can be uncovered in any specific act of pastoral care. But granted that, it is also apparent in the record that even those whose motives were pure—or as pure as human motivation can be—found that there was really no agreement among them as to what should be done with, to, or for any particular brother in any particular situation. Good intentions there were aplenty, but then, as now, they simply were not enough.

It would, of course, be an oversimplification to say that only in the twentieth century has serious attention been given to the study of pastoral care. Neverthless, there is a sense in which the emphasis since World War II has marked an approach not seen before, at least in its present form. One way to get at this is to ask the question, "How do you complete the sentence, 'We now know . . .' ?" Put in this form, it is apparent that the sentence is not completed by such things as "God's love for us is revealed in Jesus Christ" or "We have the responsibility to care for our brothers" or

"Pastoral care should be carried out in the context of every experience of life and not just those that can be identified as 'religious.'" What is genuinely new in this century is the emphasis on procedure, the evaluation of specific case material, and the development of principles by means of which students may learn effective strategies of pastoral care at the beginning of their ministry and ministers may constantly evaluate their pastoral experiences as a means for increasing their ability to be of help in all sorts and conditions of life. Another way to put this is to recognize that there have been great pastors through the years (i.e., the twentieth century is not the first to witness effective pastoral care), but in general their effectiveness often grew gradually by painful trial-and-error experience which could be evaluated primarily on pragmatic bases in terms of unexamined criteria. Opportunities for learning were usually confined to imitation in a kind of apprentice fashion or utilizing various formulas for this or that distress as in the days of the penitentials. There is little if any record of a systematic analysis and evaluation of the principles underlying the practice of pastoral care or the sense in which the "what" of the gospel and the "how" of the gospel bear a primary relationship to each other.

The emergence of using case material as the means for developing more effective pastoral care has many springs and tributaries. It is likely that clinical studies in the behavioral sciences provided the basic thrust, although this type of investigation has passed through various stages. As is well known, Freud resisted any attempt to describe or analyze what actually "went on" in the psychoanalytic hour, and in all his voluminous case studies the inclusion of what has come to be called "verbatim" material is conspicuously lacking.[2] In contrast, Carl Rogers, more than any other one person, has been responsible for opening the door of the therapeutic room and inviting analysis and criticism of the process of helping.[3] In the theological world Anton Boisen pioneered in bringing students to the clinic as a means for deeper understanding of religious experience and the meaning of man's struggle toward health. Curiously enough, however, Boisen stands in the tradition of Freud in his resistance toward describing and analyzing what actually happened in the pastoral interview. It is somewhat amazing that Boisen as the "founder" of the clinical training movement which has gone forward on the wings of the "verbatim" did not, in his major publications, deal specifically with this aspect of pastoral investigation.[4] At about the same time that Boisen was writing the account of his own religious pilgrimage, Russell Dicks, together with Richard C. Cabot, published *The Art of Ministering to the Sick*.[5] His use of case material, notes written at the time of the interview, as the data for investigation foreshadowed what was to become the principal strategy for teaching and learning pastoral care. Since most ministers today have long since known that Dicks pioneered in the use of "case notes," it might be surprising to many to examine the first edition of *The Art of Ministering* and discover that all the "verbatim" material is in an appendix! In those early days, this material had not made its way into the actual structure of the discourse.

In the same year that Boisen and Dicks published the books already noted, Seward Hiltner published "Case-work Technique and the Therapeutic Use of Religion," in *Spiritual Factors in Social Work*, which reported the Church Conference on Social Work held in 1935.[6] He was at that time executive secretary of the Council for Clinical Training of Theological Students (later the Council for Clinical Training and now merged into the Association for Clinical Pastoral Education). He had been graduated from Lafayette College in 1931 and pursued his studies at the University of Chicago. During these years he was secretary of the Westminster Foundation at the University of Chicago and in the summer months participated in clinical training. I have never had an opportunity to examine this volume on social work and thus am uncertain as to the approach Hiltner made to "case-work." Even so, whatever use he assigned the material, it is significant that one of his first publictaions had to do with concrete data in the light of religious experience. His first book, *Religion and Health*, appeared in 1943.[7] Significantly, it contains no "verbatim" type case material. Nevertheless, the importance of this type of data for pastoral improvement is evidenced in such notations as the following: "If careful records were kept on ministry to a few patients, and some person especially expert were consulted even by mail, much could be accomplished. It sounds brash to suggest improving ministry to the sick by correspondence courses. The note-writing itself would be of great value, but the comments of someone else would, of course, be of greater value if they came in the course of a personal interview. But any objective comments would be worth something." [8]

During the 1940's Hiltner's concern for "verbatim" reports became more evident in his publications.[9] When in 1949 his substantive book in pastoral counseling appeared,[10] he was firmly committed to the method of examining specific cases to discover general principles which could then be brought to bear on future pastoral experiences.

It was about this time that he became pastoral consultant for the newly launched periodical *Pastoral Psychology*.[11] It was this journal, more than any other single channel, that was to be the instrument by which Hiltner could communicate with his growing audience of ministers interested in pastoral care and counseling. Many chapters that later appeared in his *The Counselor in Counseling*[12] had first been "tested" in the pages of *Pastoral Psychology*. For nearly twenty years Hiltner's influence has been exerted through editorials and essays in this journal, a contribution appropriately noted by Simon Doniger in the foreword of this volume.

In the light of this brief sketch it is clear that Hiltner has been singularly involved in stressing the use of case material in pastoral studies even though he was not the only one to mark the importance of this procedure for the nurture of ministerial effectiveness. The significance he placed upon this type of learning is clearly spelled out in an article which he published in *Theologische Literaturzeitung*[13] in 1963 and a somewhat modified form of the same thesis in 1965.[14] In writing to his European audience, Hiltner noted the basic distinction between the approach there and that of the American understanding of pastoral care. He pointed out that whereas in Europe the primary questions were

"What is the problem?" and "What is the authority for its solution?" in America the central concern emerged from the questions, "What happened?" "What was done?" "What were the events?"

Significant as this emphasis in Hiltner's approach is, there is a still deeper concern which makes his work of primary importance in contemporary pastoral care. It is well known that in the early days of the emergence of specific investigation of pastoral practice, any theology present was on the whole reductionistic. There are, to be sure, exceptions, but the number is not impressive. Various reasons have been explored to account for this obvious fact. It is noted that the researchers in case material were by and large persons who had become disenchanted with the organized church. It was perhaps natural that they would be less concerned with the perspectives of theology (which they, to some extent, had already rejected) than those which came from the behavioral sciences. Moreover, the atmosphere of the clinic was all around them, and it is understandable that they would make use of principles from psychology, psychiatry, and sociology to sort out the data they were uncovering in their investigations. As a consequence, most of the early writing is nontheological on the whole, and in those instances where theological concepts are introduced, they are made subservient to the psychological or psychotherapeutic principles which apparently seemed more relevant to the data.

It would not be accurate to say that Hiltner escaped this pitfall at every point. He too was a product of his time, and the thrust of the movement in which he had found significance and meaning naturally affected his formulations. Nevertheless, whether by reason of his Calvinistic background or some other, he most assuredly came closer than any other writer to dealing forthrightly with the theological implications of the empirical data. He was not only aware of the theology of the "Fathers" but saw the importance of maintaining a theological perspective at every point in the investigation of experiential material. Significantly, he wrote in February, 1968, an editorial in *Pastoral Psychology* calling attention to the tremendous contribution of Paul Tillich to the field. Toward the end of the editorial he said, "In America our fields of pastoral psychology and pastoral theology have been built in recent years largely through close inspection of the case or other concrete situation, standing in its uniqueness. We have been short in general theory especially of a theological kind that can interpenetrate with the concrete observations; and it is perhaps the most obvious contribution of Paul Tillich to our field that he helped to correct that procedural imbalance." [15] Hiltner goes on to comment on the strengths and weaknesses of Tillich's approach for the pastoral field. But the point is that in noting, correctly, that scant attention had been paid to the theological dimensions of pastoral care, he (understandably) does not draw attention to his own work. In 1958 he had published his now well-known *Preface to Pastoral Theology*, which opened untapped resources and which today stands as a landmark in the whole matter of the theological investigation of concrete material. Because James Lapsley gives pointed attention to Hiltner's position in the development of pastoral care in the first essay of this volume, I shall not press the point here. Suffice it to say that many of the current seminal investigations exploring the relationship between psychotherapy and theology[16] stand in the line of Hiltner's pioneering thesis.

Following his work with the Council for Clinical Training, Hiltner moved to the (then) Federal Council of Churches, where he served with several departments, including being secretary of the Department of Pastoral Services as well as of the Commissions on Religion and Health and Ministry in Institutions. During these years he was lecturer in pastoral counseling at Union Theological Seminary in New York and at Yale University Divinity School. The responsibilities connected with these assignments provided a wide range of contacts with clergymen and social scientists, yielding opportunity for continual evaluation and investigation of the hypotheses already taking shape in his own research. When in 1950 he returned to the Divinity School of the University of Chicago (then the Federated Theological Faculty) as professor of pastoral theology, the fifteen-year interim since his student days had seen the maturing of those concepts which had been nascent in his undergraduate work. It is notable that he was tapped by the university even though his highest academic degree at that time was the A.B., which he had received from Lafayette College in 1931. So certain was the university of his ability that the traditional "union card" of the Ph.D. was waived, albeit provisionally. His doctoral dissertation, interestingly enough, was in the field of ethics, and prior to his receiving the Ph.D., he had been honored by his alma mater with the Doctor of Divinity degree. Since 1961 Hiltner has been professor of theology and personality at Princeton Theological Seminary, and for many years he has served as theological consultant to the Menninger School of Psychiatry in Topeka, Kansas. As my purpose here is not to give a detailed biographical account, I have sketched in only the barest outline of Hiltner's professional career. A complete listing of committees, commissions, boards, lectureships, and foundations with which he has been associated would tax the space available in this volume. Moreover, it is likely that these data will one day be gathered into a systematic delineation of his life and work.

It is ordinarily a risky exercise to single out one aspect of any person's professional career as his unique contribution and legacy, and to do so with regard to Hiltner's work is no exception. Nevertheless, with considered awareness of his activities as a teacher, administrator, counselor—and the list could run on—I am persuaded that it is through his writings that he has left us most deeply in his debt. The January, 1968, issue of *Pastoral Psychology* carried his complete bibliography to that date, and to say that it is impressive is to comment on the obvious: nine major books (not counting *Ferment in the Ministry,*[17] which has appeared since the listing was compiled); editor of six additional books, for most of which he prepared one or more articles; contributions to thirty-five volumes compiled or edited by others, including forewords and introductions; over a score of pamphlets dealing with a wide range of subjects in the field of psychology, social work, and pastoral care; and in addition a list of articles in periodicals and journals that fills thirteen pages and includes not only those appearing in *Pastoral Psychology* but also in such a variety of publications that only a sampling can be noted here: *The Christian Century, Presbyterian Life, Religious Education, Journal of Social Hygiene, The Church Woman, Christianity and Crisis, Crozer Quarterly, Theology Today, National Council Bulletin, American Journal of Orthopsychiatry, Journal for the Scientific Study of Religion,* and on and on.

In addition to the sheer number of books and articles listed in Hiltner's bibliography, the wide range of topics is also worthy of comment. A random selection illustrates the point: alcoholism, the death of God, ministry to the sick, four letter words, Christmas cards, communion, city and suburbs, suicide prevention, the pastoral care of Dean Rusk, and innumerable comments on the life and contribution of the great and near great in the field of the social sciences and pastoral theology. Everywhere and often in the most unlikely places his creative imagination found grist, and his disciplined mind ground it into the product that made it available to hosts of consumers. In anticipation of writing this introduction I have been reading through back issues of *Pastoral Psychology* to taste again the flavor of Hiltner's style. There is always a nugget, a kernel, a substance that has inherent significance; there is clarity, an orderly presentation with transitions easy to follow; there is a perception which throws light on this or that facet of the thesis together with a pointing to relationships and implications that might otherwise escape attention; there is erudition attesting to wide study and research and a storehouse of information available for use in penetrating thorny and complex issues of the day; and always, either apparent or just beneath the surface, there is wit, a profound sense of humor that gives life and zest to the data and enables the reader to move more easily through the reasoned arguments. As I write these words, I am quite aware that they represent impressions shot through with subjective dimensions, but I am content with that and quite willing to leave a more formal analysis of Hiltner's writing to another time or another person. It has often been remarked that Freud obviously had something to say but that he might never have attained his position of prominence in psychiatry had he not been a superb writer. In much the same fashion, I am convinced that apart from his ability to write, Hiltner would never have gained the attention which his substantive work in pastoral theology deserved. There is no doubt in the minds of those who have been closely associated with Hiltner that he is able to write in the kind of closely knit, scholarly, and formal style traditionally associated with Germanic theologians; nevertheless, as noted by Simon Doniger in the foreword of this volume, his passion has been to keep much of his writing on the level that would make genuine scholarship available to a wide variety of readers whose background and experience might make difficult the following of highly abstract arguments and esoteric terminology.

It is fair to say that this decision has been the occasion for criticism through the years by those who took the position that such a style tended to stray from true scholarly pursuits. I have no intention here to debate the point one way or another. From a purely pragmatic point of view, it is certain that Hiltner has reached a wide audience. The nature and the permanence of his influence can probably be assessed accurately only after the passage of time has swept away the distortion of proximity.

It would not be appropriate to leave the matter of Hiltner's writing without noting one recurring dimension which has been singularly characteristic through the years. I am referring now to his practice of devastating critique leveled at the positions and publications of those with whom he did not agree. Sometimes taking the form of pulling out the "stackpole" and watching the structure tumble, at other times following the painstaking and painful dissection of each aspect under scrutiny, Hiltner's attacks make use not only of carefully reasoned argument but also include irony and at times ridicule. Many instances of this procedure come readily to mind, but a few excerpts from his Inaugural Address at Princeton Theological Seminary suffice to illustrate the point.[18] His subject matter is anthropology, and he is deploring the scant or inadequate attention given to this matter by such contemporary theologians as Barth, Brunner, and Tillich.

He argues that Barth is by no means devoid of an anthropology but that his theological method makes it unnecessary for him to think systematically about it. As he works out his analysis, he concludes, "As any social work agency could tell Barth, the perils of a child's growing up, whether he is legitimate or otherwise, can hardly be averted by withholding a name until the child is old enough to choose a nice one for himself." [19] He then turns to Brunner, noting that he moves beyond Barth in taking "the first basic step" in the direction of specifying man's and men's nature and need in relation to God. However, he deplores the fact that Brunner stopped there, and continues, "Although his personalistic approach to theology is mostly realistic except in regard to marriage, where romanticism still prevails, his lack of specificity at the anthropological level enables him to be invoked, no doubt to his horror, by the 'Follow the Gleam' crowd on the one side and by aggressive evangelistic exploiters on the other." [20] Turning to Tillich, he expresses approval for his inclusion of data from the social sciences but complains, "His [Tillich's] own forthrightness in the procedure would better serve the future of Christian anthropology if he did not insist that all such contributions must first be filtered through philosophy to a master discipline of 'systematic theology,' after which purification rites they eventually lead, by correlational osmosis, to a superior Christian anthropology." [21]

I have dwelled at some length on this facet of Hiltner's writing and hope that the quotations are adequate to illustrate the sometimes scathing nature of his invectives. At the same time I do not wish to leave the impression that this procedure is employed indiscriminately. An excerpt from the Alden-Tuthill Lectures which he delivered at Chicago Theological Seminary in 1966 [22] gives a significant clue to the criteria for launching such an attack. He is speaking of life in the suburbs and has used various analogies to explore the meaning of this type of existence. Toward the end he says, "Before I close out this section on suffering in the suburbs, it may be that some of you are waiting for me to come to the 'afflict the comfortable' part of my speech, in which I shall lash out at the exploiters and coupon-clippers and restricted covenanters and Saturday-night wife-swappers and rich physicians and conscienceless brokers, and perhaps even ministers who have cultivated suburban paunches, pocketbooks, and pious piffles. Perhaps I ought to do this. But my heart is not in it. *When the situation seems to promise some constructive action therefrom, I think I am one of the best 'viewers-with-alarm' in the business. . . .* The real fact is that I am very dubious about the chance of a prophetic ministry today to influence the suburbs that does not enter, personally, in a fully pastoral sense with the people who are in the suburbs."

Granted the fact that the thrust of his statement is to press ministers toward pastoral involvement as a part of their prophetic function, the key phrase is the one referring to the "promise of some constructive action." Put in other words, Hiltner tends to attack persons or issues when he believes something better will come from the encounter. It can be argued that his assessment of the potentially positive results is not always accurate and even that on some occasions the very virulence of the attack has seemed to prevent the hoped-for improvement. In the excerpt quoted above, the words omitted convey a somewhat rueful acknowledgment of his own fallibility at this point. He says, "I even tried this on the Federation of Theological Schools over a good long period; but then, nobody can win all the time." [23] Even so, it seems proper to observe that the inaccuracy of judgment does not negate the validity of the distinction.

With this I conclude my comments on Hiltner's contribution to the field of pastoral theology. As indicated earlier, it has been my purpose to be suggestive rather than exhaustive—for obvious reasons. It is perhaps not too vain a hope that one of the readers of this volume may be motivated to undertake a systematic and detailed analysis and evaluation of Hiltner's life and work. Such a chronicler would find rich resources for his research. And if the results matched the wealth of the data, there is no question but that an important link would be forged in the unfolding development of pastoral care.

II

To turn now to a consideration of the essays themselves, a glance at the table of contents will reveal the overall structure of the book. At the outset it was the judgment of the *Festschrift* Committee that the essays should serve not only as a procedure for honoring Seward Hiltner but also as a means toward making a significant contribution to the emerging understanding of pastoral theology. To that end a tentative structure was devised, and essays were requested which would implement this latter concern while at the same time remaining true to the first consideration. Each author was given the privilege of suggesting an alternate proposal if at the time of the invitation he had some particularly relevant research in process of completion. It is encouraging to report that of all those invited only two found it necessary to decline by reason of prior commitments which made it literally impossible for them to submit essays within the prescribed time. In both instances these persons expressed genuine regret that their schedules would not allow them to submit an essay and emphasized their wholehearted support of the venture.

As would be expected in an enterprise of this dimension, certain persons who originally agreed to prepare essays found that their intention was thwarted by circumstances over which they had no control. It would be inappropriate here to delineate the situational obstacles encountered by these individuals; it is proper, in their behalf, to note that their truly personal desire was to give tangible expression of their regard for and appreciation of Seward Hiltner and that however much those of us who read this volume regret that they were not able to carry through on their intention, our disappointment in no sense matches their own. The readers who have been closely associated with Hiltner through the years will assuredly be able to conjecture the identity of the persons to whom I am referring. Even though they will not be named here, I would like to express on behalf of the *Festschrift* Committee our genuine gratitude for their support and encouragement.

Although I do not pretend any expert knowledge in the matter of preparing a *Festschrift*, my impression is that there are two general methods of procedure ordinarily employed in such enterprises. On the one hand, essays are invited from significant persons in (or outside) the primary field of the honoree without regard to the personal relationship of the writers to him. The other general procedure is to confine the list of those invited to submit essays to persons who have been closely associated with the honoree. As has already been noted, this latter course was selected by the Hiltner *Festschrift* Committee precisely because of a desire to give tangible evidence to the fulfillment of his wish that his students and colleagues engage in publication as a means for continuing the necessary dialogue for the enhancement of pastoral understanding. So it is that the large majority of the essays included herewith are written by students of Hiltner who in this fashion and in other writings attempt to carry forward the work in which he has been so effective a pioneer.

The twenty-four essays fall into three broad categories: "Pastoral Theology: Implications and Development," "Pastoral Theology and Theological Education," and "Pastoral Theology and Pastoral Care." There may be some significance in the fact that the first and third are each approximately twice as long as the second, but I shall not speculate on possible reasons. The arrangement of the essays is designed to facilitate discussion and dialogue on the part of theological students as well as ministers, and it is the hope of the *Festschrift* Committee that the order will be of value in stimulating genuine involvement on the part of the reader. However it is obvious that those who desire to investigate particular dimensions of pastoral theology can do so without regard to the sequential ordering of the several essays. Moreover, an index has been prepared to facilitate the exploration of various topics or areas of particular interest.

Appropriately enough, the first piece in the book is a personal word from Simon Doniger, who until January of this year was editor of *Pastoral Psychology*. It is likely that no other person has been so closely associated with Hiltner over a twenty-year span, and the fact that his affection and regard for Hiltner are mutual can be verified by reading the lead editorial in the January, 1969, issue of *Pastoral Psychology* in which Hiltner describes his appraisal of the long-time relationship.

The initial essay in Part I is a general survey of "Pastoral Theology Past and Present," by James N. Lapsley. The author has been associated with Hiltner first as a student at the University of Chicago and more recently as a colleague on the Princeton faculty. He identifies four "essentials" of pastoral theology which emerge from Hiltner's work and uses them as criteria for examining the adequacy of various formulations in the field. Noting that the time may be at hand for an expanding theory, he suggests three focuses as guidelines for such a venture. Broadening the horizon, Graeme Griffin explores the development of pastoral theology and pastoral care overseas, focusing primarily on his own land of Australia while noting particular approaches in Europe and Asia. Following this, Donald A. Groskreutz examines the relationship between modern pastoral theology and the Christian tradition. In his essay he notes the sense in which there is a necessity for a realistic relationship between the past and present and a necessity for a continual evaluation of contemporary procedures not only in the light of that which has been but also in terms of that which now is. These three essays set the basic context for the remainder of the book.

Representative of the rich contributions which have come to the field of pastoral theology from related disciplines, the chapters by Daniel Day Williams and Gardner Murphy illustrate relevant data from theology and psychology. Williams' essay examines the meaning of identity and the quest for "being" in a Christian context and relates his findings to psychological and existential concepts. Murphy's thesis sets forth the necessity for examining and rethinking many of the old truisms in arriving at a responsible understanding of religious experience.

The next three chapters continue the investigation of data outside the field with particular reference to implications for constructive theory and practice of pastoral theology. Robert Bonthius describes the "explosive mix" in contemporary urbanization, including population growth, racism, the cybernetic revolution, and secularization, and then draws provocative conclusions for pastoral care and the role of the churches. This is followed by Don S. Browning's essay, which pursues the thesis already set forth in his *Atonement and Psychotherapy*. Here Browning delves into the implication of phenomenological psychology for theology and argues for a more adequate ontology of the human to provide the basis for deeper theological constructs. Finally, Leland Elhard draws on the implications of existentialism as the basis for encouraging persons to stand forth in the midst of life, eschewing any sort of desire for a life of ease, devoid of struggle and stress.

The concluding chapters in Part I look into the future with the purpose of suggesting guidelines for continued exploration and research. James G. Emerson identifies a theology of discipline as promising for a refining and deepening of present constructs. From another perspective, Coval MacDonald suggests that the time is at hand to make use of the data emerging from general systems theory in somewhat the same fashion that Hiltner made use of field theory in his *Preface to Pastoral Theology*.

In Part II the essays are concerned with the implications of investigations in pastoral theology for various aspects of theological education. Leighton McCutchen picks up the general principles set forth in the first description of the religion and personality field at the University of Chicago in the early 1950's. Applying these principles to the concept of "dialogue" in the religious academy, he suggests that if religion is the mother figure and psychology the child figure in the relational construct, there is need to identify the father figure. His tentative proposal provides provocative material for further exploration. Paul Irion, from a different perspective, looks at the place of pastoral theology and the "practical" fields in theological education. Currently president of the Association of Theological Professors in the Practical Fields, Irion rehearses the significant factors in the development of this area of theological education and notes that the task ahead is to develop new and more effective strategies for the education of theological students.

The last three chapters in Part II deal with issues surrounding the crucial matter of field work and competent supervision in theological education. James Spicer argues that experience-oriented teaching is the most crucial need on the contemporary scene. Both Lowell G. Colston and John H. Patton deal with the particular significance of clinical training in the wide range of field-work experiences. Colston notes that pastoral theology cannot ignore process and describes the characteristics of process-oriented theologizing, including criteria for assessing strengths and weaknesses at any point along the way. Patton, as a certified clinical supervisor, explores the principles of supervision in pastoral education. He makes use of Paul Tillich's concept of "Christ as the New Being" as a clarifying analogy in this process and illustrates his thesis with brief excerpts from clinical data.

The initial essay in the third division turns our attention from theological education to pastoral care. Joseph Havens draws on long experience in the Quaker tradition to provide the basis for group relationship and the mutual caring of one person for another.

The next two articles complement each other in assessing some of the primary factors in effective pastoral counseling. LeRoy Aden examines the implications of Rogerian therapy for devising process and criteria in optimal counseling. From another perspective Robert Elliott suggests that in addition to the factor of unconditional acceptance the parishioner also requires the kind of relationship which issues in respect. Referring to the work of Mowrer, Glasser, and others, he develops the thesis that attention should be given to the "fatherly" as well as the "motherly" mode of pastoral care.

The college campus provides the context for the following two essays. Clyde J. Steckel believes that a new form of ministry is required to meet the needs of the student today, involving a new form of clinical training to prepare persons for this ministry. He draws implications from pastoral theology and applies them to religious work on the campus, and in the same manner he argues that work on the campus has significance for reexamining pastoral theology. Dealing specifically with the counseling of college students, William R. Rogers identifies three areas as being of crucial importance: (1) identity, (2) emptiness and meaning, and (3) nihilism and morality. Citing specific aspects of student unrest, he makes a case for the type of counseling relationship which avoids all superficial approaches to presenting problems.

Continuing an exploration of pastoral care for persons in particular circumstances or situations, Kenneth Mitchell examines the problems and opportunities inherent in any kind of dealing with peers or superiors in professional relationships. Making use of data obtained from experiences in training and sensitivity groups, he spells out implications both for the ministry and pastoral theology. Thomas Klink, long associated with Hiltner in work at the Menninger Foundation, discusses the sociological, physiological, psychological, and spiritual dimensions of ministering to the dying patient. Finally, Frank M. Bockus describes the process of guidance with particular reference to mental health units and other local groups designed to enable persons to cope with the pressures and problems of life.

The concluding essay is, appropriately, centered on the meaning of the blessing or the benediction. Paul Pruyser writes as a nonordained churchman who, like Thomas Klink, has worked with Hiltner through the years at Topeka. He sees the blessing and the benediction as clues to pastoral identity involving providence and grace.

III

In November of this year Seward Hiltner will celebrate his sixtieth birthday. It is this event which has been the underlying focus in the preparation of the *Festschrift*. These essays represent a genuine expression of appreciation not only by the authors themselves but in a vicarious way by those countless persons whose lives have been enriched through Hiltner's work in pastoral theology. In paying tribute to him, we join not only in gratitude for that which is past but also in eager anticipation of a future which will continue to yield the creative results of his research and writing.

Notes

1. E.g. John T. McNeill, *A History of the Cure of Souls* (New York: Harper, 1951); William A. Clebsch and Charles R. Jaekle, *Pastoral Care in Historical Perspective* (Englewood Cliffs, N.J.: Prentice-Hall, 1964); H. Richard Niebuhr and Daniel D. Williams, eds., *The Ministry in Historical Perspectives* (New York: Harper, 1956); C. W. Brister, *Pastoral Care in the Church* (New York: Harper, 1964); Carl J. Scherzer, *The Church and Healing* (Philadelphia: Westminster Press, 1950).
2. Toward the end of the final lecture in *A General Introduction to Psychoanalysis* ([New York: Garden City Publishing Co., 1943], p. 398) Freud refers to his reason for this procedure. Cf. also his "Further Recommendations in the Technique of Psychoanalysis," *Collected Papers,* Vol. II (New York: Basic Books, 1959). In this same vein, several persons invited to submit case material for inclusion in *Case Studies in Counseling and Psychotherapy,* edited by Arthur Burton (Englewood Cliffs, N.J.: Prentice-Hall, 1959) stated categorically that there was no way, verbatim or otherwise, to reproduce what actually "happened" in therapy.
3. Rogers' first major book, *Counseling and Psychotherapy* (New York: Houghton Mifflin, 1942) included a lengthy transcript of phonographically recorded material. This procedure has been continued in subsequent publications, e.g., *Client-Centered Therapy* (New York: Houghton Mifflin, 1951), *Psychotherapy and Personality Change* (co-editor with Rosalind F. Dymond [Chicago: University of Chicago Press, 1954]), etc.
4. E.g., Anton T. Boisen, *The Exploration of the Inner World* (New York: Willett, Clark & Co., 1937); *Religion in Crisis and Custom* (New York: Harper, 1955); etc. Of course Boisen used notes and case material in teaching theological students, but I have never read anything by him that moves in the direction of verbatim analysis as it is usually defined. I can well remember one evening in Seward Hiltner's apartment in Chicago when Boisen was meeting with a group of us. No matter how hard we pressed him to describe what he actually "did" with a patient in the interview room, he successfully avoided any explicit description.
5. Richard C. Cabot and Russell Dicks, *The Art of Ministering to the Sick* (New York: Macmillan, 1936).
6. Worth M. Tippy, ed., *Spiritual Factors in Social Work* (New York: Federal Council of Churches, 1936).
7. Seward Hiltner, *Religion and Health* (New York: Macmillan, 1943).
8. *Ibid.*, p. 249.
9. E.g., "How to Make an Evangelistic Call" (New York: Federal Council of Churches, 1946).
10. Seward Hiltner, *Pastoral Counseling* (Nashville: Abingdon Press, 1949).

11. Manhasset, New York.
12. Seward Hiltner, *The Counselor in Counseling* (Nashville: Abingdon Press, 1952).
13. Seward Hiltner, "Theology and Pastoral Care in the United States," *Theologische Literaturzeitung*, LXXXVIII (1963), 502. Reprinted in *Pastoral Psychology*, November, 1967, pp. 15-21.
14. Seward Hiltner, "Integrity in Pastoral Care," *Princeton Seminary Bulletin*, 1965, pp. 39-48. Reprinted in *Pastoral Psychology*, November, 1966, pp. 17-26.
15. Seward Hiltner, "Pastoral Psychology—After Paul Tillich," *Pastoral Psychology*, February, 1968, p. 6.
16. E.g., Don S. Browning, *Atonement and Psychotherapy* (Philadelphia: Westminster Press, 1966), and various essays included in this present volume.
17. Seward Hiltner, *Ferment in the Ministry* (Nashville: Abingdon Press, 1969).
18. Published in *Theology Today*, July, 1963, pp. 242-57.
19. *Ibid.*, p. 246.
20. *Ibid.*, p. 247.
21. *Ibid.*
22. Published in *Princeton Seminary Bulletin*, June, 1966, pp. 54-78. Reprinted in *Pastoral Psychology* under the general title, "Troubled People in a Troubled World," in three parts, as follows: "People in the Suburbs," February, 1967, pp. 14-21; "People in Cities," April, 1967, pp. 20-27; "People at Work and Play," May, 1967, pp. 36-43. The reference here is to the February, 1967, issue of *Pastoral Psychology*, pp. 19-20. (emphasis mine).
23. *Ibid.*, pp. 5-7.

I. Pastoral Theology
Implications and Development

Pastoral Theology Past and Present

James N. Lapsley

In speaking of pastoral theology past and present we run immediately into the problem of what is meant by the term, for its meaning has been far from stable. Hence we must begin with an attempt to say what it means without being too arbitrary on the one hand, or so inclusive on the other, that nothing in the life of the church is excluded. In doing this I am also stating a thesis regarding the present situation in pastoral theology, since the changes that have taken place in the meaning of the term essentially embody the history of the discipline. Thus I inevitably am putting the cart before the horse from a historical point of view since my definition must be a contemporary one.

To begin with, all who have used the term agree that it refers in some way to the pastoring dimension of the ministry. In the past some have held it to be another name for doing something—for the kinds of *activity* involved in this dimension, though few would hold this today. Beyond these points there is little consensus. Some would, as in the past, hold pastoral theology to be the study of all the functions of ministry (with the possible exception of homiletics) inasmuch as all are essentially pastoral in the sense of exercising concern for the flock or individuals in it. Others wish to focus upon those aspects of ministry in which the minister's (whether ordained or lay) "tender and solicitous care" is the primary phenomenon to be studied. This activity or aspect of ministry has generally been called pastoral care, and hence in this view pastoral theology is the theory of pastoral care.

This latter view of pastoral theology as the study of pastoral care forms the historical basis upon which the thesis of this essay rests although it is not in itself sufficient. The elements which go into the construction of an adequate contemporary view have many sources, both inside and outside the discipline itself. Focal, however, is the position set forth by Seward Hiltner in his seminal work, *Preface to Pastoral Theology* (1958). Hiltner held to the narrow focus of pastoral theology but recognized that if the definition applies only to a certain kind of activity, the result is a compartmentalization of ministry which contradicts the inherent wisdom of the broad view that there is indeed something pastoral about the whole of ministry. To meet this problem Hiltner conceived his now well-known "field-theory" or perspectival model of ministry, in which "shepherding" (or pastoring) becomes one "perspective"—along with communicating and organizing—on ministry as a whole. In this view every act of ministry can be understood to have some effect, positive or negative, on all three of these dimensions of ministry—although one perspective is dominant over the others on a moment-by-moment basis according to the valences of behavior and intention.

Hiltner also emphasized another point of great importance. This is that pastoral theology is a definite "branch" of theology—albeit an "operation-centered" branch as distinguished from the "logic-centered" branches of the traditional disciplines. Hence it proceeds by the asking of theological questions of the pastoral "data" and moving toward theological conclusions regarding these, thereby making a contribution to theology as a larger discipline. His formal definition of pastoral theology thus runs: "that branch or field of theological knowledge or inquiry that brings the shepherding perspective to bear upon all the operations and functions of the church and the minister, and then draws conclusions of a theological order from reflection on these observations." [1]

Not explicit in this definition is another point of great importance in Hiltner's view. The personality sciences are accorded a major role in understanding the data of the "shepherding perspective." Although Hiltner is not precise in his treatment of this role, he strongly suggests that it may even be determinative in some respects. "This knowledge is about more than methods and techniques. It may teach the spiritual shepherd the equivalent of how to prevent the grass from disappearing from a green pasture through knowledge of irrigation, crop rotation, and tree planting." [2]

While not contenting for the complete adequacy of Hiltner's definition (as will be made clear), I hold that it does embody the essentials of any viable approach to pastoral theology. These are (1) a basic focus on the caring, helping, healing, and sustaining aspects of ministry as data of the inquiry, (2) recognition of the pervasiveness of these aspects or dimensions of ministry, which are nevertheless not exhaustive of it descriptively, (3) the theological character of the discipline—which means that both the starting point and the conclusion of inquiry in pastoral theology are theologically oriented with implications for broader theological understanding, and (4) the use of the personality sciences and related disciplines as important tools in the inquiry.

The thesis of this essay is, then, that these four essentials provide a rough criterion by which any approach to pastoral theology may be examined. In its light we shall first look at the past and then the present.

I. Pastoral Theology Before World War II

I shall make no attempt at a detailed report of the history of all that has been called pastoral theology or the cure of souls. The works of Kemp, McNeill, and Clebsch and Jaekle may be consulted for the full story of pastoral care.[3]

Rather it is enough to note that since the term came into use about 1750, no work devoted to pastoral theology as the writers understood it fulfilled all four points of the criterion, although at least two works devoted to topics tangential to, or including pastoral theology, contained adumbrations of all four. A rather large group represented by J. J. Van Oosterzee[4] dealt with pastoral theology as an aspect of practical theology, which they regarded as theological understanding applied to the practice of ministry. They saw pastoral theology as concerned with the personal aspects of ministry and thus met the first point of criterion. Moreover they were theological in their approach even though they failed to meet the third criterion because their aim was merely practice rather than the enhancement of theological understanding in the light of practice. W. G. T. Shedd [5] represented a view especially prevalent in America that pastoral theology had to do with everything a minister does except preaching. His work fails to meet any of the four points. Later around the turn of the twentieth century, more attention was paid to the sciences and other cultural disciplines, which is related to the fourth point, but this tended to be coupled with less and less systematic and theological interest. Relevance became the dominant concern at the expense of responsibility to theory or, in the long run, to persons.[6] A more sophisticated variation of this approach from a psychological point of view is found in the work of John G. MacKenzie, who represented the trend toward the use of dynamic psychology. Although more systematic in some respects, MacKenzie failed to integrate his insights with a theological approach.[7] This trend continued to grow during the 1930's and has, of course, persisted strongly until the present. In the more conservative traditions there were also works appearing toward the end of this period which attempted to hold theology and psychology in some kind of tension. But these manifested little interest in learning from the concrete pastoral situation and none in feeding back contributions to theology. The work of William Goulooze represents this trend and also shows how too great tension between disciplines can help lead to an approach that is little more than a catalog of resources.[8]

Of all these works in the general area of practical or pastoral theology, only one, to my knowledge, genuinely foreshadows the developments which have occurred in recent years. This is *An Introduction to the Study of Pastoral Theology* by Clement F. Rogers. Published in England just prior to the outbreak of World

War I, this work is virtually alone in advocating that ministers develop "laws" of pastoral theology by studying their own practice in the light of secular and theological knowledge. Rogers viewed theology as a science which studied "man's share in his fellow-man's relation to God." [9] Although Rogers did not distinguish pastoral theology in just the way I have suggested in setting up criteria, he nevertheless saw it as dealing with what we would call the personal elements in ministry, which are pervasive of the whole. The only place where Rogers failed clearly to meet my criteria was in the absence of any discussion of how the laws of pastoral theology might make a contribution toward the understanding of theology as a whole. He even foreshadowed Hiltner's perspectival approach in his discussion of the "elements" of ministry, one of which may predominate while others are not entirely absent.[10]

Turning now to the two works that more clearly suggest the kind of approach set forth in the opening pages of this essay, let us first look briefly at F. E. Schleiermacher's posthumously published *Pracktishe Theologie,* in which he set forth a systematic and unique approach to practical theology growing out of his systematic theology.[11] Schleiermacher defined practical theology (of which pastoral theology was an aspect dealing with *seelsorge*) as the "technique of the maintenance and perfection of the church." [12] This rather pedestrian definition is elsewhere amplified to include study of the following five elements: (1) the Christian disposition, which participates in the guiding activity of the church, (2) the historical setting, (3) understanding of task and goal of anticipated impulses in a general theological culture, (4) developing the rules for the execution of action that really corresponds to the reality being dealt with, and (5) special talents that minister and people have.

Although my paraphrase of Groskreutz' report may appear somewhat opaque, it does indicate that Schleiermacher wished to include a study of the personal and cultural (historical) aspects of the situation and that he saw practical theology as a genuine branch of theology. It is not clear from these elements whether he held that practical theology might also make a contribution to the whole discipline of theology, but in the following passage he seems to open the way for just this kind of development:

> Improvement of dogmatics purely out of itself has nothing to do with practical theology. But if we examine the things in their direct bearing upon the church, then the development of dogmatics for the integration in which the relation of this science with the church lies, it is not indifferent, notwithstanding the scientific nature in itself, *and there practical theology* grasps into the scope of dogmatics.[13]

It would be saying too much to insist that Schleiermacher saw implications of what may have been only a passing thought, not clearly embodied elsewhere. Nevertheless, the great theologian did see, even if momentarily, where one must move if he takes practical theology seriously as a discipline. His insight was not acted upon either by himself or anyone else in the nineteenth century, so far as I know.

The other precursor of great importance is, of course, Anton T. Boisen, whose life and work are so well known to most readers of this volume that I shall not rehearse them here. It is enough to note that it was Boisen who put concrete meaning into the study of theology through the use of "human documents," even if Clement Rogers had used the phrase earlier (cf. note 9 above). Hiltner records his debt to Boisen in the following words: "Boisen has not himself been concerned to work out a systematic pastoral theology, but the basic clue to the systematic construction of this author has come from Boisen." [14] In his *The Exploration of the Inner World: A Study of Mental Disorder and Religious Experience,*[15] Boisen described his approach to the study of mental illness based on his own experience. His advocacy of a case study method using psychological insights but aiming beyond psychology toward morality and religion made a profound impact upon Hiltner, who sought to develop this side of Boisen's contribution. Utilizing the technique of the verbatim report developed by

Russell L. Dicks, whose distinguished career spanned the first three decades of the movement, the clinical training movement came, even before World War II, to give expression to the practical implications of Boisen's work for ministry. Through many vicissitudes, including the division of the movement in the 1940's occasioned by the organization of the Institute of Pastoral Care as, in part, a protest against the lack of theological perspective in the original Council for Clinical Training, this movement is again united in our day as the Association for Clinical Pastoral Education.

II. World War II to the Present

Although, as we have seen, there were anticipations of a modern conception of pastoral theology in the period before World War II, they were virtually lost with the exception of the work of Boisen. The war itself was a tremendous stimulus to the development of pastoral care and counseling and hence indirectly to pastoral theology. Chaplains for military service had to be quickly trained, as did ministers to work with men returning from the war. The influence of Carl R. Rogers was, of course, to begin its nourishment of the pastoral care movement at this time—an influence which is only now beginning to wane.

A development of the 1940's, equally important, was the establishment of professorships in the pastoral field which would be filled by men who had been nurtured in the clinical training movement. Four of these were to become of special significance in the postwar decades. Paul E. Johnson became professor of the psychology of religion at Boston University (later professor of psychology and pastoral counseling), Carroll A. Wise began to teach pastoral psychology and pastoral counseling at Garrett Biblical Institute (now Garrett Theological Seminary), Wayne E. Oates became professor of psychology of religion and pastoral care at the Southern Baptist Theological Seminary, and slightly later (1950) Seward Hiltner began to teach at the University of Chicago, subsequently becoming professor of pastoral theology.

These four men and their institutions became the principal resources for advanced training in the pastoral field until about 1957, when they began to be joined by others. In 1961 Hiltner moved to Princeton Theological Seminary, where he became professor of theology and personality, and in 1965 Johnson retired. Wise and Oates continued at their posts.

As may have been noted, Hiltner is the only one of these to have the word theology in the title of his professorship. While Paul Johnson worked easily within the pervasive personalism of Boston University developing his "responsive counseling" approach, he did not focus explicitly his conception of how pastoral care was to be understood theologically, in spite of a great interest in and sophisticated approach to the psychology of religion.[16] He, along with Wise, centered primarily on the psychological understanding of pastoral care and counseling. Wise has also made a significant contribution to the understanding of religion from a health point of view.[17] Nevertheless he has taken an explicit stand that theology has nothing to offer pastoral care, although it may have value in its own right as interpretation.[18] His view of theology as doctrine essentially divorced from life appears to have been determinative at this point, preventing his seeing that pastoral care can make a dynamic contribution to theological understanding and that it in turn needs to be informed by theological inquiry. In view of these considerations we must conclude that as great as the contributions of Johnson and Wise have been to the pastoral field generally, their contributions to pastoral theology have been indirect, through the stimulation they have given students and readers, rather than direct.

The stance of Wayne E. Oates has been quite otherwise. Although early in his career Oates seems to have been primarily interested in getting his students and readers (whom he regarded as probably conservative in their orientation) to accept a psychological view of pastoral work,[19] he always maintained a strong view of the minister as a representative of Christ and his word. This interest has resulted in recent years (along with some alarm lest pastoral work become overly psychologized) in an increasing emphasis on the theological understanding of pastoral work. His *Protestant Pastoral Counseling*[20] is, to use phraseology which he prefers, his theology of pastoral care. In this book Oates shows how his understanding of pastoral care and counseling is related to and in some respects derived from the free church tradition. He generally eschews the term pastoral theology,[21] and this may be a clue to a basic tension which appears in his work. For as concerned as Oates is to understand pastoral work theologically, he does not explicitly say that pastoral understanding can or ought to lead directly to increased theological understanding, although much of *Protestant Pastoral Counseling* can be so understood.[22] While he does not explicitly oppose this kind of effort, his wariness of the psychological sciences and of psychoanalysis in particular[23] may have led him to hesitate at this point for fear of contaminating the revealed truth. No one has surpassed Oates in his fruitful grappling with the implications of the theological tradition for pastoral care, but his vision of the implications of pastoral care for the tradition is less clear.

In arriving at the conclusion that in order to have integrity as a discipline, pastoral theology must be in a position to make a contribution to the whole body of divinity, Seward Hiltner was applying the general principle upon which the whole tradition of the Divinity School of the University of Chicago rested for more than a generation. This should be kept firmly in mind in attempting to understand Hiltner's now demonstrated virtual uniqueness on this point. He alone among the leaders we have discussed stood in this tradition. Shailer Mathews, Henry Nelson Wieman, Charles Hartshorne, Bernard Loomer, Bernard Meland, and Daniel Day Williams—to name only a few of the more prominent of Hiltner's teachers and former colleagues—all stood in a basic way for the application of the empirical principle in theology. There were great differences in the ways in which and the degrees to which they applied it, and Hiltner clearly belongs to the more dialectical group along with Hartshorne and Williams, as distinguished from the more thoroughgoing empiricism of Wieman and Meland. Nevertheless the basis for this kind of thinking as a whole is what made possible the rather easy juxtaposing of scientific, pastoral, and theological materials in *Preface to Pastoral Theology*, a juxtaposition still baffling and somewhat disturbing to those schooled in traditions where religion is one thing and science is another. It is possible that Hiltner's own schooling in empirical theology made him more oblivious to the jolt that this approach would cause others; even so there is much evidence in the book that he was keenly aware of this problem and tried to meet it by concrete discussion of cases and issues rather than by polemics about methodology.

However this may be, Hiltner's approach represents a fusing of the Boisen legacy of a clinical approach to theology with the more philosophically based empiricism of the later Chicago School. As I have suggested earlier in this essay, this is a fortunate occurrence and represents the base upon which the progress of the discipline depends. Nevertheless I must point out that publications representing this kind of approach have thus far been few, either by Hiltner himself or by those influenced by him.[24]

Publication alone does not, of course, tell the whole story. Several generations of theological students in a dozen or so institutions have been exposed to this general approach in classroom, seminar, and clinic. What the impact of this exposure will be upon them as ministers remains to be seen although there are signs that the conceptual grasp of ministry afforded by the perspectival "two-way street" model contributes to a sense of professional self-confidence in the parish, where it has been so sorely lacking, in that it provides a more adequate understanding of ministry than the models previously available. Using this approach, a minister can provide himself with the conceptual tools to analyze what he is doing moment by moment, even though it does not necessarily tell him what he *should* be doing.

Thus far my focus has been on the stream of pastoral theology to which Hiltner has made the most definitive contributions. Nevertheless no treatment of the topic can omit entirely the developments in Europe and among Roman Catholics. In Switzerland and England we must take note of the emergence of pious (in the best sense of the word) physicians in the field. Paul Tournier is the best known, though Théodore Bovet is in my judgment the more responsible scholar of these two Swiss physicians.[25] Both these writers take seriously the findings of modern psychology and employ them directly in attempting to understand and help persons in distress, in contrast to Eduard Thurneysen, who represents the more normative and strictly theological approach of continental pastoral theology.[26] Among the British physicians who have taken a keen interest in pastoral concerns are Robert A. Lambourne and Frank Lake. Both share a christocentric piety which colors their approaches markedly, although Lambourne is concerned to develop this communally,[27] while Lake, in his monumental *Clinical Theology*, has focused upon the meaning of the suffering and death of Christ for individuals in distress.[28] Lambourne, writing out of a background of general practice and also holding a theological degree, stresses the role of the community in illness and healing while deprecating psychotherapeutic approaches and especially psychoanalysis. Lake, an admitted amateur in theology, presents a wealth of clinical detail from his dual background in parasitology and psychiatry. Despite the fact that his theology is rather narrow and only partially related to his clinical material, he has enriched the literature in the pastoral field by his great knowledge and insight into the early months of life, reflecting the influence of Otto Rank and Melanie Klein.

None of these writers has directly suggested that his work might be useful in constructive theology, although the data presented by Lake in particular and his reflections on them are an important resource for others who are interested in making this kind of contribution.

Although the pastoral care movement is further advanced in the Netherlands (among both Protestants and Catholics) than in any other country in Europe, to date the concentration has been on the training of ministers and priests in pastoral care—or pastoral conversation, as they prefer to put it—rather than upon the development of a pastoral theology of the comprehensive type which could take this into account but move beyond it.[29] In time we may expect that significant contributions will be forthcoming.

In the Roman Catholic tradition pastoral theology has had a more definite and stable meaning than in Protestantism. It referred to the whole work of the priest as a theory of teaching, ruling, and administering the sacraments in a parish—all of which was thought of as the cure of souls (moral and ascetical theology are parallel disciplines). Recent developments have come mostly in the adjunct discipline of pastoral psychology, which undertakes to provide psychological understanding of man's ills and their alleviation in a proximate rather than ultimate sense. Charles Curran, W. C. Bier, Raymond Hostie, and Andre Godin have been among the pioneers in this area. To date, however, they have not ventured into the field of pastoral theology as it is understood in this essay, even though they have made contributions to the field in the sense of applied theology.[30] Outside the pastoral field Catholics have made contributions to the growing literature relating psychology as such to theology. The works of van Kaam and Daim are of more than Catholic interest.[31] However, the gap between pastoral operations understood psychologically and dogmatics is only beginning to be bridged.

III. Pastoral Theology and the Current Crisis in the Church

Before concluding, I shall try to state my understanding of the most crucial issue confronting pastoral theologians, namely the question of how their discipline can make a significant contribution toward reconstruction in theology as a whole. We are all very much aware of the crisis of values in our culture and the fact that the church is participating in this crisis, uncertain of its direction. It is this current crisis that has been in my thinking in insisting that the essentially theological character of pastoral theology must be central to a proper understanding of it. For pastoral theology, alone among theological disciplines at the present time, has both the practical and theoretical resources to make the kind of contribution needed. This is not to say that it is all that needs doing but that it can make the kind of contribution that other theological disciplines need to learn to make: to bring the fruits of critical reflection upon the concrete data of acts of ministry in the church to the task of theological reconstruction.

If pastoral theology is going to do this, however, increased effort and hard thinking on the part of those who profess it are necessary. First there is the problem of trying to define adequately what is meant by pastoral theology. Hiltner's definition, however much it conveys to those who understand the perspectival model, suggests to others that pastoral theology is only a way of looking at something and that it lacks the integrity that data of its own can provide. The term shepherding, too, has proved problematical in some respects. The ordinary usage in Roman Catholic pastoral theology is that "shepherding" refers to the work of the priest as "ruler" of the flock, whereas some writers, like Carroll Wise, have seen in it a regressive image unsuited to an urban culture. The field theory model, upon which the perspectival approach rests, is thought by some to lack the heuristic value it once had, and according to some a new model—drawn perhaps from cybernetics—is needed.[32]

These considerations do not invalidate Hiltner's way of defining the discipline, but because of linguistic shifts and instability, it will be better for the purpose of highlighting the theological character of the discipline to define it more simply as *the study of all aspects of the care of persons in the church in a context of theological inquiry, including implications for other branches of theology*. This definition lacks the precision of the perspectival approach properly understood but avoids the misunderstanding conveyed to many by that language. It emphasizes pastoral theology as inquiry, but does not preclude the drawing of conclusions of a proximate sort as to what is and is not sound ministry to persons. In speaking of aspects rather than perspectives the emphasis is upon the behavior observed, although, to be sure, it still is seen from a certain perspective by means of which it is identified and evaluated.

Now I wish to state briefly three directions in which I think the discipline needs to grow if it is to fulfill its task.

1. Pastoral theologians need to focus more directly upon the *data of ministry* itself rather than upon the data and thinking of other disciplines. This is to say that, in my view, too much attention is being given to "theology and psychology" and not enough to pastoral care and related aspects of ministry. I am convinced that the churches will listen to us much more readily if our focus is upon the ministry itself rather than upon other professional forms, such as psychotherapy, however analogous they may seem, or theoretical formulations, as interesting as they are. This is not a plea for an approach which leaves out scientific understanding but for a use of that understanding in illuminating pastoral work.

Along with this focus on the data of ministry must come increasing sophistication in methods of empirical research. Some pastoral theologians are quite sophisticated in this area already, but others are not. I suspect that one reason there is so much interest in correlational studies involving psychology and theology is that these do not usually involve the entanglement, false starts, and frustration that hypothesis-testing by quantification approaches ordinarily entails. Yet the yield from this kind of study in pastoral theology counts far more in the intertheological marketplace.

2. The need for increased attention to the communal aspects of life in church and society alike is facing us squarely, but we have been slow to rise to the challenge. Our concern is still too much the one-to-one relationship, even though we know we must give attention to group approaches in pastoral care and to the relevance of personal help in a society whose structures are trembling. Wayne Oates has made a beginning in the attempt to explore the relationship between pastoral care and social issue, but he relies primarily on the one-to-one model.[33] We need attention particularly to the ways in which the whole communal (tribal) or affiliative urge of contemporary man affects our understanding of

personal help and how this in turn affects our theological understanding of man. We need also to study the social action field to learn how our understanding of healing is affected by a radical emphasis upon self-giving (not exactly a new idea in our tradition, but one which we have not always held in focus). Joseph Havens has pointed out that our discipline came of age in the waning period of individualism in our culture,[34] and he makes a start toward showing how the pastoral understanding of small-group life can contribute to the needed reconstruction in theology. R. A. Lambourne, while he has not drawn theological implications from his approach, has shown more clearly the full implications of the communal emphasis for pastoral care than has anyone else.[35]

These efforts are obviously only a tiny vista on what is still virtually an unknown territory. But anyone who is in contact with young people knows that the old superego structures and strong sense of drive for individual "self-realization" to which we were wont to appeal (either positively or negatively) are not the same anymore. We must learn to relate to communal man or find that we have by degrees become completely irrelevant.

3. Pastoral theologians will have to become sophisticated philosophically and learn to use their sophistication without apology. Schleiermacher observed over a century ago that the relationship between practical theology and the church is essentially a philosophical question.[36] While many pastoral theologians have acknowledged this insight as true and have been able to use the "right" philosophical language in the company of their peers, they have been hesitant on the whole to come to grips with the epistemological problems inherent in relating the findings of one discipline to others.[37]

My own preference is for the kind of position built upon Whitehead's metaphysics, which is only now coming into its own in theology through the works of John B. Cobb, Schubert Ogden, and Daniel Day Williams, whose recent volume, *The Spirit and the Forms of Love*,[38] should do much to get this point of view clearly before the general theological reader.

Nevertheless pastoral theologians cannot expect such men to do their philosophical homework for them; only they can know the special problems that their discipline presents. No ready-made philosophy is going to meet precisely the particular needs we face in relating disciplines, however suggestive it may be. We must be prepared to dig into these mines to find the one we need and refine it to suit our purposes.

All this adds up to a formidable assignment, and some specialization of interest and function is inevitable, even desirable. Still no one who wishes to be a responsible pastoral theologian will be able to ignore any of the three areas of growth which I have sketched. Only those who feel strongly attracted to the Christian tradition and to the personal values embodied in the pastoral care movement are likely to undertake the task. Yet I believe there are many who sense their responsibility to this hour by virtue of ability, special training, and experience. It is to them that we look with confident expectation.

Notes

1. Seward Hiltner, *Preface to Pastoral Theology* (Nashville: Abingdon Press, 1958), p. 20.
2. *Ibid.*, p. 25.
3. Charles F. Kemp, *Physicians of the Soul: A History of Pastoral Counseling* (New York: Macmillan, 1947); John T. McNeill, *The History of the Cure of Souls* (New York: Harper, 1951); William A. Clebsch and Charles R. Jaekle, *Pastoral Care in Historical Perspective* (Englewood Cliffs, N.J.: Prentice-Hall, 1964).
4. J. J. Van Oosterzee, *Practical Theology* (New York: Scribner's, 1878).
5. W. G. T. Shedd, *Homiletics and Pastoral Theology* (New York: Scribner's, 1867).
6. Cf. e.g., John Watson, *The Cure of Souls* (New York: Dodd, Mead, 1896).
7. John G. Mackenzie, *Souls in the Making: An Introduction to Pastoral Psychology* (New York: Macmillan, 1929).
8. William Goulooze, *Pastoral Psychology: Applied Psychology in Pastoral Theology in America* (Grand Rapids: Baker Book House, 1950).
9. Clement F. Rogers, *An Introduction to the Study of Pastoral Theology* (Oxford: Clarendon Press, 1912), p. 36. In this connection he used the phrase "a student of human documents," p. 96.
10. *Ibid.*, p. 99.
11. F. E. Schleiermacher, *Pracktishe Theologie* (Berlin: G. Reimer, 1850). For information regarding this work, including the translation of portions of it into

English, I am indebted to Donald A. Groskreutz, whose A.M. thesis at the University of Chicago (1958) consisted of a careful study of this work and translation of parts of it.

12. Donald A. Groskreutz, "A Critical Study of Frederick Schleiermacher as a Pastoral Theologian" (A.M. thesis, University of Chicago, 1958), p. 22.
13. *Ibid.*, p. 22.
14. Hiltner, *Preface to Pastoral Theology*, p. 51.
15. Anton T. Boisen, *The Exploration of the Inner World: A Study of Mental Disorder and Religious Experience* (New York: Willett, Clark & Co., 1937).
16. Paul E. Johnson, *Psychology of Religion* (rev. ed.; Nashville: Abingdon Press, 1959), and *Personality and Religion* (Abingdon Press, 1957).
17. C. A. Wise, *Religion in Illness and Health* (New York: Harper, 1942); *Psychiatry and the Bible* (Harper, 1956).
18. C. A. Wise, *The Meaning of Pastoral Care* (New York: Harper, 1966), p. 40.
19. Wayne E. Oates, *The Bible in Pastoral Care* (Philadelphia: Westminster Press, 1953); *The Christian Pastor* (rev. ed.; Westminster Press, 1964).
20. Wayne E. Oates, *Protestant Pastoral Counseling* (Philadelphia: Westminster Press, 1962).
21. However, he does use it in discussing the needed response to the crisis of pastoral care (*Protestant Pastoral Counseling*, pp. 23-34).
22. E.g., his discussion of "time," pp. 113-16.
23. E.g., *Protestant Pastoral Counseling*, pp. 38-39.
24. Perhaps the clearest embodiment of Hiltner's approach which he set forth in *Preface to Pastoral Theology*, written by himself, is in his article "Clinical and Theological Notes on Responsibility," *Journal of Religion and Health*, October, 1962, pp. 7-20. James G. Emerson's two volumes, *Divorce, the Church and Remarriage* (Philadelphia: Westminster Press, 1961), and *The Dynamics of Forgiveness* (Westminster Press, 1964), are both partially reflective of Hiltner's approach, despite Emerson's explicit redefinition of pastoral theology to pertain to the whole work of the parish in the second of these (pp. 24 ff.). I have contributed one article which was intended as an essay in pastoral theology in the sense in which we have been using the term, that is, an inquiry beginning with a theological question, moving to pastoral data interpreted with the help of the personality sciences, and attempting to answer the original question in the light of these data ("Reconciliation, Forgiveness, Lost Contracts," *Theology Today*, April, 1966). Don S. Browning's *Atonement and Psychotherapy* (Westminster Press, 1966) embodies the spirit of this approach, although the data employed are psychotherapeutic rather than pastoral, and Kenneth R. Mitchell has applied aspects of this approach to the problem of multiple-staff relationships—an issue in the "organizing" perspective (*Psychological and Theological Relationships in the Multiple Staff Ministry* [Westminster Press, 1965]). This account is not necessarily exhaustive but does include most contributions related to the pastoral theology of Hiltner's *Preface*. The commemorative volume, *The Dialogue Between Theology and Psychology*, Vol. III, edited by Peter Homans (Chicago: University of Chicago Press, 1968), contains contributions that are somewhat related, but for the most part they deal with the relationships between theology and psychology without reference to pastoral operations. The contributions of Charles Stinnette, Joseph Havens, and LeRoy Aden are the most germane. Edward E. Thornton, although a student of Oates rather than Hiltner, produced a book which in several respects reflects a dialogical point of view (*Theology and Pastoral Counseling* [Englewood Cliffs, N.J.: Prentice-Hall, 1964]).

25. Théodor Bovet, *The Road to Salvation: A Handbook on the Christian Care of Persons,* trans. F. A. Baker (Garden City, N.Y.: Doubleday, 1964).
26. Eduard Thurneysen, A *Theology of Pastoral Care* (Richmond: John Knox Press, 1962).
27. Robert A. Lambourne, *Church, Community and Healing* (London: Darton, Longman, & Todd, 1963).
28. Frank Lake, *Clinical Theology* (London: Darton, Longman, & Todd, 1966).
29. E.g., Heije Faber and Ebel van der Schoot, *The Art of Pastoral Conversation* (Nashville: Abingdon Press, 1965).
30. E.g., Andre Godin's *The Pastor as Counselor* (New York: Holt, Rinehart & Winston, 1965) has been well received by Catholics and Protestants alike.
31. Adrian Van Kaam, *Religion and Personality* (Englewood Cliffs, N.J.: Prentice-Hall, 1964); Wilfried Daim, *Depth Psychology and Salvation,* trans. Kurt F. Reinhardt (New York: Frederick Ungar, 1963).
32 Coval B. MacDonald, personal communication. MacDonald is presenting his approach to method elsewhere in this volume.
33. Wayne E. Oates, *Pastoral Counseling in Social Problems: Extremism, Race, Sex, Divorce* (Philadelphia: Westminster Press, 1966).
34. Joseph Havens, "Religious Awareness in Small Groups: Warmth vs. enlightenment," in Homans, *The Dialogue Between Theology and Psychology,* III, 263-84.
35. Lambourne, *Church, Community and Healing.*
36. Groskreutz, "Critical Study of Frederick Schleiermacher," p. 9.
37. This is a strong point of the volume in the series commemorating the one hundredth anniversary of the Divinity School of the University of Chicago (Homans, *Dialogue Between Theology and Psychology,* III) though as has been noted, this volume focused more upon the relations between psychology and theology as disciplines rather than upon pastoral theology.
38. Daniel Day Williams, *The Spirit and the Forms of Love* (New York: Harper, 1968).

Pastoral Theology and Pastoral Care Overseas

Graeme M. Griffin

In recent decades both the practice of pastoral care and theological reflection upon that practice have received new impetus, taken new forms, and forged new directions. And this phenomenon is worldwide. It need no longer surprise us to find a pastoral counseling service in Singapore or in Scandinavia, nor yet to hear that a supervisor in Korea has received his own clinical training in Japan and that a New Zealand lecturer in pastoral theology received his in Australia. In 1968 the Scottish Pastoral Association has increased its operating branches to twelve, and the Clinical Theology Association in Great Britain has enrolled over 1,000 persons, mainly clergy, in its seminar courses. A clear index of the extent of this concern is the fact that the American Association of Pastoral Counselors has been able to place nearly one hundred names on its list of international affiliates, persons working in some identifiable way in the field of pastoral counseling in twenty-one countries and five continents outside North America.

The literature reflects this new internationalism. One of the best recent textbooks in pastoral conversation has come to us from Holland,[1] and a new and locally produced work on pastoral care will shortly be available in the Thai language.[2] One British publisher has already issued four titles (with another five in course of preparation) in a "Library of Pastoral Care,"[3] and journals have appeared in both Britain and Australia. And these are only samplings.

A great deal of this resurgence of interest is directly traceable to the pastoral care movement in the United States—and the closely associated development of clinical pastoral training there. The writings and personal travels of leading figures in this movement have excited interest overseas and attracted students to the U. S. This influence has perhaps been most strongly felt in Asia and in Australasia but is also apparent, alongside the relatively independent local movements, in both Great Britain and Europe generally. Thus, for example, when Heije Faber and Ebel van der Schoot published *Het Pastorale Gesprek* in 1962, it was "a first attempt in a European country to stimulate interest in the problems of pastoral conversations and the possibilities contained in the 'clinical training' movement." [4] The book was widely and well received in Europe as, indeed, the English translation has been outside Europe since its release in 1965. Similarly, and at about the same time, Ian McIntosh was building on his American experience in a pioneering development of clinical training in a parish context in England.[5]

I

These comments are unabashedly written from the point of view of an Australian working in the field in his own country and with all the advantages and disadvantages that follow from such geographical detachment. This may help account both for some notable omissions from the story and for some strange emphases. But an Australian point of view cannot be fully appreciated without some background to the Australian situation—and this will also help orient us to the position of pastoral theology in the antipodes.

A. G. L. Shaw has written, "This is the century of the common man, and perhaps in Australia he attained his goal earlier than in other countries. Here he has created his society." [6] This comment provides an essential clue to an understanding of Australian life, including the life of her churches. For generations Australians have harbored a deep suspicion of the highly educated, the intellectual, the expert, the specialist, the original thinker, and indeed any nonconformist to the pattern of "the common man." Although now breaking down under the sheer pressures of the twentieth century, this attitude has by no means disappeared. The romantic illusions of equality and "mateship," derived from the rigors of life in "the bush," assumed an almost religious intensity at precisely that point in her history when the bush was no longer typical of an Australia in process of becoming one of the most urbanized of all societies.

Alongside this there rapidly developed the conviction that anything imported must be, *ipso facto,* superior to the local product —but never immune to either criticism or suspicion by virtue of its very foreignness. These basic insecurities have been firmly woven into the national life-style.

One of the earliest victims of the egalitarian spirit was the Church of England's monopoly on religion and education. In the mid-1800's anti-clerical liberals, opposed to privilege, autocracy, and all the other abuses (real or imagined) thought to flow from the English social system, found common cause with the free immigrant adherents of the national churches of Scotland (Presbyterian) and Ireland (Roman Catholic) and of the dissenting churches of England. Without losing their suspicion of each other they were united in their opposition to Anglican domination. Part of the price paid by the sectarians for their share in this "victory" was the gradual secularization of the colony through its educational institutions.

One important consequence of this was that theological studies were deliberately excluded from the curricula of Australian universities from their foundation—and continue to be so to this day with only minor exceptions. The result has been the proliferation of small theological colleges on a denominational basis, inadequately staffed and financed (a familiar complaint elsewhere) and tending to be on the periphery of the critical interdisciplinary exchanges characteristic of a university context at its best. There is, for example, only one Australian theological college (Protestant or Anglican) which has so far given evidence of meeting the fairly modest standards for accredited membership of the Association of Theological Schools in South-East Asia.[7] Some of the Roman Catholic seminaries are rather better endowed with resources, but it is only now that any real planning for cooperation between Catholic and non-Catholic training institutions is taking place. No seminary is able to offer a regular program of studies beyond the B.D. level, and for many years only the Presbyterian Church and the Society of Jesus normally expected that men entering their theological training would have undergone at least three years of prior university training.

These factors have tended to inhibit the development of any vigorous and indigenous style in theological thought. The issues for debate and controversy have largely been imported along with the traditions which have shaped the stance to be taken on the issues. Or at least so it has been with pastoral theology.

Up until the 1950's one could more or less accurately judge the state of pastoral theology in Australia by asking what that state had been a decade or so previously in England (for the Anglicans and Methodists), in Scotland (for the Presbyterians), and in Ireland or Rome (for the Roman Catholics). These four denominations make up nearly 90 percent of the local church population.

From England we had learned to appreciate that modern psychology may have something to contribute to the practice of pastoral care. Leslie Weatherhead, for example, mentions no fewer than eight different Anglican and Methodist movements in Britain between 1905 and 1946 which shared something of this conviction.[8] In Australia an Anglican medical practitioner, W. L. Carrington, was lecturing to a small group of theological students as early as 1940 and introducing both European and American insights on psychotherapy into his course on "pastoral psychology and practice."[9] One early vision which may have resulted in a genuine pastoral theology was dimmed with the untimely death of John F. Williams, who had secured medical and psychiatric training following his ordination as a Methodist minister and had planned an integration of these disciplines in his ministry.

But from Britain also we had learned a certain reticence, and many a minister could appreciate the words of a Scottish writer who said in 1947, "We are a shy race, and our people do not naturally open their hearts to their pastor or come to him in difficulty." The same writer spoke very hesitantly of the acknowledged responsibility for "spiritual guidance and direction of souls" and warned his ministerial colleagues to use what psychological knowledge they might have "only as a help to know the 'anatomy of the soul.'"[10] Thus when Eduard Thurneysen's great work, *Die Lehre von der Seelsorge,* was translated into English as *A Theology of Pastoral Care* in 1962,[11] many found articulated for the first time a basic methodological position which they had long held. Implicitly or explicitly they too had placed "all responsibility for communication on the Holy Spirit,"[12] and what little pastoral theology was taught in non-Catholic theological colleges in Australia tended firmly to be under the domination of homiletics. In the Roman Catholic tradition the liturgy and the sacraments of the church provided the focus for pastoral concern.

In the 1950's the Church of England in Australia began to recognize the possibilities of clinical pastoral training on the American model for the Australian scene. This church already had a long tradition of supervised in-service training with its curacy system and a compulsory three years of postordination training, and it was becoming clear that supervision was a task requiring special skills and training. In 1956 W. H. Graham visited the United States for both training and investigation. Subsequently two priests from the same diocese of Melbourne have acquired supervisory credentials. A small group of other clergy have since experienced clinical training in the States and returned to chaplaincy positions. Others received a rather similar order of training with the marriage guidance movement.

Thus a clinical dimension began to enter into the training of clergy and the experience of chaplains in hospitals and other institutions. By the time of the second National Clergy-Doctor Conference in Adelaide (1966) elements of clinical training were in evidence in four of the six states of the commonwealth and in all major denominations. But these were still largely pilot programs, and the great majority of clergy and theological students have had no exposure to them. It was not until 1967 that anything as extensive and intensive as the basic thirteen week full-time clinical training course could be offered anywhere in Australia. This program, at the Austin Hospital in Melbourne under the supervision of Chaplain Roy Bradley, is recognized by the Association for Clinical Pastoral Education in the United States.

A major boost was given by the visit of Seward Hiltner in 1959. This opened up in a serious way the possibility of a "new style" pastoral theology to inform, undergird, and learn from the reawakened concern for pastoral care. In distinction to Thurneysen, Hiltner sought to derive theological insights from the participation in and examination of particular human situations—experiences of "shepherding"—illuminated by whatever disciplines may contribute to their understanding. He argued for a facing up to the problems of communication in the caring situation and was against both imperial subjection and pretensions among theological disciplines.[13] His visit was followed in due course by visits from Granger Westberg and Howard Clinebell, who each brought his own inspiration. One direct consequence of the Hiltner visit was that the writer, an Australian Presbyterian minister, completed the doctoral program in pastoral theology at Princeton Theological Seminary and returned to Australia in 1964 to teach. Among other things this has assisted in keeping clinical pastoral training in touch with seminary teaching and vice versa.

Meanwhile the Barthian sun was going into eclipse in Europe, and the voice of Paul Tillich was being heeded there and heard in Australia. Where Thurneysen had wished to preserve a sense of a great gulf fixed between "natural exploration and experience of our life" and that knowledge of man derived "through Christ" which alone has final theological validity,[14] Tillich was acutely aware of the existential questions arising from culture and sought to correlate these with answers derived from the revelation. The basic methodological positions of Thurneysen, Hiltner, and Tillich remain the major significant and articulated positions, so far as I can determine, both within the United States and beyond its shores.

In 1961 Francis Macnab, another Presbyterian minister, returned to Australia after doctoral studies in Aberdeen. His book *Estrangement and Relationship*,[15] based on his experience with schizophrenic patients and their relatives in a Scottish hospital, makes effective use of Tillich's correlational method. It also goes a long way toward meeting the traditional American criticisms of British or European ventures in pastoral theology. It is concrete; the theological and psychological reflection is firmly anchored to the therapeutic situation in which the author was involved, and he displays no reluctance to explore and present for criticism by others the nature of his own involvement in the dynamics of the process. On his return Macnab founded the Cairnmillar Institute,[16] a very exciting marriage between a local congregation and a psychiatric and pastoral clinic with an educational mission. In 1964 the Cairnmillar Institute commenced publication of *The Journal of Societal Issues* "for all concerned with counseling and total care."

Since then two other significant steps have been taken toward the further development of pastoral theological thought. One was the establishment in 1967 of a full professorial chair in the area of pastoral theology in the Theological Hall at Ormond College.[17] The other was the inclusion for the first time of a subject entitled "Theology of Pastoral Care" in the syllabus of studies for the B.D. degree at the Melbourne College of Divinity (one of only three bodies in the country to award this degree) and the receipt by the same college of a first doctoral thesis in the area.[18]

II

The taking over of insights from one culture to another is not without its dangers or difficulties. Medicine is not the only discipline to come up against problems of rejection in transplantation. Different traditions can prove massive obstacles. Both Hiltner and Faber have explored, deftly and briefly, the differences between the American and the European scenes[19] so that need not detain us here. But in Asia, where Christianity itself is seen as an import from the West, other problems arise. Two examples must suffice.

A seminary professor in Thailand reports that the shortage of pastors there makes it very hard to develop any real concept of pastoral work and to give theological students opportunities for adequate field education. But at a more fundamental level the traditional Thai society is built around a concept of human nature and of community which is different from that of Western culture. The Buddhist priest is not usually thought of as a "pastor" in the Western sense and "doesn't ordinarily think of himself as the one to whom a congregation has been committed. . . . The traditional way of meeting problems in Thai society is to withdraw from them and try to find an inner core of peace. The withdrawal is usually done without much concern for the other party or parties involved." [20]

In Singapore also the local culture has forced modification in the pattern of pastoral caring although here it is interesting to observe that another American model has been substituted for the earlier Rogers-with-a-dash-of-Freud approach. Writing immediately prior to his return to the U. S. after spending a year as clinical director with the Churches' Counseling Service in Singapore, Chester A. Raber comments: "With the Asian authoritarian system so deeply forming the structure of life here, there is simply insufficient time by the tremendous press on the counselor and insufficient internal motivation and courage in the counselees and too little experience of 'caring' in the whole society for the client-centered approach to work. Clinebell's approach is much more useful and possible here." [21]

Australia, of course, is Western and does not share these particular cultural features with her Asian neighbors. Indeed she is tempted to ignore the fact that Asia and New Zealand are closer neighbors than either Europe or America! But Australia has her own problems. Churchgoing is not a fashionable activity here, and while the reticence of people to speak to their pastors has proved largely illusory (if the pastor demonstrates that he can listen), there remains a strong residue of the "stiff upper lip" philosophy. In my judgment the suspicion is greater here than, say, in America, that to seek help is an unfortunate admission of weakness. Provincialism and denominationalism have taken their toll, and already one of our very few pastoral theologians has felt himself forced back to the United States. The men who are currently receiving advanced training overseas can have no guarantees that there will be either structures or positions open to them within which they can make best use of their qualifications on their return.

But difficulties also breed possibilities, and one local experiment, now in its fourth year, deserves mention. On one-half day a week (four hours for each of some twenty-five weeks) a group of twenty-four ministers and deaconesses in parish and chaplaincy appointments in Victoria meet for "training in pastoral consultation." These weekly sessions feature clinical group experiences based on the students' own verbatim reports of pastoral contacts made in the context of their own ministries. They also include straight didactic elements (both psychological and theological) and a further group experience with more directly therapeutic goals. This particular coat has been cut from the available supervisory cloth and has now expanded to the point where second and third years of training are offered and a group of six locally trained supervisors will shortly graduate.

We may hope that the emerging openness of theologians the world over to the possibilities of genuine dialogue between theology and secular disciplines may lead to some more direct confrontation of the methodological issues in pastoral theology in the near future. In this connection it is of more than passing interest to observe the experience of the Western European and Northern American Working Groups on "The Missionary Structure of the Congregation," as reported in the W.C.C. publication *The Church for Others*. While the Western European group approached the subject in a more formal and traditionally "theological" manner than the North Americans, "the theological developments shared by both groups kept pushing them both toward a process of 'reflection-upon-action.'" Regional characteristics did not become lost in this process—the reflective side was still more dominant in the European approach, and the "arenas of action" made more immediate appeal to the Americans—but the stress is laid in the reports on "the remarkable commonality of theological emphases between the two groups" and their genuine openness to the sociological discipline.[22] The recent W.C.C. consultation on "The Teaching of Practical Theology" also points hopefully toward a new era of mutual communication and respect.[23] Both these documents are being studied with interest in Australia.

Local exposure to American thought and style, both Hiltnerian and Tillichian, is likely to minimize the impact here of Frank Lake's monumental new work on *Clinical Theology*.[24] His presentation lacks neither case material nor some awareness of the limitations imposed by the counselor himself on the helping process. But these things tend to be spoken *about* rather than confronted in their concreteness in the manner we have come to look for and expect. Some important insights, both theological and psychological, are hidden by sheer prolixity, and the total effect illustrates what the American worker in the field, in his more bloody-minded moments, regards as "typically British." It is still tempting for the Australian to operate pastorally with the right hand and theologically with the left, but it is no longer the only available option.

Theological awareness of a secular world is breaking down the old suspicion that pastoral counseling in the American mode is necessarily ambiguous in its setting forth of the claims of Christ and the gospel. We in Australia await with interest reports of the recent conference between American and British pastoral counselors and theologians;[25] at the same time we also look forward to the development of our own style suitable for our own situation. But we have learned we cannot do that in isolation. Meanwhile the peculiar status of pastoral theology here may be summed up in the comment from the chair at a recent meeting of chaplains at which the present writer presented a paper on forgiveness. The chairman, an experienced chaplain, summed up his feelings by saying, "We have all heard many talks on forgiveness before, but we have never heard anything like that!" The remark is capable of other interpretations, but the lecturer chooses to believe that any uniqueness the paper may have possessed arose from its being—in intent at least—theological as well as both pastoral and clinical. The hopeful sign is that, like Oliver, they asked for more.

Notes

1. Heije Faber and Ebel van der Schoot, *The Art of Pastoral Conversation* (Nashville: Abingdon Press, 1965).
2. Thailand Theological Seminary, Chiang Mai, is hoping to publish in book form a series of lectures by Wichean Watakicharoen, general secretary of the Church of Christ in Thailand.
3. S.P.C.K. Titles include Norman Autton, *The Pastoral Care of the Bereaved,* 1967.
4. Faber and van der Schoot, *Art of Pastoral Conversation,* p. 12.
5. Ian F. McIntosh, "Clinical Training in the Parish," *Pastoral Psychology,* April, 1966.
6. A. G. L. Shaw, *The Story of Australia* (2nd ed.; London: Faber & Faber, 1962), p. 297. Gordon Greenwood, ed., *Australia: A Social and Political History* (Sydney: Angus and Robertson, 1955) confirms the basic historical sketch outlined here. Shaw's work in particular is an excellent introduction for the general reader.
7. Ormond College, the Presbyterian theological college in Melbourne. The standards include six full-time faculty members and a working library of at least 5,000 volumes. See G. M. Griffin, "The Making of a Minister," in *The Age* (newspaper, Melbourne), April 5 and April 19, 1968.
8. Leslie D. Weatherhead, *Psychology, Religion, and Healing* (Nashville: Abingdon Press, 1952), pp. 222 ff.
9. The substance of these lectures was subsequently published in W. L. Carrington, *Psychology, Religion, and Human Need* (London: Epworth Press, 1957).
10. J. W. Baird, "Congregational and Parish Work," *The Minister's Manual,* ed. W. S. Buchan (Edinburgh: Church of Scotland Committee on Publications, 1947), pp. 116 ff.
11. Eduard Thurneysen, A *Theology of Pastoral Care,* trans. J. Worthington *et al.* (Richmond: John Knox Press, 1962).
12. The phrase comes from the Report (duplicated, n.d.) of an ecumenical consultation on "The Teaching of Practical Theology" held at Bossey, Switzerland, August, 1967. One group listed the reaction against this type of thinking as a significant factor in bringing practical theology into focus today (p. 12).
13. See e.g. Hiltner's *Preface to Pastoral Theology.*
14. Thurneysen, *Theology of Pastoral Care,* pp. 62 ff.
15. Francis Macnab, *Estrangement and Relationship* (Bloomington: Indiana University Press, 1966).

16. The name of the Institute itself strikes an interprofessional note. It was named for Macnab's mentors in Aberdeen: David Cairns, professor of practical theology, and W. M. Millar, professor of mental health.
17. The only other full-time position in the field in Australasia was created in 1967 in New Zealand.
18. Theological degrees in Australia are not awarded by the teaching seminaries but rather by outside examining bodies. The majority of theological students would not take out a B.D. since it requires another degree as a prerequisite.
19. Seward Hiltner, "Theology and Pastoral Care in the United States," *Pastoral Psychology*, November, 1967, pp. 15-21 (reprinted from *Theologische Literaturzeitung*, LXXXVIII (1963), 502.); H. Faber, *Pastoral Care and Clinical Training in America* (Arnhem: Van Loghum Slaterus, 1961).
20. Personal communication to the writer.
21. Personal communication to the writer. The reference is to Howard Clinebell, *Basic Types of Pastoral Counseling* (Nashville: Abingdon Press, 1966). The permanent staff of the Churches' Counseling Service are western, but a genuine effort is being made to train Asian counselors and assist in the training of local pastors.
22. *The Church for Others: Two Reports on the Missionary Structure of the Congregation* (final report of the Western European Working Group and Northern American Working Group of the Department of Studies in Evangelism; Geneva: World Council of Churches, 1967), pp. 57-58.
23. This consultation brought together persons engaged in practical theology, including pastoral theology, from Great Britain, Europe, Africa, Asia, and North America. See also note 12 above.
24. Frank Lake, *Clinical Theology* (London: Darton, Longman & Todd, 1966). The more than 1,100 pages of this book are devoted to the subject matter presented in the first twelve seminars of the courses conducted by the Clinical Theology Association in Great Britain. Some thousands of clergy have attended these courses since 1962.
25. Organized by the American Association of Pastoral Counselors in conjunction with the Clinical Theology Association, the Scottish Pastoral Association, and the Institute of Religion and Medicine for Summer, 1968.

Modern Pastoral Theology and the Christian Tradition

Donald A. Groskreutz

It seems plainly indicated that there is a widespread consensus among prominent and responsible spokesmen in the field that there exists a historically identifiable "modern pastoral theology." The appearance of this volume rests on that assumption. Just as self-evident, it seems clear, is the fact that the subject of "tradition" has become the focus of considerable attention in contemporary theology, together with the fact that at least one necessary implication of this term is a reference to the historic past that is sharply in contrast with what is referred to as modern.

My purpose in this essay is to show that there is also a basic interrelation between "modern pastoral theology" and the Christian "tradition," the investigation and interpretation of which can contribute depth, power, and meaning to both without compromising the integrity, truth, value, or meaning of either. The elaboration of this thesis is predicated on the assumption that it is a theological discussion[1] and that in our reference to modern pastoral theology and the Christian tradition we are not working only with theological concepts but also with the realities of history.[2]

I. Preliminary Definitions

To clarify the discussion we shall begin with a definitive description of the major constitutive elements that comprise the content of modern pastoral theology and of the Christian tradition as we refer to them in this discussion.

By "modern pastoral theology" we mean to refer to a historical theological discipline. We define it as the study of the theory and practice of the Christian affirmation of the fundamental reality and value, as well as concern for the wholeness and well-being, of *persons*.[3] We regard it as an inherently theological discipline and assert that what makes pastoral theology distinctively and truly modern includes at least the following:

1. The implementation of pastoral concern in accordance with the best information, insights, and understandings of both needs and available resources for meeting those needs, irrespective of the specific historical identity of the source. The "best" here refers to freedom of discussion and inquiry, the need for clarification and identification of needs, the identification and development of pastoral resources and technical skills, and the value of research and of openness to its results. It assumes a dialogical understanding of interprofessional relationships with the freedom and responsibility to explore and to clarify issues and relationships between the "secular" and the "religious." It thus posits fundamentally a dialogical understanding of the relation between faith and culture, and it assumes that the fundamental intention of all dialogue in which pastoral theology is involved is the attainment of clarity, understanding, and appropriate activity toward the fulfillment of objectives implied in the definition of pastoral theology.

2. The programing and actualization of pastoral work in a context of mutually informative inter- and intraprofessional and inter- and intradisciplinary relationships. This includes a notable reference to the standing of pastoral theology as one among other specialized aspects of the total complex of theological disciplines, as well as to the clinical professions, especially of psychiatry, clinical psychology, and social work and to the medical and nursing sciences and professions. This assertion refers us to a team concept of pastoral ministry that is expressive of the pastoral concern and work of a historically extant Judeo-Christian community. It also assumes responsibility for the clarification of basic theological issues and concerns in this context. It thus sets before us the chal-

lenge of making good the inference that our own pastoral concern and ministry are also the concern and ministry of the historic Judeo-Christian community, in the face of the exigencies and vicissitudes of the concrete processes of living and working.

3. Predication of pastoral work in view of the pluralism of contemporary culture that emanates in a pluralism of constitutive elements and vital forces comprising the content of personal life, a pluralism of contemporary society, and a pluralism of religious institutions and theological viewpoints. This pluralistic culture becomes the historical arena in which the theory and practice of pastoral work are developed and actualized. To illustrate, this includes among other things a phenomenologically honest interpretation of the life and work of Sigmund Freud in conjunction with the affirmation of the responsibility to set forth the meaning of pastoral theology in a unified and communicable way, as *theology*[4] in the fundamental sense of the term. It also includes the positing of the theory and practice of pastoral care, including pastoral counseling, in an awareness of the fluidity of a contemporary dynamic society. This implies the task of a disciplined attention to the dynamics of personal development as focused in the dynamics of social change.

This brief description of what is meant here by modern pastoral theology may seem variously too inclusive or too exclusive. I am aware that there are versions of pastoral theology on the contemporary scene that could not be included, but my point is that they are not "modern" in the distinctive sense of that term. Much that might be included has been omitted, but I think it is also clear that much more could be said by way of an elaboration of this brief description. Whatever modern pastoral theology is, I am saying, it is at least this.

Any approach to the concept of Christian tradition is beset by a host of complex problems arising out of the accumulated complexities of historical discussions of the subject. Ignoring all this complexity for the moment, and at the risk of some oversimplification, I offer the following descriptive assertions about the way in which we refer to the Christian "tradition" here:

1. The primary meaning of the word, as disclosed in its derivation from the Greek, is a reference to "that which is handed over" or to "that which is passed on." We shall adhere closely to this meaning of the term as we use it in this discussion.

2. The "Christian tradition" as it is used here refers indiscriminately to all that is identified as the heritage of the past, all that which is "passed on" from the past to the present by all those who identify themselves as Christians. The term therefore does not include the assertion of a claim to supremacy, exclusiveness or authenticity of a particular version of what Christianity is, in antithesis to other versions. It includes the Scriptures, religious institutions, rituals, symbols, creeds, written documents, stored historical knowledge and information, liturgical forms, physical structures and property, religious orders, beliefs, attitudes, unwritten content that is transmitted orally, and other elements comprising the identifiable historical continuity of Christianity in its totality.

3. The "Christian tradition," it will become clear, refers not to a whole but to a totality. What makes the diversity of content that is referred to by this concept *a totality* is that it includes everything that is explicitly identified as being handed over from past to present by those who identify themselves as Christians and thus that it is all considered the result in some way or another of the historical reality and influence of a person—Jesus of Nazareth. One might add that the wholeness of this totality is to be understood in relation to the contemporary historical reality of the person of Jesus, but only with the qualification that the place and significance of all the diversified content of the Christian tradition in relation to this personal presence remain far from clear. When we are dealing with the Christian tradition, therefore, we are dealing with a totality, the wholeness of which is a matter of concern.

4. But the Christian tradition is not simply "something," or an aggregate of things which are handed over and which assume the character of accumulated property. It refers us not only to what is passive and impersonal but also to that which actively influences

us in a personal way. It determines the course and shape of our lives. The Christian tradition refers us fundamentally to a person who is the source of its accumulated variegation, whose identity is always involved somehow in that which is handed over, and so fundamentally a person who gives himself as he is presented in the passing on that takes place as the Christian tradition. The historical person of Jesus thus becomes the essential reality in which is given the wholeness as well as the intent of the diverse elements of the content of the Christian tradition, in relation to whom the unity of the Christian tradition is sought and given in the study and contemporary interpretation of the Christian tradition.

With this discussion of our preliminary description of the meaning of the two concepts in the background, our attention turns to a consideration of some of the possible relations between modern pastoral theology and the Christian tradition.

II. Some Possible Relations

A consideration of possibilities as to the kind of relation that is posited theologically between modern pastoral theology and the Christian tradition discloses at least the following alternatives:

1. *Traditionalism.* The reality of tradition sometimes assumes such proportions that it becomes the overarching and exclusive determinant of authority, social sanction and structure, personal integration, and the like. The "tradition-directed" social character of David Riesman[5] is one in which social systems and institutions as well as individuals tend to be dominated in a pervasive way on the basis of a simplistic reference to the established way of doing things, which is understood as being carried on in a unilateral way from the past through the present without a significant reference to the passage of time or the occurrence of change. It will be readily apparent that such a concept of tradition is inimical to the way in which we have conceived it here. Moreover, a relationship between tradition and modern pastoral theology becomes virtually unthinkable, for such a concept of tradition stands un-

alterably opposed to anything that is specifically identified as modern. The assertion of tradition in this sense leaves the only thinkable mode of the relation between it and modern pastoral theology as one in which the "modern" in pastoral theology is continually eradicated or expunged.

2. *Anti-traditionalism.* Another option is to reject the legitimacy of any notion of tradition whatever in favor of an appeal to modernity. That this also plunges us into a methodological dilemma can be exhibited in the fact that when this alternative is chosen, the understanding of not having a tradition, including sometimes the aphorism "we have no tradition," tends to assume the character of tradition itself, being handed over from one to another among those who thus identify themselves. Furthermore, it becomes a fairly easy matter to point to attitudes, practices, policies, institutions, and beliefs, etc., which are in fact "handed over" and comprise a tradition even when the existence of a tradition is denied. Observation thus teaches us that tradition is inevitable, even though in given instances its denial eliminates the concept that is appropriate to what it involves. The assertion "we have no tradition" becomes in fact a negative tradition which rests on the more basic positive assertion of the reality of tradition, against which it traditionally aligns itself. Another problem that arises is that such a stance tends to identify something as modern without a sufficient methodological basis for determining with clarity what it really is about it that is modern, or that it refers to change and the changing world without sufficient reference to the constancy on the basis of which change itself is perceived. The result is that constant change exhibits a sameness which tends to deprive change of its significance, with a concomitant loss of power and depth that leads to a kind of monotony. The investigation of this alternative hence leads us to the decisive conclusion that there is but one alternative to a good concept of tradition in theological method, i.e., a poor one.

3. *Objectified Tradition.* The historical continuity of Christian faith and life has cometimes been referred to in terms of objectified tradition, usually alongside other objectified source constit-

uents of Christian history such as church, scripture, the episcopacy, confessions, the papacy, or some divinely inspired extra-scriptural book. Sometimes the implication is that the continuity of tradition in this sense is a historical positivism involving a mere and self-contained technical competence of a theologian who is working with objective sources or deposits. Where tradition is conceived alongside other such authoritative sources in the past, the others are always necessarily conceived of as being something more or other than tradition and thus stand in various combinations of authoritative and functional relation to it. This conception also stands in sharp antinomy to the Christian tradition as we have conceived it here. The objectification of tradition by itself is simply a contemporary and sometimes sophisticated repristination of traditionalism. The objectification or reference to other authoritative sources from the past alongside or exclusive of tradition represents a false abstraction from the totality of what is being handed over. As a result it obscures the clarification of what in fact really is in specific historical situations being handed over. Because it marks a departure from the time progression that is implied in the word tradition, reference to other concepts alongside tradition creates a vantage point above time and a built-in ambivalance toward anything that is identified as progress or modern. One could also ask whether the methodological separation of authoritative constituents from the past from the reality of what is in fact being passed on obscures the true humanity of Christian history, the true humanity of Christian life and of the church, and thus assumes the character of Docetism. Anyway, our investigation of this alternative has led to the conclusion that it leaves us amid an unresolved ambivalence and even ambiguity as to the relation of the Christian tradition to modern pastoral theology. Most crucially from the standpoint of our definition, it misses the issue of understanding and interpreting everything that is handed over as a reference to the one whose influence is thus historically expressed and whose intention it is freely to give himself in the handing over of the contents of the Christian tradition.

4. *Personalized Tradition.* An alternative we will suggest in the hope that it may prove more viable is to propose that in every instance of an actual relation between modern pastoral theology and the Christian tradition we have the occasion of a *personal transaction,* which is always in a basic sense simultaneously intrapersonal and interpersonal in dimension and scope. To make this assertion is not to deny the reality of the transpersonal in the organization of bodies of knowledge, in community organization and action, in the constituency of culture and of the forces of nature, or in the reality of God, and therefore also of the totality of the influence of that which we have identified as the Christian tradition. It is merely to affirm that the reality and category of the personal is fundamental to our understanding of the interrelation between pastoral theology today and the Christian tradition. This interpretation enables us to make the following assertions:

a. The reality of tradition and the deployment of a concept of the Christian tradition as a fundamental theological concept can be affirmed without prejudice to the contemporaneity of tradition and without prejudice to the modernity of contemporary pastoral theology. It recognizes the determinacy, whatever it be, that is indicated in the totalistic reference of the Christian tradition as we have defined it. But within this determinacy it also gives us existential freedom to select, evaluate, and interpret the tradition not merely in opposition to it, but in fundamental responsibility toward it and in dialogue with various specialized disciplines which are concerned with various aspects of the tradition. It thus affirms not only the inevitability of tradition but also the inevitability and responsibility of the interpretation and of the reinterpretation of tradition. This places us in a position to seek and to possess the riches of the heritage of the past in the most genuine manner possible and simultaneously to give expression to the Christian tradition in a fully contemporaneous way.

b. At the same time it enables us to interpret pastoral theology today in a way that is equally both fully modern and fully traditional. It represents tradition in a way that no questions are barred from being asked and fairly considered, whatever the viewpoint expressed. It represents pastoral theology in a way that basic theological concerns are necessarily dealt with as an essential reference to the reality of the divine, but not in a way that it is a departure from a simultaneous reference to the reality of the human. It thus identifies itself as theology in the most fundamental sense of the term and saves itself from a mere practicalism or from the notion that it is only an area of study the intention of which is to find occasion for the "application" of theological data and material derived elsewhere. It is fully modern in the sense in which it is open to the best and the latest by way of insights into and information about human nature in the concrete. And it does not get theological by becoming antiphenomenological or antihumanitarian, by obscuring issues as to the reality of man, or by refusing or neglecting to bear burdens in a significant and creative way.

III. Some Implications

Our discussion has implied that actually the disciplined concern of pastoral theology moves in two directions. It relates to the Christian tradition by way of a participational concern for the wholeness of this totality in relation to the person of Jesus Christ. And it relates to the contemporary scene as a contemporary interpretation of traditional Christian pastoral concern, as a concern for the wholeness of persons. It thus participates in the ambiguities and pluralisms of the time in intentional conjunction with the affirmation of the unity of personal life in Christ.

We have indicated that we are not dealing only with abstract theological concepts but with historical realities. This means that neither the formidable problems confronting pastoral theology today as we have defined it nor the peculiar *kairos* of its current opportunities are intended here to be obscured.

The problems are real, complex, and formidable. There was a time when most major theologians produced works on pastoral theology. That time is past, and with it the time of formalistic theories by which pastoral theology is constituted along with other theological disciplines on a singular and unilateral basis. The result is that currently we have a pastoral theology whose authenticity as theology is suspect in some other theological quarters and an academic theology whose concern for human beings is sometimes suspect. The bifurcation between pastoral theology and other facets of the theological disciplinary complex needs to be bridged in genuine, earnest, and clarifying dialogue. Otherwise theology tends to lose or to downgrade pastoral concern, with the inevitable implication that in theology we are concerned about matters which are exclusive of concern for the welfare of human beings in the concrete; and pastoral theology tends to lose its "theologicity," with the inevitable implication that in pastoral theology we are concerned with the welfare of human beings in the concrete in a way that is not theological. This dialogue necessarily involves us in complex and sensitive issues regarding the contemporary interpretation of the Christian tradition as pastoral concern and of its expression in pastoral work.

To illustrate, I will plunge directly into the sensitive subject of the contemporary meaning of the Reformation doctrine of total depravity. Is this concept a symptom, or is it a formidable vehicle by which we are enabled to interpret our common human life in a powerful and creative way? The concept goes back to Augustine. Whether it originated with him is the historian's story, but it is quite clear that it attained prominence there and that its use in the Reformation theology is at least in large part a result of Augustinian influence. It may be significant, therefore, that Augustine thought in a Neo-Platonic mentality that denied the real existence of evil, while the Reformers thought in a different context—they were convinced of the objective reality of evil in the papacy and in Roman teaching and practice. Equally significant may be the fact that Augustine's Neo-Platonism includes a determinate need to think in puristic and absolute concepts, as well as the fact that in Augustine the knowledge of God and self is essentially a private matter. These and other such matters are surely germane to any consideration of the possible meaning and value of the concept of total depravity today. Any consideration of them will greatly influence the way in which the doctrine is interpreted and used, if it is used at all.

Other similarly important questions are: What is the significance of the specific theological context in which the doctrine is phrased? What are the specific dynamics that are implied both inter- and intrapersonally in the way in which the concept is interpreted and used? Does it obscure or does it shed light—and in what context and under what conditions? Do students of pastoral theology misinterpret in the sense that they are responding to a distorted meaning or formulation of the doctrine? Do other theologians misinterpret in the sense in which they are oblivious to real issues that are being raised out of a context of the realities of the psychodynamics of human development? Can this doctrine be possessed in a contemporaneous way that contributes understanding and effective power, in pastoral theology as well as elsewhere? These and similar questions could only be clarified and possibly answered in the course of earnest discussion that directs some disciplined attention to the question of the significance of the way in which we use words and which persists in seeking clarification. It can proceed where there is a readiness among representatives of the traditional past with specialized competencies to risk the possibility of a radical reformulation and even the loss of the doctrine of total depravity to the contemporary interpretation of tradition and where there is a readiness of modern pastoral theologians to risk the discovery of a possible deepening and correction of pastoral concern through a contemporary pastoral interpretation of the traditional doctrine of total depravity. Such a procedure assumes that we have a pastoral theology which is both fully modern and traditional, and a Christian tradition which expresses itself as an intention to be fully contemporaneous and to move from a totality to dynamic wholeness.

Dialogue of a disciplined and scholarly but vital and intentional nature is, we have said, needed. We have illustrated by referring to only one issue, and only briefly at that. Discussion on this as well as a multiplicity of other important questions would offer the promise of an increase in the sensitivity, vitality, and power of the Judeo-Christian community which is concerned with the wholeness and well-being of human beings and which in its very coming to a more distinctive wholeness is centered in a point of common identity in Jesus of Nazareth, truly a Jew, truly the one whose influence has brought the Christian tradition. It is assumed that this unity promises to multiply the effectiveness of pastoral work of the kind for which modern pastoral theology stands. For this reason and in this wise, the work of pastoral theology, which we have said moves in two directions—concern for the wholeness of the tradition and concern for a contemporary expression of the tradition for the wholeness and well-being of persons in the best and most modern sense of that phrase—is fundamentally one enterprise. It would be unrealistic to deny that many vicissitudes lie before the continued practical realization of this unanimity of purpose. But to faith the future holds promise.

It therefore seems indicated that among the promising prospective lines of development for the future are the following: (1) Increasing recognition of the reality and value of and the concern for the wholeness of persons as we are best able to describe and understand them in a theological context as human beings. (2) Continuing development in the direction of the unity of the Judeo-Christian community, of which pastoral concern and work are here understood to be expressive. (3) Developments in the direction of the realization of the personal wholeness of the total Christian tradition, interpreted as the self-consciousness of the contemporary Judeo-Christian community. (4) Integration of the total complex of theological disciplines as a specialized phase of the life and work of the Judeo-Christian community. This would be based on the principle that the pastoral is everywhere and always an essential aspect of all theology and theological education in the best sense of those terms and that pastoral concern and work of a specialized order, in the best sense of these terms, includes responsibility for dealing explicitly with basic theological issues. (5) We will also hazard the prediction that a person-centered pastoral theology will play an increasingly important role in the engagement of the Judeo-Christian community with the people of non–Judeo-Christian religions and of atheism and secularism.

In the pastoral theology that is in the best and deepest sense both fully modern and fully traditional—as well as in other aspects of the contemporary interpretation of the Christian tradition—there are occasions that call for celebration in the classical sense of that word: the recalling of the goodness of specific past events because of their great significance for our present and for a future that beckons with promise.

Notes

1. A suggested definition of theology: the disciplined and intentional self-consciousness of those whose being is constituted in and by the revelatory activity of God in Christ.
2. "History" is here restricted to the history of man. Theology is understood to include the history of God's dealings with man but never in such a way that the account is not also truly human history. A suggested definition of history as *history* is: the concourse of human events. As a definition of history as a discipline I am suggesting: the concourse of human events become self-consciously and precisely intentional. Theology is in this context regarded in all its aspects as a historical discipline.
3. "Persons" means here simply human beings, including the idea of distinctive personality and identity of each individual.
4. The crucial point here is that "theology" indicates some kind of necessary and intelligible reference to the reality and significance of the divine in human life.
5. David Riesman, Nathan Glazer, and Reuel Denney, *The Lonely Crowd: A Study of the Changing American Character* (New Haven: Yale University Press, 1950).

A Theological View of Identity

Daniel Day Williams

Methodological questions are immediately raised in a theological analysis of identity, for "identity" as usually interpreted is not a theological category. It is derived from the psychology and sociology of personality. A philosophy of identity is not necessarily opposed to a theological perspective, but it may have a different context. Erikson defines identity thus: "Within historical actuality it is the sum of all images, ideas, and forces which —roughly speaking—make a person (and a people) feel more 'like themselves' and act more 'like themselves,'—which means in historical terms: like what they have come to consider their historical selves. By the same token, identity confusion defines what will make individuals and peoples feel that they are betraying their core and losing their grip on 'their' times." [1] Thus understood, identity belongs to the structure of every human life. It is empirically identifiable, within limits, and its meaning can be pursued in psychological and social structures. Erikson shows, however, that identity points toward ultimate questions when he speaks of "the core of the self" and "the times." The real self involves the meaning of history.

Theologically we can ask about identity in the biblical experience, but the biblical account of identity cannot be restricted to cultural and existential categories. The biblical context presupposes that the culture and the times are transcended, though not negated, by the relation of God and man in the history of salvation. The Bible knows no answer to the question "Who am

I?" apart from the history of the God-man dialogue. Our problem, therefore, is to relate two perspectives on human existence, one theological the other psychological. Our attention in this essay is focused primarily on the theological perspective. Whatever significance theology may have for psychology can become clear only if theology clarifies its own perspective and criteria, and the same is true of psychology.

There is a further methodological point to be made. Theology always interprets the biblical faith in relation to a world view, which means a conception of being and a criterion of truth, which are not derived solely from the biblical revelation but from the critical inquiry after truth in all reason and experience. There are theological methods which deny this, but here I can only record my dissent from them and say that the interpretation here given of the biblical categories involves a judgment about the history of Christian thought which can be summarily stated: the Christian doctrine of man as we have inherited it is derived both from the Bible and from the metaphysical interpretation given to it within the Hellenistic world view. The doctrines of the soul, of freedom, of the relation of mind and body, of immortality, of sin and grace, of the individual and society, were woven together partly out of the ancient supernatural world view, partly out of the biblical understanding of God's self-revelation, and partly out of Greek metaphysics. I believe that today this traditional synthesis has to be revised and our doctrine of God and man reconstructed. In giving, then, a Christian interpretation of the doctrine of man, I shall seek to get at its core, that is, what makes Christianity Christian, but I shall do this with conscious acceptance of the new metaphysics of process, of becoming, in which God is related to his world in social interaction so that time and history are real for God as well as for man. What follows, then, is not *the* biblical interpretation of selfhood. It is a theological interpretation from a point of view. In this point of view human nature is in process and exhibits both perennial structures and creative novelty.

First, then, we encounter the theme of God and man in history. I shall try to show how the biblical interpretation of man leads to the christological question. Human life is set within a history which begins with God's creation of the world and man and ends with God's final acts of judgment and redemption. For every man then the question "Who am I?" is bound up with the question "What is God doing in his creation and in our history?" In this perspective personal identity can never be discovered solely within the individual and his immediate personal relations, however important these are, because every man is in a history which embraces the whole creation, and what his life means is bound up with that history. It is true that Augustine says he wants to know only two things—the soul and God—but it is also clear that, in *The City of God,* Augustine had to reflect upon the entire history of salvation in order to say what the relation of God and the soul really is. Consider three aspects of this history.

First, the search for identity always takes place within the history of a people. In the biblical view God engages in a history with the whole creation, and within this history he elects a people to live in a special relationship to him. The witness of Israel is concerned with the life of a particular people under God. In our age of social relativism we are perhaps more prepared to consider seriously the significance of this doctrine. No one belongs only to humanity in general. We live in communities with concrete traditions, values, and faiths. The search for identity involves the search for the people to whom one belongs or can belong. Martin Buber insists that there is here an insight in Judaism which Christianity has never reached. He says: "Reverence for the absolute without the use of an intermediate agency is the principle of Israel's everlasting life. . . . To this day, however, we have not yet learned to revere the absolute by our very existence. What has kept us alive until now is the task itself—not its fulfilment, the task which burns in our blood like a fire, and will not die down. . . . A people has only one means to point to God, and that is through life lived in accordance with his will." [2] He thinks that Christianity has never quite understood the significance of the people as over against the individual.

The issue here has an important bearing on the new nationalism. Innumerable people in our culture find their personal identity in the spirit of nationalism, including American nationalism. The constructive and destructive aspects of nationalism are obvious features of our present situation. Christian interpretation of nationhood still has some critical issues to face. Idolatries, like that of national socialism, fall into a special category perhaps, though let us remember that even that was swallowed by some Christians at certain stages of its development. The passionate new nationalisms, such as some in Africa, which assert the freedom, equality, and dignity of all people require a different analysis. The question of racial identity is often involved. In any case, the biblical view has a kinship with all doctrines of the self which recognize the significance for personal identity of the history of a people.

Consider secondly, sin and grace. To be in human history is to manifest an estrangement from God and our intended being. The estrangement from God is both individual and collective, diverse in forms, but identifiable as unbelief or refusal to trust, hubris, and concupiscence.[3] In the Christian view, I know myself when I know myself as estranged, and in this knowledge I am in some sense one with every man. I participate in a history which is given its character not only by my finitude but also by my sin. In this history the meaning of every individual life and of the collective life involves the history of God's actions of judgment and redemption and of man's response. Therefore in the Christian interpretation the wrestle of the prophets with the meaning of God's redemptive action drives toward the question of his future action, the hope for his kingdom. In the Old Testament there are the first glimpses of a christological answer, especially in Daniel and in the suffering servant figure, though what is to be identified in the Hebrew Bible as Messianic in the strict sense is still a matter of considerable discussion. Thus the history of sin and grace as understood in the biblical perspective drives toward the question of Christology. As Paul Tillich formulates it, it is the question of the appearance in history of a human life in which the break between essential human nature and existential estrangement is overcome within the conditions of existence.[4] This is the third aspect of the bearing of history on identity.

In the Christian perspective my identity is discovered and bestowed (both words must be used) through the action of God in the historical Person, who is not myself but who is every man's elder brother and who stands in a different relation to every man from that of father, mother, siblings, friends. "He who loves father or mother more than me is not worthy of me." (Matt. 10:37.) It is this christological structure we have now to explore.

At this point our theological method opens the way for conversation with those who approach identity psychologically. We may look for analogies to the christological structure in the psychological understanding of identity. There is much theological significance in the remarkable address of Eric Erikson to the American Psychoanalytic Association in 1961 under the title "Psychological Reality and Historical Actuality." Erikson says, "Historians *and* psychoanalysts must learn to grasp fully the fact that while each individual life has its longitudinal logic, all lives lived interdependently within a given historical period share a kind of historical logic—and a-logic. Much of this is contained in the way and in the images by means of which men identify with each other, . . . identify themselves with their leaders and their leaders with themselves, and how, as they thus identify, they repudiate . . . their adversaries and enemies." Erikson develops this theme in relation to the psychoanalytic method and says, "We cannot escape, then, the major task of our time—a task which we have helped to shape—namely, that of participating in historical actuality more consciously and thus responsibly than have the generations before us." He discusses the guilt of passing over the meaning of destructiveness in history, and concludes, "In this time of a tragic confrontation of 'selfless' and 'objective science' with its murderous results, however, it may well be up to psycoanalysis to initiate a self-scrutiny of the scientific mind." [5]

Where is the healing or reconciling reality in the actuality of history as Erikson sees it? It appears in his hope that individuals will "transcend the remnants of the past, and mobilize and cultivate more rational outlooks for the sake of a wider and more inclusive identification among men—such identification as provides the leverage for decisive deeds." Erikson looks for leaders who possess superior gifts and who "create a joint future out of a combination of their own pasts and the typical pasts of the led, and thus acquire and provide a conception of truth in action." [6] We cannot say that this is a christological statement made from a psychological point of view. The frame of reference does not permit that. But it is Erikson's answer within his framework concerning the center of meaning and truth in history. Erikson recognizes that the identity problem requires a historical answer, and he is, so far, close to the biblical perspective.

We can now state more formally a Christian view of the source and structure of identity. The Christian perspective locates the center of identity neither in the individual nor society but in a relationship between persons and the one Person who represents human nature in history and who is the bearer of reconciliation in the midst of alienation. This is the christological structure of biblical anthropology. I know who I am through another who is not myself but who in some way is the key to every self. The main features of this christological structure can be stated under four headings.

I. The Person in History

The God of Christian faith acts in history. He is known through his acts. The context of every assertion of the Christian faith is the history of salvation within the concrete historical life of the world. In this history the center is found in the life of the man Jesus of Nazareth who lived and died in Palestine about A.D. 1-30. There are important issues in this claim.

First, there is the nature of the Gospels, the historical record. They give a report of events, but as seen through the eyes of faith and as interpreted. The debate about the kind of history we have in the Gospels is crucial for the Christian faith. If Jesus is not really there in history, then the Christian understanding of God and man is not true. Yet the record gives us little biographical information about Jesus by himself. It is a record arising from the witness of men to the new reality they found in Jesus and using the symbols of their culture to express that reality. The personal relationship to Jesus Christ is always constituted in part by the symbols by which the meaning of his life is grasped.

A second aspect of the personal relationship has to do with the way in which Jesus is remembered. He is known as the risen Christ, the ever present Head of the Church. He lives "not after the flesh," as Paul says, but in a new kind of memory. All the christological symbols, images, and doctrines enter into the personal relationship in which he is known. Their diversity and mystery constitute both a richness and a problem for the discovery of the true meaning of the Christ. John Knox has put the actual situation of the believer who finds his identity through Jesus Christ in this way: Jesus is known as he is remembered, interpreted, and experienced in the ongoing community which shares in and lives by the faith given by his life and its meaning.[7] Thus Jesus confers personal identity on individuals always within the community which bears the meaning of his life through history.

This raises sharply of course the question of uniqueness and finality in the Christian revelation. Is there no other way by which we may come to personal identity? Is the personal identity known in Christian experience completely different from all other identity? Arnold Toynbee says it is megalomania to say that the meaning of existence must be confronted only in one place in the universe and one point in history.[8] The issue of whether Christianity separates man from every other center of meaning or whether in Jesus there is the center of a historical meaning which embraces all others is a crucial one. I take the view that to assert the finality of Christ is not to reject meaning in other faiths. The Christian finds a solidarity with all others, including unbelievers, through his relation to Christ. The meaning known in Jesus Christ must be reflected in all history if it is valid in any history.

II. Love as *Agape* and as *Eros*

The content of the Incarnation is the love which the New Testament knows as *agape*. It is love given in the midst of alienation. It is forgiveness. It is the basis of the real universal community. It is grace. The question of the relation of love as *agape* to the human loves becomes critical for identity, for if a man is constituted by his loves, as I take it most psychologies would assert, then if there is a love other than human love, it becomes of fundamental importance for the Christian's identity. The question "Who am I?" as a created, loving, sexual being—loving persons, loving the world, art, work, and play—is bound up with the question "Is there another love beyond these?" Now the argument of Nygren in *Agape and Eros* that these are two utterly different loves, that *agape* is different in origin and structure from the human loves, states a radical problem for Christianity. Nygren, to be sure, does not say *agape* rejects the human loves, but *agape* is something utterly different. It moves from God to man exclusively and is the one possible ground of reconciliation for man and, therefore, of human integrity. What shall we say to Nygren's position?

Agape is not the same as *eros*. It does not depend on any particular structure of human relations as does *eros*. It does not have the distinctive emotional components of *eros*. It comes at the edge of human love as a new possibility, and it comes as grace, as undeserved, leading to a reconciliation with others and within the self. It is of critical importance, therefore, to show how *agape* can incorporate the freedom and vitalities of *eros* and not reject them. I am agreeing with Paul Tillich against Nygren here.[9] An absolute separation of *agape* and *eros* is fatal to the possibility of uniting Christian faith and human existence. The direction of the solution is that love as *eros* is never completely self-contained. All *eros* pushes toward the point where the meaning of *agape* looms up as its judgment and its completion. *Eros* does not turn into *agape* automatically, but it can reach toward *agape*. On this point the possibility of the unity of *agape* and the loves of the self depends.

Agape is known within the Christian faith as the love which God has shown in Jesus Christ. It has a center in history, and its definition and power are derived from this historical Incarnation. In Jesus' teaching there is no rejection of the human loves. They are often seen as parables and analogies of *agape* as in the story of the prodigal son.

A further point concerning love involves the historical community which Buber insists is the key to biblical faith. The Christian perspective agrees with this but asks, "Where is that community within which man can find his authentic being?" In the New Testament the community has to be understood in a new way. It is the church, the body of Christ. This new people has a concrete life. Its members are members one of another as participants in the new life which has come through Christ. Since, however, this community is in its meaning and intent the community of the whole creation under God, it is a community of the spirit and cannot be limited to any historical form as defining its boundaries. Here identity becomes an ecumenical issue. It is also an issue concerning recognition of the holy catholic church and its authentic existence wherever the work of love is getting done. Not only is Christ in the least of these who are ministered to, but he is present incognito wherever the way of *agape* is being broken open in the midst of all the human loves. We cannot say that the problem of identity for the Christian can always be resolved within the form of the church as we know it. The real depth of the empirical church is discovered where within it we see the possibility of the spiritual community which transcends the forms in which it lives.

III. Eschatology

Our third topic is the significance of eschatology for a theology of identity. It may be that theology here makes a special contribution to identity theory. Jürgen Moltmann's *Theology of Hope* has become significant for contemporary theology because he has stressed the eschatological dimension in the New Testament.[10] Christ points toward the end of history and time, the completion of meaning. He gives not immediate realization but the promise of a fulfillment yet to come. The very meaning of the cross and resurrection points toward a consummation which is known only in hope. Christ must reign until he has put all enemies under his feet, and the last enemy which shall be destroyed is death (I Cor. 15:25-26).

This eschatological dimension reflects itself in each individual's existence. The life of faith is a progress toward the new life as well as a realization of it. If personal identity is self-discovery through the image of God, the New Testament transfers this identity to the image of Christ and declares we are being transformed into his image. Our becoming has a new structure which is not consummated. We are perplexed but not in despair; cast down but not destroyed; we know in part, and it is only at the end that we will know as we are known, as Paul says (II Cor. 4:8-9; I Cor. 13:12). Identity in the theological sense, therefore, can never be identified with the cultural images and values which enclose us in a particular time and place. From the Christian point of view this given cultural identity is something less than the authentic reality of our being. It is not too strong to say that the Christian gospel introduces a new kind of alienation into history and into the life of the individual. If "alienation" suggests something pathological, then discard the word, but the life of faith involves a break with the enclosure of the present culture and its symbols. It introduces a new element of criticism into all self-definition.

The history of sin does not end with the revelation of grace. It takes on a new character, but it is still present. What ought to be an increase in self-knowledge and in the power of *agape*—love to fulfill the human loves—is at the same time within the mystery of evil and freedom a new temptation. Therefore, the Christian distrusts the identification of his identity with the present structure of his being. In faith he becomes an alien to every cultural satisfaction that seeks to enclose the meaning of his life. He expects his identity to be disclosed, and its essence is "life in love," but its shape and definition are not solely in his hands nor in the hands of any culture, and this includes Christian culture itself, insofar as that is an object which can be identified with particular concepts, institutions, and symbols. There are modern humanisms and other perspectives which have analogous insights into radical freedom.

IV. Vocation and Identity

The christological approach to identity issues in a concept of life as vocation. What is called "vocation" in a secular sense enters powerfully into the identity quest in every human life. We may come to self-knowledge in relation to significant work. In the Christian view there is a vocation within every vocation, that is, an ultimate calling within the specific tasks of life. I shall call this ultimate and unifying vocation the Calling and discuss it as form, as spirit, as suffering, and as decision.

The source of the Calling is given within the christological structure. The Word of God comes to man in Jesus Christ as an offer of grace that summons man to response. Jesus himself is called to his vocation. He is the "elect Man," the elect of God for his task in history. He calls others to follow him, to bear their burdens, to take up their crosses. This is the familiar structure of Christian discipleship. Let us ask about its relevance to the dynamics of the search for identity today.

The Calling involves a definite form of existence. Paul speaks of the Calling as the *locus* in which one hears the gospel. This seems to be the original sense of the statement in I Cor. 7:20, "Let every man abide in the same calling wherein he was called" (KJV). What I am to become in the response to the summons of Christ involves my specific existence in the world with its form, its limitations, and its history. I cannot jump out of this or ignore it and achieve the new being in some unhistorical way. The history of the interpretation of Paul's dictum is of course a long one, bound up on the one hand with the Roman Catholic tradition that only the religious have a special Calling and on the other with the Protestant Reformers' secularizing of the conception to regard every legitimate profession as a Calling. The Reformers, unfortunately, tended to combine this doctrine with the idea that God has decreed the circumstances of every life, and I believe we must reject that doctrine. Process theology can help here, for it asserts that there is a real history and becoming not only for man but also for God, so that no present form of existence should be absolutized as a block against the creative possibilities pregnant in every situation. We are called in a world which has both freedom and form, and we lose our identity if we do not come to terms with this fact. None of this is meant to exclude the truth in the Reformer's emphasis on the providential character of the Calling. There are possibilities of good which God wills amid all the givens in life. We are masculine and feminine, of this race, in this culture, in this time, with this body-mind and this emotional inheritance. Personal identity involves coming to terms with this givenness and yet finding within it that which is not merely given but which can be shaped by courageous response, discipline, and faith.

This reshaping may take the form of rebellion. The Christian view of the Calling cannot be identified with either the conservative or the radical stance. Gauguin leaving his banker's world for Tahiti, Eugene O'Neill leaving family and school to knock around the world on sailing ships—these are authentic contexts of the discovery of identity and vocation. There is no Christian norm which judges as appropriate or inappropriate any human decision apart from its human context and motivation and its relation to love and lovelessness. The Christian faith leads to an acceptance of the givens in any personal destiny, but it sees God himself interacting with the world and with men in the concreteness of circumstances to change them. This is one reason why the identity crisis at age forty can be just as traumatic as the one at adolescence.

The Calling comes from spirit to spirit. Paul speaks of one

Spirit and one Calling just as there is one baptism (Eph. 4:4-5). He treats the question of individuality in vocation through the doctrine of the one spirit with a diversity of gifts. I Cor. 12 is a fundamental New Testament text on identity. The diversity of gifts involves psychological factors, for Paul does not rule out natural and tempermental differences, but these are explained theologically. God has called some to be prophets, some apostles, some teachers. The metaphor of the organism with its various members is here, as everywhere, fundamental for him. The consequence is that the Calling is not to a new life in general but to a new existence in Christ and therefore in the church. That is, the meaning of every calling is disclosed within the history of redemption. Here we encounter the question of finding a new vocation. The break with the old life means the discovery of a new structure of vocation. To be called out of darkness into the marvelous light is also to be given a new path to walk.

Just here the Reformers' doctrine of the Calling is pertinent. They did not reject the secular callings. The work of the world has to be done, and that work includes all the services men may reasonably and effectively render one another. Yet the identification of each vocation as a Calling from God now has a new interpretation. The call to the building up of the body of Christ cannot be separated from the forms of the world's work. We must acknowledge that the actual estrangement in life as men seek meaning in their work is very deep. The present concern with the secular may help eradicate vestiges of irrelevant pietism and simple moralism in talking about Christian Calling. The categories of the Calling in the church, with its witness, discipleship, stewardship, will have to be rediscovered and brought into some kind of unity with living in the world.

The Calling involves suffering. No one has to be called to suffer, but one may be called to suffer in a certain way and for a cause. Paul describes his life as bearing about in the body the dying of Jesus, that the life of Jesus also may be made manifest. The call to the new life has come to the world through the self-giving of

Jesus. Hence life in the church is the sharing of suffering. When one member suffers, all suffer.

Suffering may lead to self-discovery. The suffering which attends the working out of the Calling is one element in the disclosure of the meaning of the Calling. No one really understands a way of life who does not know what it costs. Hence we need to see the significance of suffering not simply at the dramatic level of major crises and tragedies but in the recognition of the omnipresence of suffering in all human response to Calling. Every decision for a vocation is an acceptance of limitation, narrowing of attention, the sacrifice of other goods to this good, and the opening of one's spirit to be reshaped by the experience. When suffering clarifies who we are, what we are serious about, and what we can celebrate, then it may become a healing power.

The second aspect of suffering in vocation is related to conflict with enemies, both without and within. Erikson remarks that a large element in the discovery of identity is the demarcation of what one is against. This belongs to the characteristics of a severe identity crisis. The Christian faith has always provided for this power of opposition in the Calling. Christ's vocation is realized in conflict with principalities and powers which he in essence defeats but which still work in life. Paul's statement that neither life nor death separates us from the love of God is rightly recognized as assurance. It is not so often noted that it is a call to combat.

Finally, the Calling requires decision; this element has been implicit throughout. This must not be obscured by the traditional doctrines of election and predestination. Election is God's affirmation of human destiny as communion with him, and it is meaningless without the free response of man. There is decision at every point, in the acceptance of what must be accepted, in the rejection of what must be rejected, and above all in the risk to face the undefined and open possibilities of the future.

Existentialism has had its powerful impact in facing the actuality of the human situation with the call to assume it with courage and in insisting that man must realize his own becoming without guidelines or guarantees. Sartre says "man is only what he wills himself to be." [11] A contemporary theology, while it will by no means accept the extremism of Sartre's view (which he himself qualifies in all sorts of ways), must assert human freedom and personal creativity in bringing the new into being. Personal identity is not something which God gives simply as it is, but it is discovered and created in a free, hopefully faithful, response to God and the world. To be free, conscious spirits having an identity is to be able to say "yes" or "no" to the forms of our existence as they are and in dependence on grace, to will into being the person we are not yet. That is the ultimate risk of love: to let the other become what he will become—and God has taken that risk with us.

Notes

1. Erik H. Erikson, *Insight and Responsibility* (New York: W. W. Norton, 1964), pp. 203-4.
2. Martin Buber, *Israel and the World* (New York: Schocken Books, 1948), pp. 198, 200.
3. Cf. Paul Tillich, *Systematic Theology*, II (Chicago: University of Chicago Press, 1957), 44-58.
4. *Ibid.*, Part II.
5. Erikson, *Insight and Responsibility*, pp. 207, 211, 212.
6. *Ibid.*, p. 205.
7. John Knox, *Jesus: Lord and Christ* (New York: Harper, 1958).
8. Arnold Toynbee, *An Historian's Approach to Religion* (New York: Oxford University Press, 1956), p. 138.
9. Tillich, *Systematic Theology*, Vol. I.
10. Jürgen Moltmann, *The Theology of Hope* (New York: Harper, 1967).
11. Jean-Paul Sartre, *Existentialism* (New York: Philosophical Library, 1947), p. 18.

A Note on Method in the Psychology of Religion*

Gardner Murphy

To anyone deeply concerned with religious experience and eager to understand it as fully as he may, there are likely to be two meanings of the phrase "the psychology of religion." The term may refer to all the experiences known as "religious," or it may refer to the *steps* by which religious experience can come to be *known*. The first problem is substantive; the second is procedural. The double usage is similar to that which obtains in studies of history. If I say with Emerson that "man is explicable by nothing less than all his history," I mean that everything that has happened to man is part of human development on the face of the globe. If, however, I say with Carlyle that history consists of "the lives of great men," or quote Thucydides, who wrote, "My history is an everlasting possession," the problem is the selection, the ordering, the discovery of meaning in an otherwise tangled system of events.

I

I think that failure to make this kind of distinction between raw realities and human interpretations of them is still quite currently found in discussions of the psychology of religion, or in-

* Written in March, 1968, before receiving Paul W. Pruyser's *A Dynamic Psychology of Religion*. A true milestone. Thus my little contribution may be regarded as a part of the pre-Pruyserian era. About forty years ago I wrote "A Note on Method in the Psychology of Religion" (*Journal of Philosophy*, 1928). I seem to meet myself coming back—changed a little perhaps!

deed of politics or art. When Walter Lippmann writes on *Public Opinion,* he does not mean to discuss all the stuff that makes up the world of public opinion but rather seeks some guidelines to its total complexity, and when Rudolf Arnheim writes of *Art and Visual Perception,* he does not mean to describe all the perceptual responses that enter into the understanding or the enjoyment of art but rather seeks the small, clear, and orderly activities of science which make possible the understanding of art through the study of visual perception. The psychology of religion similarly must not be attacked or reviled simply because it "leaves out" vast areas of human experience in the religious field. It cannot possibly do justice to all the substantive realities. It must discover a method, develop it, apply it, learn from mistakes, improve the method, and ultimately try to see how psychology can actually be useful.

If the comment be made: "But there are many other ways of looking at religion—indeed, many better ways than you psychologists have used," the reply must of course be vigorous agreement. The psychology of religion is not—and cannot be—a compendium of all available information about religious experience. It is concerned with method and with the improvement of that particular method which is useful in psychology. Or rather, it seeks a systematic *integration of methods* which have been derived from the biological and the social sciences, while emphasizing both collective and individual experience and reaching out imploringly toward other biological and social sciences and indeed toward epistemology, logic, and metaphysics, in the attempt to work toward an ultimately sound and unified method for the study of religious experience.

If a feather is allowed to drop through a vacuum tube for the sake of studying gravity, one must not berate the physicist for using "artificial isolation," neglect of total contexts, arbitrary selection of problems to be studied and of observations which will clarify those methods. The physicist will reach out to the geologist and astronomer for the context in which specific events occur.

Similarly, the psychologist will reach out to the anthropologist, the historian, the philosopher, for other considerations that relate to contexts. The psychologist has a job to do, and he must not try to do all human jobs at once.

Does this mean that the psychologist is ready to try simultaneously all the methods that have ever been found useful in psychology? He has never found a way to do this. While breadth is commendable, the real issue is relevance, and not all methods are appropriate for all problems. Indeed, we must not only lop off much of the content of religious experience as being beyond the scope of a modern psychology of religion, but we must lop off at the other side a wide variety of methods which, however promising, are not demonstrably relevant to the critical issues. If, then, we ask the broad question: "What *kind* of psychology enters usefully into the psychology of religion?" the answer must be that many divergent psychological preconceptions and methods have at various times influenced those who have studied the psychology of religion. This will quickly reveal that the enterprise is a highly biased one—biased from the point of view of the sociology of knowledge; biased from the point of view of the specific kinds of religious experience which were of interest to scholars; biased in terms of the kinds of psychology available at the time and place the studies were made; and biased, above all, in terms of the personalities, the developmental foibles, the critical warp and woof of the texture of the psychologist's mind.

We might protest: "But there is surely a better hope for science than all that!" The reply is that this better hope can indeed come into existence in time as a wider content and a more sophisticated selection of methods may develop. The psychology of religion is at the present time simply a series of efforts to observe, describe, and interpret certain classes of religious experiences that happen to have met all the above mentioned criteria of interest and relevance, and the empirically oriented student must enrich the areas covered, and polish the tools used, to secure a wider array of better-authenticated data relevant to the goal of understanding.

II

Nineteenth-century German philosophers taught us to think about natural science and cultural science (*Naturwissenschaft* and *Geisteswissenschaft*), and the two were separated by a gulf of misunderstanding, particularly abetted by the greater prestige which *Geisteswissenschaft* received in the university. The greater prestige of natural science in the United States has often led us to forget the form and function of this status differential. The kinds of information we have about the psychology of religion are, however, profoundly influenced by this dichotomy. When in the first flush of experimental psychology of the thought processes Girgensohn made experimental studies of religious consciousness, practically no one, of course, except the laboratory psychologists of the era and in the particular universities concerned, paid any attention. "What! Experimental studies of religious experience?" Yes. Exactly that. Similar experimental studies on the emotional life brought a little more status to the investigator, partly because experimental studies of the physiology of the emotions were in their heyday as a result of the spread of evolutionary theory. Developmental studies of religion, as in the hands of G. Stanley Hall, and the marvelously suggestive studies of childhood and adult religious experience from the clinical-developmental point of view developed by Freud, produced a sharp dichotomy in response—some being enthusiastic, others appalled. Yet in the long run, the approach, being empirically and conceptually far-reaching, led to the general recognition that the clinical-developmental point of view was of great value, and therefore swept the new psychology, the laboratory-based psychology, into recognition of this additional field of concern.

At the same time, the cultural anthropologists, with part of their advance based upon *Geisteswissenschaft*, influenced the slowly developing social psychology in the early years of the century and even succeeded, as in the work of George A. Coe, in influencing the outlook of those who taught social psychology in American universities. The integration of a psychology based upon biological sciences and a psychology based upon the social sciences was slow in coming. It was due rather largely to the genius of Kurt Lewin; to the experimental skills of F. H. Allport, with his behavioristic experimental social psychology in the 1920's; and to Muzafer Sherif, a decade later, with his skill in transforming problems of cultural anthropology into miniscule laboratory settings.

It cannot be honestly claimed that natural and cultural science approaches to social behavior are yet ready for unification. But massive efforts have been made, notably by Gordon W. Allport, whose recent posthumous volume *The Person in Psychology* shows, as does his work over several decades, a very deep concern with religious experience as representative both of "individual men in their solitude" (William James) and of man as a symbol of a community. The movement toward integration will continue.

This, from the scientific point of view, is of course a gain. There are at the same time some very real risks. Take the matter of value judgments. It is generally agreed that the scientific enterprise in the biological sphere is a fact-finding, not a normative, endeavor. One does not get bogged down as to whether it is "right" to destroy pathogenic bacteria. One may indeed raise the question whether large-scale attacks upon pathogenic bacteria will lead to mutations and at a later point in evolution result in individual human beings who cannot defend themselves against the lethal strain. Even so, however, these are factual issues ready for scientific consideration. They are not in the ordinary sense normative issues. They do not "puzzle the will" as it deals with problems of right and wrong. Immediately, however, as the issue is referred to the Surgeon General, to the medical public, or to the general lay public, as to whether threats, insinuations, false encouragements, etc., can appropriately be used with human subjects in an investigation related to human health, there will be huge movements and countermovements concerned with the gravest questions of personal and social ethics. Experimental studies of religious experience, such as response to indoctrination at a very early age; the problem of misinformation and of double standards in right and wrong as differentiating adults from children; questions of digging deep, research-wise, into the unexpressed thoughts of small children; questions of the soundness or unsoundness of letting children develop rich and complicated fantasy worlds, space worlds, space-time worlds, such as many of them (both normal and abnormal) are prone to do—all these are issues which would hardly come up in the study of religious experience from a biological point of view, but which certainly *do* come up in a study of religious experience from a social science point of view. The reason lies to some degree, of course, in the greater objectivity of biological information, but it lies very largely, I believe, in the normative character, the right-and-wrong character, the better-and-worse character of the generalizations so often encountered in the social sciences.

We might as well say directly: Is religious experience a good thing? How absurd this sounds from the earlier stance, the stance of biological, fact-finding science! From the point of view of most social scientists the question whether religious experience is good is immediately transformed into questions like "good for what," "good under what circumstances," "good for whom," and the real confrontation with the nature of the good goes off into the high uplands of philosophy, in which we frankly agree that we have left the field of scientific investigation as such. It cannot then be honestly claimed that the fusion of the biological science and the social science approaches to religion has been achieved, or even that one knows quite how to achieve it as long as the former issues are factual and the latter issues are frequently normative.

I might summarize up to this point by saying that there is a strong temptation to think of the psychology of religion as a full-bodied psychology, a systematic mobilization of all psychological resources—substantive and procedural—which would suddenly make religious experience take on the fullest possible meaning. We simply do not have the knowledge or the wisdom to do this. We have limited knowledge of facts, limited conceptual tools, and limited methods of investigation. We must indeed be hospitable to all facts, all interpretations, all methods that may help us outgrow the narrowness which still characterizes our work. We have an infant science, a toddler science. We may indeed try to run fast and far, but we shall need to be picked up and helped to realize where we can go and under what conditions. The psychology of religion will indeed ultimately become as mature and as complete as the psychology of personality, but the psychology of personality is itself only a little more mature, and he who confidently interprets religious experience may err both by claiming a completeness for which there is no warrant and also by failure to use such specific findings and methods as are already at hand.

III

And this points to a still larger failure arising from ignorance of what the psychology of religion can do. It is not only weak on many aspects of the content but particularly ignorant of the *ecology* of the religious experience; that is to say, we frequently do not know to what environment the individual is responding. *Primitive Traits in Religious Revivals* was a popular book title of over a half-century ago. Primitive, however, with respect to what? With respect to what situational pressures, what potential meanings? Unless we know *how* a little child perceives a situation, we cannot tell whether he is irrational or more "infantile" than we would like him to be. For the most part religious experience is studied by those who do not fully share it, possibly even by unfriendly observers; they draw a line around it, using, we might say, the "cookie cutter" technique. For we think *for us* to have these ideas and to be caught by *these* snares would be childish. But the man who studies an experience must fully know to *what situation* his subject is responding. The ecology of religious experience belongs to some degree to cultural anthropology and to history and to some degree to the biographer and the novelist and the dramatist. The psychologist, as such, usually has no special knowledge or skill in this area; in fact, he is likely to be woefully defective. The psychology of religious experience can fall flat on its face by making three extraordinary assumptions: (1) the assumption that all the parameters of response are known; (2) the assumption that all the parameters of stimulation, or ecological pressure upon the person, are known; (3) the assumption that whatever transcends our knowledge of ecology is metaphysics. I would like to spell out now where I think these blindspots work their most devastating effects.

The investigator, especially if he emphasizes the experimental method, is almost sure to believe he has his eye on the main independent variables which may be responsible for an observed result. He starts with what he knows, then narrows it down to make it maximally appropriate to the situation he is studying *as he sees it,* and then drags out or whisk-brooms off all the "disturbing" factors which may "contaminate" his result. This is entirely consistent with his desire to discover truth and also with his specific desire to make a scientific contribution. His colleagues will read the material and approve of it insofar as they have similar purposes and preconceptions, but if they have different preconceptions, they are likely to be even more hostile to the result than a relatively neutral person would be because the "power field" which they have defined as their own may be jeopardized or invaded by certain special assumptions of this special investigator whose work they are reading.

The sad thing, in terms of the human need for maximal reality, is that many of the essential predisposing conditions or even the essential measurable parameters of response cannot at present be known. The result of the investigation will be to show, perhaps in beautiful detail, what follows from certain specific parameters when *other* parameters, large or small, are ignored or—as is more likely the case—when their effect is real though their presence is unsuspected. The psychology of religion can be almost all things to all men or all things to all epochs and regions not because of prejudice or banality but because the situational factors at a given time and place or the broad ecological factors for an era and a region are not known or even suspected.

When research studies are not successfully replicated from

one laboratory to another, it is quite common to hear that investigators can agree on sheer facts but cannot agree on "metaphysics"; or that investigators' business lies in the scientific study of facts and not a normative study of values and their application; or that the scientists, with limited goals, cannot be concerned with the broader reaches of logic or epistemology. While all these defenses are reasonable, they do not really touch the essential issue, namely that from the point of view of psychology itself there is no reason to believe that studies of different populations, at different times and places, by different investigators, would all give identical or even closely similar results. The trouble is not metaphysics; it is the fact that we simply do not know enough to set out appropriately the broad ecology, the specific situation, and the particular person-to-person interactions which occur in the investigation which someone else tries to replicate.

When I was teaching the psychology of religion at Columbia in the 1930's, our graduate students of psychology were rather disturbed as to whether William James's individualistic approach was "sound," or whether Ames and Coe, with their social emphasis, were nearer to the truth about the nature of religious experience. It did not seem to occur to most students that James was looking down a particular tunnel, and Ames and Coe, with their social emphasis, were looking down quite a different tunnel. Then when the students encountered Codrington's study of *The Melanesians*, with its emphasis upon the pervasive force of "mana," they wondered whether here was something which other observers had "missed," or whether the nature of animism, magic, and depersonalization had all been developed in inappropriate directions because the concept of mana had been "overlooked." I think we may all realize how the anthropological approach, the psychoanalytic approach, and indeed the Schweitzer or Tillich or Niebuhr approach could have been stated so as to be more "sound." The nonspecialist using anthropological material is almost certain to find in Margaret Mead or Abram Kardiner the thing which he is tempted to apply to some other primitive society, or even to our own. Genius, as William James says, is the capacity for a far-reaching generalization; but perhaps one such generalization out of a hundred is well enough oriented in reality to be worth emphasizing.

The same applies, I think, to psychoanalysis. We are basically dealing with observations made in clinical settings in Western European culture, and we do find some important therapeutic, educational, and theoretical facts which result from ideas thus gleaned from a certain kind of reality. Supporting data for some of these concepts appear in cross-cultural studies and may appear in developmental studies, even in animal studies, and in a few controlled laboratory studies. The effort to make psychoanalysis a system, in the sense in which Newton's physics was a system, is still being pursued though, I think, not with the enthusiasm or confidence of ten or fifteen years ago. That there is vastly more and wider observation to be carried out and systematization to be attempted seems to be more and more generally recognized by analysts. Suppose we confront a proposition to the effect that superego, a technical formulation of the concept of conscience, is derived from and represents a continuing expression of Oedipal conflict. Suppose we apply this concept to the President's conflict about sending more and more young men to Vietnam. In what ways is this conception useful in understanding the President, and indeed American character types and American social and international dilemmas? Much damage can be done by narrowly conceiving and applying this concept. But gently and tenuously woven together into a carefully considered pattern, these ideas may add great beauty and strength to the texture.

IV

Psychical research, or parapsychology, the study of telepathy, clairvoyance, precognition, and related processes, is another outstanding example today of observed data which can be applied or misapplied in dozens of ways, depending upon the soundness of the observations and especially the social science perspective of the observer. If Jesus is reported to have known what happened to a centurion's daughter, and to have been capable of playing a part in the restoration of her life, or if he could, by asking a man with a withered hand to stretch forth his hand, cause a restoration of function, how far can we go in saying, "Why the first is just like clairvoyance and telepathy, the second like a psychosomatic healing!" With the limited knowledge of today one usually has before himself a pile of jigsaw pieces and general conceptions of where he is going, and he begins to push the pieces into places where they may or may not belong so as to get a supposed unity. But one has to know the literature of psychical research quite well in order to know how to apply it. The situation may often be the reverse of what is commonly assumed by those who plead for larger use of materials from this curious and challenging field. Long-distance telepathy, for example, being systematically examined by sending observers around the world who are ascertaining the effect of distance between "sender" and "receiver" upon the strength of the telepathic messages, is a legitimate and necessary experimental adventure. But to apply the findings of such an experiment to the episode of the centurion's daughter is a very far cry—except in one very important sense, namely that a certain boldness is necessary in willingness to consider many kinds of new observations. Psychical research can add modern clinical and experimental material warranting the belief that there are many sorts of strange events relating individuals to other individuals, or individuals to distant events, regarding which we have only the most primitive knowledge. What is needed here is not brilliant, far-flung generalization but the willingness to settle down to study psychical research seriously and to look carefully for a genuine articulation between these data and other data from experience in which one has some expertness. Cross-cultural biases and the "idols of the den" will as usual give different scholars different suggestions as to the implications of this new field—all the way from the view that we are finding out new things about the physics of human communication systems to the view that we are transcending physics altogether. With data so poorly articulated, how can we answer questions like this?

V

I am afraid that all this may offer only vague though necessary precautionary notes on the relations of a science of the psychology of religion to the educational and counseling functions which can be helpful to a religiously perceptive individual. Knowing rather little about the deep roots of religious experience in a specific young man or woman, and indeed relatively little about one's own religious potentialities, one has the problem of giving specific and helpful advice which will have immediate likelihood of being understood. One must, moreover, gear in with the latent potentials that are surely going to emerge and take shape as new interpersonal relations and new ecologies develop and as the person counseled encounters fresh forces which one has relatively small likelihood of foreseeing. So how can a *general* psychology of religion, so far indeed from an organized field of dependable human knowledge and skill, be helpful in an interpersonal transaction, the parameters of which are poorly defined? One can hope, one can work, one can make self-fulfilling prophecies. If one's broad human wisdom is sufficient, one may dare to try a few concepts from psychology here and there. Modesty in the definition of what is known and broad-range and affectionate concern for other human beings offer a context in which religious counseling may slowly add something here and there from a very immature and incomplete psychology of religion.

But the main need is for a research orientation, both biologically and socially oriented, cautious and at the same time tolerant and generous, recognizing both the great strengths and the great limitations of that method to which we apply the term *science*.

The Impact of the Urban Crisis on Pastoral Theology

Robert H. Bonthius

The urban crisis is worldwide. It constitutes a revolution in human community, a revolution in the nature of human existence. The revolution affects the smallest community, but it comes to its most dramatic expression in great metropolitan centers.

This is why the word urban is inadequate when it comes to suggesting the profundity of the change that is taking place in history. Still it is useful because "city" is the name of the new community. The logic of existence on this planet is one vast city, though to make "city" a useful symbol we must see urbanization as a patterned process which is not a matter of any one city's becoming physically central to man, useful as the New Jerusalem may be symbolically. Cities around the world are gathering more and more of the peoples. They are reaching out so far in some cases that they touch other cities through their respective satellite towns.

But the urbanization process for which the word city stands as symbol is not physical concentrations of people alone—crucial as this development is for man's future. It is the transformation of feeling, thinking, acting. It is nothing less than change in the meanings that are possible to find in earthly life. Everything will be shaped by this growing interdependence for which the cities stand.

I. Urbanization: An Explosive Mix

Urbanization is an explosive mix made up of many ingredients. Each of the ingredients can be found anywhere in some strength—

not just in cities. Each ingredient contributes to the mix called urbanization. When all are brought together in highly concentrated form, we have what is called the urban crisis, exhibited in the cities of the world. These ingredients are not bad intrinsically. To say they are explosive when brought together in large amounts does not mean that only disaster is ahead for mankind. Dynamite is used for peaceful purposes as well as for war. If the mix is handled carelessly or if it is allowed to fuse without control or if it is directed by powers which are bent on protecting themselves and the *status quo,* it will be incalculably destructive. If the mix is understood and wise catalysts work with it, it will produce a new type of society, freer and more creative than any periof of past history.

Population Growth

One ingredient in the mix that makes up urbanization is population growth. Lloyd Rodwin, editor of *The Future Metropolis,* predicts:

> It appears that these metropolitan complexes will become the dominant environment, at least in the most highly developed regions of the world, for they contain the bulk of the population, and they produce and consume most of the goods. The living space will become a set of such areas, at times separated by areas of low population that provide raw materials. The metropolitan regions may be very large, even grouped in chains several hundred miles long; but they will be more or less continuously urbanized, however low their suburban densities may be. Each one will display a continuous dense web of facilities for communication, within which the population will be highly interdependent on a daily basis in terms of supply of information and of commutation to and from work. Such a society will be intricate, and its means of communication will be increasingly mechanized and depersonalized. Most likely it will be mobile and egalitarian. This type of mass habitation and this kind of inhabitant may well become a world-wide pattern.[1]

We are talking about twice the number of inhabitants in the cities of the future that we have on earth at present. The world population increases about 2 percent a year, and the rate is going up. United Nations experts believe that the next forty years will see a doubling of the present 3 billion—6 billion by 2010!

Population increases fastest in countries least urbanized, least mechanized, least prosperous. China will have one third of the world's population by the year 2000. It is barely possible that China and other nations like her will be able to find and to impose the means of controlling their rising birth rates and feeding the added numbers. But even the most optimistic predictions give us little more to hope for than that they can hold their own—which means a constantly growing population and a continuously malnourished one. A well-fed world is not likely in light of the fact that North America, with 10 percent of the population and 31 percent of the world's food supply, has not found the means of preventing tens of millions of its people from hunger. In the United States alone somewhere between 25 and 60 million people are living below the minimun standard of health and decency ($3,350 for a family of four). United Nations studies show that the Far East, the most densely populated area of the world, would have to increase its food production 475 percent by the year 2000 in order to meet what we in the West regard as below-minimum standards of health and decency. At present "over half the people now alive will die before their time because of malnutrition." [2] It is not likely that this shocking condition will be materially changed, at least for the better, forty years from now when the world population has doubled.

In the technically advanced countries most of the hungry people are found in the cities. In the United States the majority of the 25 to 60 million poor are urbanized. They are members of the following groups: Negroes, the aged, the foreign-language groups, the unemployed of all backgrounds, those living in broken homes, and those living in families where the wife is the sole wage earner. The majority of these poor are living in what Harrington calls "the economic underworld" of America's metropolitan centers.[3]

It does not take much imagination to visualize what crowding does to people. The poor arrive in larger and larger numbers in the cities of the world. The affluent in the cities tear down the slums to build highways, stadiums, gasoline stations, and office buildings, thus crowding the poor even more. Human congestion is at its worst in the inner cities. Perhaps rat experimentation does not help us to understand human behavior, but an experimenter with rat populations found that the more he increased the density of the animals, the more "social pathology" appeared among them. It was particularly high among the females! It became increasingly difficult if not impossible for the adults to build nests, let alone for the mothers to care for their young. It became almost impossible to secure food and water. Both fighting and apathy increased with the population.[4]

In spite of all difficulties population growth as it develops in metropolitan centers is not entirely threatening, particularly in the technically advanced nations. Multitudes survive, and many improve their living conditions in urban settings. Most of these are not the ones who have migrated to the cities. They are those who have grown up in the cities or their satellites, grown up with a sufficiently good inheritance to ensure their physical health, their education, and their entry into the job market at a skilled level. In the advanced countries those who make it are more in number than those who do not. Therefore it is possible to speak of the poor as invisible. What is more, relatively speaking, the poor in an affluent land are not as poor as those in underdeveloped countries. Even though the concentration of people in metropolitan areas in a nation like the United States is marked (40 percent of the total population in 1900 when it was 75,994,575 as compared with the 1960 figure of 70 percent [est.] of the total population when the total was 179,323,175), it does not begin to approach the problems experienced in most Asian, African, and Latin American countries. Population growth as a threatening ingredient in the urbanization mix is not felt as keenly in the industrialized countries. Yet even in these the density in the cites has so far outdistanced social planning that whole societies of poverty exist within societies of plenty.

Racism as an Ingredient in the Mix

Pride of religion, culture, class, and race and the consequent exclusion of men on these bases are volatile elements around the world. The situation is seen most clearly in the urban areas where people of all kinds come together. Call it racism for short. The cities of the world are cockpits of repression and revolt. Frantz Fanon of black Algeria calls it the "natives" against the "colonialists." Whatever name is given it, there is the determination of those who had control in the nineteenth century to keep it in the twentieth and there is the determination of those whose parents and grandparents were controlled then not to be controlled now.

The black power emphasis in the United States is one of the many forms the struggle takes. In many countries, where one of the antagonistic forces is native to the land while the other is foreign to it, the conflict takes the form of national unrest and uprising, covert, overt, or both. One of Fanon's descriptions suggests the consuming power of these forces. Speaking of the native, Fanon writes, "He is overpowered but not tamed; he is treated as an inferior but he is not convinced of his inferiority. He is patiently waiting until the settler is off his guard to fly at him. The native's muscles are always tensed. You can't say that he is terriorized, or even apprehensive. He is in fact ready at a moment's notice to exchange the *role* of the quarry for that of the hunter."[5]

In the urbanized parts of any land these forces come into conflict most often and most violently. These are the places where the largest number of "natives" are. The black population of this country was once predominantly rural. In 1910, when there were 10 million black Americans, three out of four lived on farms. Today there are over 20 million black citizens. Three out of four live in the cities. Negroes are the most urbanized of all Americans. Virtually all the population growth among them (and they are outstripping the whites) is in the central cities of the North. By 1985 blacks in America will number 30 million, and they will be the majority in eleven of the largest cities. (It is not insignificant that young Negro males constitute 20 percent of the U. S. Armed Forces in Vietnam. They are returning, mainly to ghettos, with combat experience!) If white Americans continue to run the systems of the land primarily for the benefit of white people, we can expect a continued increase of the spirit Fanon describes—"ready at a moment's notice to exchange the *role* of the quarry for that of the hunter."

It is hard to know how pervasive the polarization of the races is in this country or elsewhere in the world. One sees increasing polarization here. Middle-class blacks sense their identity with poor blacks. They can remember their past, and they know discrimination in the present. A common sense of alienation, already far advanced in Africa for example, appears here among most black Americans. The most general canvass is that of the Kerner Commission. It has warned the United States that the division will be unbridgeable in twenty years unless giant steps are taken by white power structures to provide equal opportunity.[6] Possibly reflecting on what has happened elsewhere in the world, the commission observed, "If the Negro population as a whole developed even stronger feelings of being wrongly 'penned in' and discriminated against, many of its members might come to support not only riots, but the rebellion now being preached by only a handful." [7]

While racism is by no means the sole ingredient in urbanization, it is the most prevalent. It permeates the entire community of man and threatens to destroy it piecemeal if not *in toto*.

The Cybernetic Revolution

Cybernation is a part of the mix that makes urbanization so formative for the future of mankind. It promotes urbanization as well as receiving incentive from it. The word was coined by Donald N. Michael, who wished to avoid the problem of referring here to automation and there to computers. To avoid semantic difficulties "we invent the term 'cybernation' to refer to *both* automation and computers." [8]

The cybernetic revolution in which computers direct the machines which men have previously directed means leisure and unemployment, freedom and depersonalization. It has already led to serious demands on the part of organized labor not only for guaranteed annual incomes but for guaranteed life incomes. With regard to the poor it has raised the question of guaranteed incomes for those totally unemployed, for the part-time unemployed, and for the underemployed.

Predictions as to the effects of cybernation vary. There are ominous estimates that within ten to twenty-five years a mere 2 percent of the population will be able to produce everything the other 98 percent can consume. There are sanguine assurances that new products will be developed which will create new jobs. No one predicts that there will be jobs for all.

Unemployment is slowly but steadily rising in the United States, for example, as industry cybernates the design and the manufacture of goods. It is said that by 1985 many manufacturers will be able to go directly from mechanical drawings to finished products by way of the computer. In this country we are moving in the decade of the 60's from an unemployment ratio of 3 to 4 percent to an unemployment ratio of 11 to 12 percent. There will continue to be pages and pages of ads in the newspapers offering jobs. There will continue to be millions of men out of jobs. The reason is that the jobs available require technical skills which many now in the job market and many of those entering the job market do not have.

Seligman says there are three myths still widely believed about the cybernetic revolution: "that it upgrades workers" and that "it produces as many or more jobs as it destroys." Since these myths contribute to complacency, they are vicious, he declares. "The third myth is that automation advances but slowly." [9]

The problem of solving unemployment can be illustrated in the recent experience of one American city. During the first half of 1968, twenty-two government and business manpower programs were in operation. They attempted to find and train jobless people. The results were:

Number of jobless people in Cleveland: 40,000 (est.)
Number of people reached by the twenty-two programs: 8,000
Number of people who actually got jobs: 2,500

Of the people who were employed, the jobs paid below-minimum wages in many cases. In some cases the jobs paid less than these people got while they were being trained for the jobs!

The 3 to 4 percent (2 million) unemployment figure quoted above is the usual federal government statistic. It does not take into account two or three times that number (4 to 6 million Americans) who have ceased to look for jobs and therefore are not on the records as being unemployed. Nor does it take into account 6½ million more who are underemployed, that is, earning less than $3,350 for a family of four—the national poverty level. Already the unemployment in this one technically advanced country is several times the official estimates. It is impossible to predict what it will be in the United States or in any other country ten to twenty-five years hence. But one ecologist has warned, "We have little enough time to prepare to cushion the shock of the cybernation revolution. If we bury our heads in the sand this time it will not be some far-off people who will pay for the willful blindness, but ourselves, in affluent and comfortable America." [10]

Secularization: Part of the Urban Mix

Another set of ingredients in the urban mix is the progressive secularization of thought and action. Macquarrie summarizes the meaning of a secularized outlook in four terms: (1) interest is in the temporal order rather than the eternal, (2) everyday activities are the concern rather than "religious" activities, (3) knowledge to be trusted is knowledge gained through human means rather than through revelation, (4) the autonomy of man is stressed rather than dependence upon God.[11]

The cities of men are the centers of this secularizing process. They exemplify man's power over nature and history. This is uniquely the case with the modern metropolis. Man has been building cities for five thousand years, but the metropolis is less than a hundred years old. Today's cities are the products of technological power. They are possible only because of man's recent inventions in transportation, communication, manufacturing, and building. Without these developments the interdependence of millions would be impossible. With them entire societies are influenced. Everything from hair styles to the cost of living is determined in these metropolitan centers. They have become the chief source of life's enhancement and its exploitation. Here the focus is on the cities as carriers of the secularizing process. Wirth has noted a number of characteristics of metropolitan centers which explain their secularizing power.

The size of the populations reduces mutual acquaintanceship, affords citizens the opportunity to meet one another in highly segmented roles, enhances personal freedom but reduces the sense of personal participation, increases the number of essentially predatory relationships, and requires organizational actions rather than individual actions.

The density of the populations puts a premium on visual recognition of persons rather than in-depth understanding, divides people into many social worlds, increases the number of physical contacts but increases also the social distance between people, accentuates individual responsibility but increases loneliness, accelerates all movements, places less reliance on voluntary cooperation and more reliance on impersonal rules and routines.

The heterogeneity of the populations breaks down the rigidity of caste lines, maximizes the possibilities of specialized development of skills and abilities, depersonalizes the individual in the process of distributing his goods and services, draws the individual into mass movements where he can both realize and lose himself.[12]

The net effect of such communities is to change the nature of human existence by requiring different responses and cultivating different abilities. The very expectations of life in an urban society change from those of rural existence.

The psychological studies of Simmel have shown:

1. "Metropolis exacts from man as a discriminating creature a different amount of consciousness than does rural life."[13]

2. "In order to accommodate to change and to the contrast of phenomena, . . . he reacts with his head instead of his heart. . . . Intellectuality is thus seen to preserve subjective life against the overwhelming power of metropolitan life." [14]
3. With money rather than goods as the medium of exchange, the "modern mind has become more and more calculating. The calculating exactness of practical life which the money economy has brought about corresponds to the ideal of natural science: to transform the world into an arithmetic problem, to fix every part of the world by mathematical formulas." [15]
4. "Punctuality, calculability, exactness, are forced upon life by the complexity and extension of metropolitan existence and not only most intimately connected with its money economy and intellectualistic character. These traits must also color the contents of life and favor the exclusion of those irrational, instinctive, sovereign traits and impulses which aim at determining the mode of life from within, instead of receiving the general and precisely schematized form of life from without." [16]

In an environment in which man is required to marshall all his capacities for scheming, in which he must produce through calculation, in which he must live by playing his part in a complex web of responsibilities regardless of his feelings, lies the principal means of genuine secularization. In such an environment secularization becomes essential to survival as well as advancement. It is no wonder that Protestants in the West, for example, have generally regarded urbanization as bad. They have seen the priorities it places upon the temporal, the everyday, human knowledge, and autonomy.

II. The Effects of Urbanization upon the Churches

Regarding urbanization as the enemy of Christian faith in God for many reasons—good as well as bad—the churches have sanctioned withdrawal.[17] The flight to the suburbs cannot be regarded as the only form of rejecting the urban task. Yet Winter is right when he makes the diagnosis: "Suburbia is symptomatic of a mass amnesia—a widespread and morbid forgetfulness by which men and women shut out the world of human reality and even the deeper aspects of their own experience." [18]

The urban crisis, as expressive of the revolutionary changes taking place in history, has disclosed the irrelevance of religious institutions to the contemporary problems of man and has called forth their interest in becoming relevant. Indeed, one way of analyzing the crisis within the churches is to say that they are torn by the values religion has for retreat from reality and the values it has for confronting it—the comfort-challenge conflict.

On the positive side—most readers know the negative side well enough—urbanization has already evoked remarkable changes in the churches as institutions. An illustration is the production and the use throughout the world of the World Council of Churches' documents on new structures for mission.[19] These documents disclose a thorough knowledge of the times and an unwavering commitment to desirable social change. They recognize that a new mode of human existence is coming into being with untold consequences for good or ill. The task of the church is to respond to what is happening, to think, to organize, and to act not out of concern for itself—it is a church for others. Churches are "to share in every truly human effort in a way that is both constructive and critical." [20] The purpose of churches, according to these reports, is to recognize and support the establishment of *shalom* in the world.

> Everything in the world may have a double aspect. Each time a man is imprisoned, tortured, or destroyed, death is at work. But each time a man is a true neighbor, each time men live for others, the life-giving action of God is to be discerned. These are signs of the Kingdom of God and of the setting up of *shalom*. One may consider examples like this: the emancipation of the coloured races, the concern for the humanization of industrial relations, various attempts at rural development, the quest for business and professional ethics, the concern for

intellectual honesty and integrity. So God, as he moves toward his final goal, is using men and women, both inside and outside the churches, to bring signs of *shalom*." [21]

The World Council reports devote the most space to structural reform of the churches. Asserting that one of the sins of the churches has been "morphological fundamentalism" (absolutizing the local congregation as the form of church life), the reports declare Christians must reform present structures and create new ones which go into the world and meet it where human need exists. The churches must renounce all "come structures" of church life which wait until the world comes to the church door or which try to persuade the world to become a part of the church. "The message and the structures of the churches can only be formulated with respect to the immense variety of actual realities amidst which we live. Hence it is the world which must be allowed to provide the agenda for the churches." [22] A sizable portion of the first report and most of the second report describe the kinds of structures that may be called for and the forms of service the churches can and should engage in if they are to be the church for others.

III. Urbanization's Impact on the Clergy

In the United States the most revealing evidence of the impact of the urban crisis upon clergymen has emerged from the civil rights struggle, now transmuted into the movement for black self-determination and the subversion of white racism. The data on clergy conflicts stemming from civil rights involvement clarify and confirm what studies there are of clergy in other situations.

High on the list of ministerial tasks is the rediscovery of the prophetic role. What is it? How can it be carried out? In the course of examining this question and experimenting with answers, American clergy have locked horns with other clergy and the laity, churches have been divided, pledges have been cut, factions have formed, and not a few pastors have lost their jobs.

The civil rights struggle has disclosed the degree to which the churches are caught between their professed ideals of brotherhood and their apartheid practices. More, it has revealed that by and large their expectations of pastors are ones of comfort rather than of challenge. Beyond the fact that no man wants to be what has crudely been called a "paid gigolo," there is the fact that few pastors, no matter how conservative, can escape some knowledge of the needs of the community. Their very contact with parishoners in trouble reveals some of the problems men face in an urbanizing world. There is, furthermore, the recognition that some aspects of society are dehumanizing. According to a recent study of theological education, the most disturbing thing about the practice of the ordained ministry today is the widespread frustration of pastors that they cannot move beyond personal help for a few to changing the structures that affect many. "He [the clergyman] wishes to touch the sources of power in American life." [23] How to aid in effecting justice in urban society—the prophetic task—is an absorbing question now.

Another effect of urbanization on clergy is the opening up of nonordained but equally significant ministries. Clergy, rejected by their congregations for their involvement in civil rights and similar social problems, have been forced to find other forms of service. Specialization within the ranks of ordained men has gone on for a long time—in one sense it began with the apostolic church—but urbanization has increased the pressures to find other avenues of service. There is now a full-fledged movement in the churches to interpret ministry to such a way as to stress God's call to the whole church as over against to certain members who become "ministers." As ministry is seen by the churches as the task of all members, the clergyman *as we know him* may vanish, as Illich has predicted. "The adult layman, ordained to the ministry [by which he means presiding in worship], will preside over the 'normal' Christian community of the future. The ministry [again, leading worship] will be an exercise of leisure rather than a job." [24] At any rate, the way in which urbanization is dividing the functions formerly performed by pastors and the pressures of fragmentation felt by clergy today combine to create a serious vocational problem as well as a host of fascinating possibilities for worldly ministries.

Urbanization may be expected to change the focus of the clergyman's job. For some time he will no doubt retain certain traditional responsibilities, but new ones will be added, chiefly in the area of community leadership (direct and indirect). These new responsibilities will be forced upon the clergyman by his own desire to be relevant, by metropolitant forces which expect help from the churches, and by at least a minority of parishioners who want direction in relating their faith to daily life. The nature of this change will be suggested in the last part of this essay.

IV. The Effects of Urbanization upon Theology

So far the most marked results of urbanization have been upon the thinking and acting of churchmen. As most studies show, they think and act like secular men. This is particularly true of laymen. One nationwide questionnaire on the beliefs of clergy and laity showed the clergy to be considerably more liberal than the laity as far as the traditional doctrines of Christianity are concerned. At the same time, the questionnaire revealed that the beliefs laymen hold have far less relevance for them than beliefs do for clergymen. The meaninglessness of traditional Christianity for both clergy and laity, however, is so widespread as to be normal. The very terms in which Christianity is being reinterpreted show this. Theological literature whether written for the scholars or for the common man is polarized between the themes of God and secularity to such an extent that all thinking in the churches is conditioned by it.

Macquarrie has shown how differently contemporary theologians go at the task of reconstructing theology. Van Buren in *The Secular Meaning of the Gospel* does it with the help of British empiricism. Ronald Gregor Smith in his *Secular Christianity* takes Bultmann's existentialism as his point of entry into a theology for today. Harvey Cox in *The Secular City* is guided principally by sociology. Van Leeuwen's treatise on *Christianity in World History* frames the problem of secularization, interestingly enough, in Barthian terms and opts for a secularized Christianity that is the new bearer of Christian mission to the world. These varying approaches demonstrate the center of gravity in theology now. It is the world revolution of which urbanization is the advance guard—a world increasingly this-worldly and drawing Christian thinkers into this orbit. It is forcing Christians to abandon or reinterpret their beliefs. It is putting them into positions of unavoidable encounter with other faiths, above all secularism (which involves the absolutizing of contemporary methods and values), and thus it requires of Christians both explanation and reinterpretation.

Winter suggests the scope of the change which urbanization has brought about when he writes: "When the churches maintained their apostolate to the world by enlisting loyalty to religious activities and institutions, the burden of Christian reflection and teaching could be carried out by religious specialists. . . . The secularization of the world terminates this traditional structure of continuity, for it rests the heavy burden of apostolate on the laity in their work in the world. The servant Church emerges as a community of highly sensitive and theologically self-conscious laymen. . . . They bear the burden of discerning the meaning of events in the human struggle." [25]

V. Urbanization and the Pastor's Role

Once again, under new conditions and for pressing reasons, the pastor must become a priest, a celebrant, a leader of worship. The era of pastoral psychology helped pastors to discover the significance of shepherding, healing individuals in inner conflict and interpersonal relations. Today the pastor begins to see shepherding in a different context—without denying the importance of this ministry to persons. He sees laity as the missionaries to the structures of this world which threaten to dehumanize all men.

His task is to help them prepare for Christian service. Worship becomes a vital means to that end.

If the church is to make a unique contribution to what happens in the urbanizing process of history, it will include helping men to discover what is *holy* about what is happening, and what is *demonic*. What is it that is happening out there? What is important in the world? What ought Christian men to be doing in it? What can they do? It will be necessary to discover, in Robinson's words, that:

> Liturgy is essentially and primarily a secular activity, as the origin of the word in the sphere of public works testifies. It is concerned . . . with matter, with society, with action—*ordinary* matter, society, and action—*at the level of the holy*, at the level at which it is touched and re-created by the transforming Spirit of Christ. It is not concerned with a special world of its own, but with the making sacred of the secular. . . . Communion has to do with the transformation of ordinary things and ordinary relationships. But this is what every celebration should be saying, and our sanctuaries are too religious for secular man to see it. This does not mean they are too holy—often far from it. But it means that the holiness that pervades them is not a worldly holiness: it does not speak to men, in Kiekegaard's phrase, of a "deeper immersion in existence," of how *their world* can be changed.[26]

The focus of this and all other roles will probably be that of enabler—H. Richard Niebuhr calls it "pastoral director." The pastor will have as his purpose in all that he does the task of the catalyst. Niebuhr sensed the change that is coming over the churches and suggested the lines along which its leadership would develop:

> In his work the pastoral director carries on all the traditional functions of the ministry—preaching, leading the worshiping community, administering the sacraments, caring for souls, presiding over the church. But as the preacher and priest organized these traditional functions in special ways so does the pastoral director. His first function is that of building or "edifying" the church; he is concerned in every-

thing that he does to bring into being a people of God who as a Church will serve the purpose of the Church in the local community and the world.[27]

Niebuhr shows how this concept of the ordained ministry shapes all functions, traditional and innovative, so that they have a unity. Preaching becomes a means of helping men to become mature in their faith and responsible in their actions. Teaching instructs those coming into the church in its true purpose and instructs the members in the ways and means of mission. Teaching teachers—laity who bring their own insight and experience to the task—becomes a role of the pastor. The leadership of worship becomes a demonstration of God's love for the world through the church (emphasizing not the old sequence, God-church-world but the new: God-world-church; "that is, God's primary relationship is to the world, and it is the world and not the Church that is the focus of God's plan."[28]) Counseling deals with personal problems but in the larger context of preparing for service. The general aim in all pastoral work, says Niebuhr, will be this: "The Church is becoming the minister and its 'minister' is its servant, directing it in its service."[29]

Urbanization's effects on man require that future ministry be to structures as well as to persons. Elsewhere I have contrasted the acceptability of the one and the unacceptability of the other:

To date, the term pastoral care does not connote any kind of ministry to the social conditions which help to create, continue, and complicate individual problems, and which are indispensable factors in the fulfillment of man's psychic needs. At present, pastoral care is quite proper when it is given to sick persons but not when it is given to sick cities. It is perfectly acceptable to give pastoral care to physically and mentally handicapped individuals. It is not regarded as true pastoral care to give the same attention to institutions which cripple individuals physically and mentally. Dying persons have the attention of pastors and this is rightly regarded as pastoral care. The trouble is that the same attention to a dying community (not to mention death-dealing institutions like war) is regarded as "meddling" when the pastor gets involved. Working with a small group of persons to enhance their insight and interpersonal effectiveness is sanctioned as proper pastoral care. Working with a group of persons to improve employment or educational or housing systems which obviously affect the social productivity, and perhaps less obviously but nonetheless surely the very life purpose of individuals, is still not considered pastoral care.[30]

The nature of existence in an urban society will require that pastors relate differently to the community than they have been. They will have to have one foot in secular agencies striving for change and one foot in ecclesiastical structures committed to change. Their link will be task forces from both communities. It is already apparent that churches alone can neither initiate nor sustain the range of action necessary to arrest a dehumanizing process or develop a human one. Churches that have been significantly involved in social change have been provoked, prodded, and enabled by some community agency. The Southwest Community Organization in Chicago, for example, began by bringing in a professional community organizer who worked with concerned people in the neighborhoods of that racially disturbed area of 180,000. It was clear that the help of the churches was needed, that they could make the difference between a community which was deteriorating physically and socially and a community which could stabilize the environment and reconcile its residents. In this situation thirty-six out of sixty-seven churches became members of the organization thus enabling it to be the area-wide means of peaceful, integrated social change.

The history of this effort shows that a community organization can become a symbol of hope in the community, provide a forum for diverse groups in the community, provide avenues for joint action, make it possible for a moral ideal to become a practical principle of action, and control or eliminate destructive elements which frequently develop in a social crisis. The churches would not have been able to produce this organization, but they were vital to its success. In turn, certain pastors played decisive roles from the beginning. Had they not identified themselves with the organization, they would not have know what was going on, they could not have confronted rumor with truth, and they would not have had the means of getting their congregations into creative service to the community.

Pastoral care in the future will be pastoral care of communities and the enabling of Christian laymen to take the lead in this care.

Notes

1. Lloyd Rodwin, ed., *The Future Metropolis* (New York: Braziller, 1961), pp. 9-10.
2. Paul Simon, *The Christian Encounters a Hungry World* (St. Louis: *Concordia*, 1966), p. 89.
3. Harrington observes, "There are tens of thousands of Americans in the big cities who are wearing shoes, perhaps even a stylishly cut suit or dress, and yet are hungry. It is not a matter of planning, though it almost seems as it the affluent society had given out costumes to the poor so that they would not offend the rest of society with the sight of rags." Michael Harrington, *The Other America: Poverty in the United States* (New York: Macmillan, 1962), p. 13.
4. Leonard J. Duhl, ed., *The Urban Condition* (New York: Basic Books, 1963), chap. 4.
5. Frantz Fanon, *The Wretched of the Earth* (New York: Grove Press, 1965), p. 42.
6. *Report of the National Advisory Comission on Civil Disorders* (New York: Dutton, 1968), p. 407.
7. *Ibid.*, pp. 397-98.
8. Quoted in Robert Theobald, ed., *The Guaranteed Income* (New York: Doubleday, 1966), p. 31.
9. Ben B. Seligman, "Automation and the Work Force," *The Guaranteed Income*, p. 78.
10. William Vogt, "Conservation and the Guaranteed Income," *The Guaranteed Income*, p. 160.
11. John Macquarrie, *God and Secularity* ("New Directions in Theology Today," Vol. III; Philadelphia: Westminster Press, 1967), chap. 3.
12. Louis Wirth, "Urbanism as a Way of Life," *Cities and Churches*, ed. Robert Lee (Philadelphia: Westminster Press, 1962), pp. 21-33.
13. Georg Simmel, "The Metropolis and Mental Life," *Cities and Churches*, p. 35.
14. *Ibid.*, p. 36.
15. *Ibid.*, p. 38.
16. *Ibid.*, p. 39.
17. Douglass records the fact: "Many leading Protestants genuinely feel that a permanent and deadly hostility exists between urban man and those who are loyal to the Christian faith and ethic; that village ways of life are somehow more acceptable to God than city ways. . . . Today one out of every eight people in the United States lives in a city of more than a million inhabitants; four out of every ten, in cities of at least 25,000; and another four, within twenty-five

miles of such cities. And from these cities spring ideas, tastes, standards, folkways, and value judgments which—through radio, television, and the mass-circulation magazines—become those of the whole nation. If Protestantism gives up the city, it virtually gives up America. Yet that is precisely what it has been doing." (Truman Douglass, "The Job the Protestants Shirk," *Cities and Churches*, pp. 88, 87).

18. Gibson Winter, *The New Creation as Metropolis* (New York: Macmillan, 1963), pp. 136-37.
19. *The Church for Others: Two Reports on the Missionary Structure of the Congregation* (final report of the Western European Working Group and the North American Working Group of the Department of Studies in Evangelism, Geneva: World Council of Churches, 1967).
20. *Ibid.*, p. 13.
21. *Ibid.*, p. 15.
22. *Ibid.*, p. 20.
23. Episcopal Church Foundation, *Ministry for Tomorrow: Report of the Special Committee on Theological Education* (New York: Seabury Press, 1967), pp. 39-40.
24. Ivan Illich, "The Vanishing Clergyman," *The Critic*, June–July, 1967, pp. 22-23.
25. Winter, *New Creation as Metropolis*, pp. 63-64.
26. John A. T. Robinson, *Liturgy Coming to Life* (Philadelphia: Westminster Press, 1964), p. xi.
27. H. Richard Niebuhr, *The Purpose of the Church and Its Ministry* (New York: Harper, 1956), p. 82.
28. *The Church for Others*, pp. 16-17.
29. Niebuhr, *The Purpose of the Church and Its Ministry*, p. 83.
30. Robert H. Bonthius, "Pastoral Care for Structures—As Well as Persons," *Pastoral Psychology*, May, 1967, pp. 14-15.

The Influence of Psychology on Theology

Don S. Browning

There has been a persistent subordinate theme running throughout the pastoral psychology and pastoral theology movements. This theme has to do with the possibility of psychology's making significant contributions to the task of systematic and constructive theology. That psychology can contribute something to theology was a possibility that did not command the attention of many people within the pastoral psychology movement. Nor can it be said that psychology, as American pastoral counselors have known and practiced it, has actually had a great deal of influence on modern theology. It is probably true that Paul Tillich, David Roberts, and Daniel Day Williams were the only American theologians during this recent period who either pursued or profited from the dialogue with the psychologies and psychotherapies popular on the North American scene. For the American pastoral counseling movement, psychology was associated with the names of Freud, Jung, Rogers, Horney, and Sullivan.

In spite of this situation, in Europe and to a lesser extent in the United States, a new kind of psychology known as existential phenomenology was gaining prominence and was destined to influence both clinical psychology and theology. I am referring to the existential phenomenology of Martin Heidegger,[1] which soon influenced the psychology of Ludwig Binswanger and Medard Boss as well as the theological ontologies of Rudolf Bultmann and Paul Tillich.

In answering the question as to what influence psychology has had on modern theology, the answer would greatly depend upon which psychology one has in mind. If one is referring to empirical psychology, the answer must be that it has had only a slight influence. But if one is referring to existential phenomenology, the answer must be that its influence has been enormous, and in some ways it constitutes the single most important cultural influence on contemporary theological thought.

I. Phenomenology and Psychology

Even though it can be readily granted that existential phenomenology has had significant influence on modern theology, it is still important to consider the question: to what extent can existential phenomenology justifiably be called a *kind* of psychology?

It is probably safe to say that in the work of Heidegger an earlier distinction made by Husserl between phenomenological psychology and transcendental philosophy (philosophical phenomenology) began to break down. Husserl understood philosophical phenomenology as a study of the pure subjectivity of the transcendental ego. In order to make such a study two reductions had to be made: the transcendental reduction and the eidetic reduction. The transcendental reduction involved the suspension of the so-called "natural attitude"—one's naïve belief in the existence of the world and its objects. The eidetic reduction involved an effort to abstract the "invariant" and "essential" forms or patterns which were manifest in the multiplicity of different appearances of the phenomenon one might be studying.[2]

Husserl distinguished philosophical phenomenology from phenomenological psychology. Phenomenological psychology was, according to Husserl, an eidetic discipline but one which sought for the essential structure of phenomena *within* the natural attitude. Phenomenological psychology does not practice the transcendental reduction: it does not suspend its commonsense assumptions about the existence of the world. Therefore it attempts to study man as being-in-the-world. This is the step Heidegger took. He attempted to give a description of the essential structures of man's being-in-the-world, the essential structures of man's subjectivity within the natural attitude.

Although Heidegger's attempt to bring to light the essential structures of man's being-in-the-world takes a step toward what Husserl understood as phenomenological psychology because of its repudiation of the transcendental reduction, it does not quite become phenomenological psychology as Husserl described it. Phenomenological psychology was an effort to describe the essential structures of *psychic* consciousness—the psychic experiences of the *human* ego. Pure phenomenological philosophy attempts to describe the essence of the larger background of consciousness which Husserl called the transcendental ego, of which the human ego is only a component. Heidegger's phenomenological existentialism is like Husserl's philosophical phenomenology in this respect: it brackets the human ego and describes the larger background of consciousness, what Heidegger called the *Dasein* or "being there" of man. This is why his enterprise is often called an ontological-existential analysis of man.

Of course, within the phenomenological tradition both phenomenological philosophy and phenomenological psychology were distinguished from empirical psychology. Phenomenologists such as Husserl, Sartre, and Merleau-Ponty tend to characterize empirical psychology as that psychology which patterns itself after the empirical methods of the physical sciences. They argue that such a method must necessarily treat man's psychical experience as a *res extensa*, as a substance which operates in analogy to physical objects in the space-time continuum. Such a psychology seeks to ground its propositions in causal-explanatory hypotheses and seeks validation through quantitative and experimental procedures.

To answer the question of how psychology has been influential on modern theology one must specify with some precision the proper domain of the use of the word psychology. If one is to enlarge the meaning of psychology to cover the study of the totality of consciousness in all its actual and potential states, then psychology can encompass everything from Husserl's philosophical phenomenology to Heidegger's ontology on down to empirical psychology. There is no particular reason to limit psychology to the specific study of the so-called "psychical" experiences of the human ego and then to assert that the larger field of consciousness is somehow the proper field of philosophical phenomenology. To suggest that one has moved from psychology to philosophy when one has placed in brackets the human ego and then concentrated on some larger field of consciousness called either the transcendental ego or *Dasein* is, it seems to me, not only arbitrary but even misleading. It may be accurate insofar as it clearly communicates that philosophical phenomenology and existential phenomenology are interested in describing the subjective and constitutive aspects of consciousness at a level which transcends specific reference to the experiences of the individual ego. But it is misleading in that it overlooks that psychology too must be interested in the wider field of consciousness, the wider structure of the human, even if it is primarily concerned with understanding the experiences of the individual ego.

For example, several American psychologists, and specifically Carl Rogers, make a distinction between the self (Snygg and Combs call it the "phenomenal self") and the larger experiential field out of which it differentiates.[3] Although Rogers is primarily interested in studying the self as an object within this field, it would be entirely possible for a psychologist of his stamp to turn to a study of the structures of the larger experiential field. To do this would be to move toward a study of what Heidegger would call the *Dasein.* Furthermore, if Rogers were to place in suspension his natural belief in the existence of the world, he would move a step closer to what Husserl would have called pure philosophical phenomenology. If, however, Rogers were to take on such a pursuit, if he were to expand his interest and study the structures of the larger experiential field, I doubt if he would be inclined to call it philosophical anthropology; he would undoubtedly consider such an interest to be well within the proper domain of psychology.

Therefore, there can be no clear demarcation between philosophical anthropology and psychology, and it can be asserted with some justification that philosophical anthropology, and especially Heidegger's existential-ontology, is a kind of psychology. Heidegger's ontology, as it was developed in *Sein und Zeit* during his earlier period is an attempt to describe the implicit and sometimes "hidden" structures of man's consciousness of being-in-the-world. It is a phenomenological description of the *a priori* structures of the *Lebenswelt*, a concept very similar to the concept of "life-space" as we have come to know the concept in American psychology through the work of Kurt Lewin.

II. Bultmann and Tillich

If Heidegger's existential-ontology is a kind of psychology, then it can be seen more clearly how this kind of psychology has been influential on modern theology. It is widely known that Bultmann's theological program is a somewhat unambiguous translation of New Testament myth and symbol into Heidegger's existential-ontological concepts. This was his widely celebrated program of demythologization in which all New Testament statements which attributed supernatural causes to natural and earthly phenomena were translated into existential-ontological statements, that is, statements descriptive of the self-understanding of faith implicit in the mythical material.[4] Bultmann believed there is a special affinity between Heidegger's ontology and the implicit understanding of man operative in the New Testament. Therefore, Bultmann found it relatively easy to restate the Pauline concept of the body into Heidegger's description of *Dasein*, the Heideggerian concept on *Befindlichkeit* into the Pauline concept of the heart, or Heidegger's concept of *Verfallenheit* into the biblical concept of "bondage to sin." Heidegger's description of *Dasein* as *Sorge* ("care") and the *a priori* existentials such as *Befindlichkeit*, *Verstehen*, *Verfallenheit*, and *Rede* constitute the *Begrifflichkeit* ("a system of basic concepts") into which the New

Testament material is translated.[5] Because in Bultmann's approach the New Testament is translated into this *a priori* system of basic concepts, it is entirely fair to say that it is a kind of existentialist psychology of religion applied to the gospel material. It is not essentially different from using the core of basic concepts typical of any other psychological system, say Freudian or Jungian, to interpret the biblical story except that Heidegger's ontological-existential concepts are phenomenologically derived and are not causal-explanatory in character. Theoretically such concepts are supposed to be more faithful to the full richness of human intentionality and therefore less reductive. But it may be that the concepts of phenomenological existentialism are reductive in a different sense, not in the causal-explanatory sense so much as in a certain "abstractive" sense which is equally distorting.

I believe that Tillich's approach to the interpretation of biblical myth and symbol is more similar to Bultmann's than is often recognized. It must be remembered that Tillich develops an ontology based upon an analysis of the self-world correlation. The self-world correlation is Tillich's way of talking about man's situation as being-in-the-world. The ontological elements which he derives from the self-world correlation—the polarities of individualization and participation, dynamics and form, freedom and destiny—are Tillich's *Begrifflichkeit*, his core of systematic anthropological concepts in terms of which he interprets biblical symbolism. In Tillich, the ontology of the human and metaphysics merge into one because it is with the ontological elements derived from man's being-in-the-world that he describes other beings besides man (even inanimate beings) as well as describing, in a symbolic and nonliteral sense, God himself.[6] Tillich proposes, as does Bultmann, that man must speak of the divine itself in analogies taken from man's own being. And although both theologians find a place for revelation, their interpretation of the meaning of revelation is stated in terms drawn from an ontology of human existence—an ontology which I have attempted to demonstrate can be justifiably called a kind of existential psychology.

III. Psychology and an Ontology of the Human

Both Bultmann and Tillich believe an ontology of man's being-in-the-world is a necessary propaedeutic to the interpretation of biblical myth and symbol. This poses several questions. First, is this true? Is it necessary to develop an ontology of the human which serves as a common anthropological base into which religious material can be translated? Second, if it is necessary, what is the best way to develop such an ontology, and what role should psychology play in bringing it about?

It should be readily admitted that there exists today new resistance to the idea that theology should be assisted by an auxiliary ontology of the human. Those theologians influenced by the later Heidegger have seemed to lose interest in the use of a general ontology for theological interpretation but rather are confronting scripture in a more Barthian-like openness to being "formed" by the language event upon which the New Testament is founded. In this view one does not need a general theory of interpretation to understand the language of the New Testament; rather, the language of the New Testament is that which opens up understanding and mediates it to the listener. Language is the "house of being," and we do not interpret language so much as language interprets us.[7]

Paul Ricoeur also seems to be moving more and more in his later works toward a direct phenomenology of the myths and symbols of evil, refraining from permitting his earlier pure phenomenological description of the will in *Freedom and Nature* and his empirics of the will in *Fallible Man* to dominate his later work in the *Symbolism of Evil.*[8] He too wishes to enrich modern language with the fullness of reality apprehended by myth and symbol. His work stands as a repudiation of Bultmann and Tillich in their interest to translate myth and symbol into an ontology of the human compatible with the modern mentality. Rather, Ricoeur is more interested in rediscovering the richness of human reality which pure "reflection" seems unable to grasp.

It is doubtless true that any general ontology of the human

arrived at by reflection, either as pure phenomenological description in Husserl's sense or through a phenomenology of the *Dasein* in Heidegger's sense, is likely to be abstractive and finally somewhat rationalistic, in spite of the attention it may pay to features of human experience such as anxiety, guilt, and death. Although existential phenomenology may not be able to provide us with an entirely satisfactory ontology, some kind of ontology of the human is needed if religious symbols are ever to make meaningful contact with other cultural disciplines. An ontology of the human is needed not so much to interpret religious and theological symbols, but to serve as common coinage for intelligible discourse between the sciences of man and these religious symbols. For instance, the pastoral psychologist and counselor would profit immensely if he possessed a common ontology which would be effective for the interpretation of both clinical phenomena and religious myth and symbol.

What I am suggesting is this. It will be almost impossible for theology to effectively relate to the other sciences of man (psychology, sociology, law, economics) without recourse to a general ontology of the human. I can agree with Bultmann and Tillich that such an ontology should provide a system of basic concepts into which biblical myth and symbol can be translated. But in contrast to Bultmann and Tillich, I also believe myth and symbol (both Christian and non-Christian) are richer than any possible set of *a priori Begrifflichkeit*. Consequently, one's ontology must never completely dominate the concrete symbolism—be it clinical or biblical—that one is attempting to interpret. Therefore, one must agree with the direction of the new hermeneutics and Ricoeur in wanting to re-create and resuscitate all modern ontologies with the reality which primordial language mediates. It should be both ways: at the same time we permit our preexisting ontologies to guide us in the interpretation of the symbolism of primordial discourse, we must permit the richness of symbolism to constantly re-create and expand our preexisting ontologies.

But I am also suggesting more. I am suggesting that phenomenology, whether it be pure or existential, cannot be depended upon to develop a satisfactory ontology of the human. I have already argued that Heidegger's ontology is a kind of existential psychology, but having made the point, it is now important to argue that this kind of ontology is not sufficient nor adequate for the many tasks it must perform. A phenomenologically derived ontology of the human is weak for the very reason it is strong. It is strong because it avoids various kinds of reductionism—reductions to childhood and infantile origins, reductions to naturalistic and physicalistic causal origins, reductions to social determinisms, etc. But it is for this very reason that phenomenology is weak. It makes it impossible to chart out the causal configurations involving infantile, biological, physical, and social factors which at least influence (although not necessarily causally determine) various human phenomena. A phenomenologically derived ontology of the human must be paralleled by a variety of empirical disciplines, and especially empirical psychology. Merleau-Ponty has advanced this thesis in his essay entitled "Difficulties Involved in a Subordination of Psychology." Here he argues that the subordination of empirical psychology to phenomenology often suggested by Husserl and further supported by Sartre is mistaken and misleading. It is too simpleminded to say that phenomenology deals with essences and empirical psychology deals with facts. Actually, empirical psychology, according to Merleau-Ponty, makes implicit assumptions about essences at the beginning of its work and often finds conclusions which are further illuminative of essences. Furthermore, the so-called eidetic essences of phenomenology are really not "exact essences" but are actually only "morphological essences" which are "inexact by nature." [9] This seems to mean that the eidetic essences are really only "idealizing fictions" which are constructed out of the concrete actualities of lived experience.[10] In order to make certain that a so-called eidetic essence does not become little more than a prejudice, one must be able to support the phenomenological description with facts and empirical observation. In addition Merleau-Ponty, as well as Aaron Gurwitsch, also stresses the need for a genetic phenomenology.[11] The idea of a genetic phenomenology, something suggested by the later Husserl, seems to recognize the fact that some of the structures of consciousness may have a developmental history and that in order to comprehend them one may need to be able to do a "phenomenology of genesis." What the boundaries would be between a phenomenology of genesis and the developmental psychology of psychologists such as Jean Piaget and Erik Erikson is at this point difficult to say.

Obviously the kind of empirical psychology Merleau-Ponty has in mind is somewhat different from the limited concept of the empirical found in the model of the physical sciences, the model which the early phenomenologists were reacting against. Merleau-Ponty has been influenced by the empirical work of the gestaltists and Kurt Goldstein. For my part the work of Erik Erikson provides a suggestive model for the meaning of an empirical psychology. Erikson never makes simple causal-explanatory statements. Instead he looks for configurations of causal factors which operate in the creation of psychic structures but which never in any rigid sense can be called causally determinative.[12] Erikson constantly shows the configurational interplay between basic bodily modes, geographical conditions, historical memory, technological procedures, and basic patterns of child-rearing. Out of this he has developed what can properly be called certain "essentialistic" concepts, mainly about the nature of ego identity and human development. In fact, his developmental stages can justifiably be called a phenomenology of ego genesis. It is my contention that Erikson's kind of configurational analysis can constitute something of a model for the kind of empirical psychology needed to supplement the existential phenomenological psychologies which have been so influential for the construction of the ontologies of the human fundamental to the work of theologians like Bultmann and Tillich.

If theology needs an ontology of the human, such an ontology should emerge from a synthesis of the following sources: psychoanalytic ego psychology, the cognitive developmental psychology of Piaget, and the existential phenomenological psychologies of thinkers such as Heidegger and Merleau-Ponty. If progress can be made toward such a synthesis, theology will have a more adequate ontology of the human to carry out the program of theologians such as Bultmann, Tillich, and John Macquarrie. In addition, all the sciences of man and all the helping professions which depend on these sciences will have a common fund of propositions about man. This common ontology would be flexible and constantly changing as deeper insights into the nature of human consciousness are discovered. Moreover, such an ontology would constitute a common clearinghouse for theology, history of religions, and the sciences of man. This ontology would help interpret biblical myth and symbol but at the same time might be deepened and enlarged by biblical myth and symbol. History of religions should also play a role in this. Not only should modern language be re-created by a recovery of archaic myth and symbol from Western Judaic, Christian, and Greek sources in the fashion of Paul Ricoeur, but it should also be re-created by non-Western myths in the manner recommended by Mircea Eliade.

IV. Correlation of Perspectives Reconsidered

Seward Hiltner's program of correlation of perspectives has constituted the model for much of the dialogue between theology and psychology on the American scene. It was designed primarily to be used with various brands of empirical psychology popular in American clinical circles. It called attention to the perspectival character of empirical psychology and theology. This approach understood both theology and psychology as intellectual disciplines which were abstracted from the full richness of concrete human events. Theology was seen as necessarily a secondary process of reflection which is abstracted from the full richness of faith and its primary witnesses. Psychology, on the other hand, was viewed as an effort to give rational articulation and order to the regularities of human consciousness and as such was also thought to be an abstraction from the concrete density of these processes. The abstractive character of these two disciplines, according to this way of thinking, tended to force recognition of the relativity of both with respect to the fullness of human truth. This gave rise to a method for relating psychology and theology which was often referred to in Hiltnerian circles as the method of "correlation of perspectives." [13]

Theological and psychological concepts can be fruitfully compared and mutually corrective, according to Hiltner's position, if the respective perspectival and relative characters of the two disciplines are both appropriately acknowledged and then bracketed or set aside. Certain presuppositions surrounding psychological and theological concepts were set aside, and a comparative analysis of the two sets of concepts was then attempted. For instance, it might be true that theology assumes that all healing comes from God while, on the other hand, psychotherapeutic psychology studies a nontranscendent type of healing involving a psychotherapist and his relation with a patient. Yet it is possible to bracket presuppositions about the origins of healing and simply study and compare the structure and dynamics of the two types of healing. This is something along the line of what is attempted in my book *Atonement and Psychotherapy*.[14] It should be recognized that this procedure constitutes a kind of comparative phenomenology of the concepts of different disciplines. Similar studies using this methodology have been made of other parallel concepts from theology and psychology, such as sin and neurosis, faith and identity, forgiveness and acceptance. This bracketing of presuppositions kept the methodology of the correlation of perspectives from becoming a psychology of religion of the crudely reductionistic kind. Yet it is clear that in many instances a comparative phenomenology which attempts to grasp the structure of concepts from some of the more rigid empirical psychologies would be limited by the narrow selectivity and rigid thematization which went into the development of the empirical concept. One might attempt to bracket these contaminations, but they have probably already done their damage.

I am suggesting that we must go beyond the method of correlation of perspectives, although at the same time I believe we cannot completely surpass it. We must take a step back toward the psychology of religion—but a psychology of religion that is broader and more inclusive than any we have had in the past. We must develop an ontology of the human along the lines of Bultmann and Tillich—but one which supplements, supports, and in some instances corrects the ontology of existential psychology with more empirical and developmental psychologies along the lines outlined above. This simply means that before psychology can make more substantive contributions to theology, some battles need to be fought within the boundaries of psychology itself between its various branches and approaches. This means that more and more instead of simply correlating theological concepts with psychological concepts we will be more directly interpreting religious concepts in light of psychological concepts, but psychological concepts that are broadened and enlarged to include the highest levels of intentionality as well as the lowest levels of the habitual and involuntary.

It may be that an empirical psychology which seeks for causal configurations without totally eliminating factors of human freedom and spontaneity can contribute greatly to broadening our ontology of the human and re-creating our language by bringing it back into contact with the richness of experience. For instance, one may be able to reclaim the archaic through depth psychology and its analysis of dreams and behavior just as easily as one can through a phenomenology of ancient myths and symbols as Paul Ricoeur proposes. For instance, Ricoeur's research into the symbolism of evil has yielded new insight into the dimension of "stain" and "defilement" implicit in most Christian views of the nature of sin—a dimension that was all but lost in later conceptions of sin which more and more emphasized ethical features of freedom, responsibility, and guilt.[15] Yet those of us familiar with the psychological works of Helen Lynd, Erik Erikson, and Jean Piaget knew that the ontogeny of moral development places the elements of shame and physical contamination prior to the emergence of more discrete experiences of guilt.[16] Hence in psychology for some years there have been efforts to save the modern sense of fallibility from a one-sided bias in the direction of the ethical.

This is just one brief example of how empirical psychology may be able to broaden our ontology of the human and enrich our language in ways similar to the historical quest for archaic origins. Ricoeur himself admits that a direct phenomenology of man's fallibility may tend to end in a bias toward the ethical. It may be a methodological limitation of phenomenology that it cannot grasp the deeper dimensions of fallibility represented by stain and defilement. This is why Ricoeur feels he must turn to the richness of the ancient symbolisms of evil. It may be that psychology itself can perform a similar service for modern man by plumbing the depths as well as searching the heights of contemporary human experience.

Notes

1. Major sources for a discussion of the influence of Martin Heidegger on European psychology and psychotherapy are as follows: Rollo May *et al.*, eds., *Existence: A New Dimension in Psychiatry and Psychology* (New York: Simon and Schuster, 1967); Jacob Needleman, ed., *Being-in-the-World: Selected Papers of Ludwig Binswanger* (New York: Basic Books, 1963); Medard Boss, *Psychoanalysis and Daseinanalysis* (New York: Basic Books, 1963).
2. For competent discussions of the distinctions discussed in this paragraph the following sources are recommended: Joseph J. Kockelmans, "Husserl's Original View on Phenomenological Psychology," and "Toward a Descriptive Science of Man," *Phenomenology: The Philosophy of Edmund Husserl and Its Interpretation,* ed. Joseph J. Kockelmans (Garden City, N.Y.: Doubleday, 1967); Aaron Gurwitsch, "The Phenomenological and the Psychological Approach to Consciousness," *Philosophy and Phenomenological Research,* XV (1955), 303-19; Aaron Gurwitsch, *Studies in Phenomenology and Psychology* (Evanston, Ill.: Northwestern University Press, 1966); and Jean-Paul Sartre, *The Emotions: Outline of a Theory* (New York: Philosophical Library, 1948), pp. 1-21.
3. Carl Rogers, *Client-Centered Therapy* (Boston: Houghton Mifflin, 1951), p. 483.
4. Rudolf Bultmann *et al., Kerygma and Myth:* A *Theological Debate,* ed. Hans Bartsch (New York: Harper, 1961), p. 16.
5. For an illuminating discussion of the translation of New Testament theology into Heidegger's existentialism, see John Macquarrie, *An Existentialist Theology: A Comparison of Heidegger and Bultmann* (New York: Macmillan, 1955).
6. For a fuller discussion of Tillich's concept of symbolism, see my article "Analogy, Symbol, and Pastoral Theology in Tillich's Thought," *Pastoral Psychology,* February, 1968, pp. 41-54.
7. Discussions of the post-Bultmannian developments in hermeneutics can be found in the following books: James Robinson and John Cobb, eds., *The Later Heidegger and Theology* (New York: Harper, 1963); see also their *The New*

Hermeneutic (Harper, 1964); and Robert W. Funk, *Language, Hermeneutic, and Word of God* (Harper, 1966).

8. Paul Ricoeur, *The Symbolism of Evil* (New York: Harper, 1967), p. 19; see also his "Hermeneutics of Symbols and Philosophical Reflection," *International Philosophical Quarterly*, II (1962), 191-217.
9. Maurice Merleau-Ponty, "Difficulties Involved in a Subordination of Psychology," *Phenomenology*, ed. Joseph Kockelmans (Garden City, N.Y.: Doubleday, 1967), p. 490.
10. *Ibid.*, p. 500.
11. *Ibid.*, p. 488; Aaron Gurwitsch, "The Phenomenology of Perception," *An Invitation to Phenomenology*, ed. James M. Edie (Chicago: Quadrangle Books, 1965), pp. 26-28.
12. Richard Evans, *Dialogue with Erik Erikson* (New York: Harper, 1967), p. 86.
13. For Hiltner's understanding of the meaning of "correlation," see his *Preface to Pastoral Theology* (Nashville: Abingdon Press, 1958), pp. 1-29, 55-69, 221-23.
14. Don S. Browning, *Atonement and Psychotherapy* (Philadelphia: Westminster Press, 1966).
15. Ricoeur, *Symbolism of Evil*, pp. 25-46.
16. Helen Lynd, *On Shame and the Search for Identity* (New York: Harcourt, Brace & World, 1958); *Erik Erikson, Childhood and Society* (rev. ed.; New York: W. W. Norton, 1963); Jean Piaget *et al.*, *The Moral Judgment of the Child* (New York: The Free Press, 1965).

The Implications of Existentialism for Pastoral Theology

Leland E. Elhard

One of the primal experiences of modern pastoral theology, the brief mental illness of Anton Boisen, has both scientific-psychological and existential dimensions. We have followed up largely on the former and ignored the latter in our recent approaches to pastoral work. It seems that no one located professionally within the field of pastoral theology has presented us with a carefully drawn picture of what the existentialistic "posture" may mean for us. Obviously these few pages are not enough for such a picture, but I do hope they may stimulate some of us to look more carefully into the implications of existentialism for the work of, and reflection upon, shepherding.

1. The more pessimistic existentialist view and commitment has nihilistic consequences, e.g., Sartre negates all theology with his militant objection to the reality of the basis for theological reflection. Faith is only man's passionate but useless desire to overcome his lack of being. Correlated with this negation is the denial of the *pastoral* dimension, "Hell is other people." [1] Sartre observes that people inevitably objectify other people, even in their moments of highest love. Obviously, then, no relationship can be pastoral. Any ministry is merely a covert way of using the other person for one's egocentric purposes; it is the subtlest destruction of the person in its denial of his only resource, the exercise of his lonely freedom. Thus a very real implication of some versions of existentialism is that it makes pastoral theology impossible.

2. Where it has more positive effects, existentialism implies that pastoral theology becomes a chief participant in a theology far more concrete, empirical, and historical. Obviously, such a theology is not yet fully developed. However, there are hints of its coming in some places, e.g., Schubert Ogden's focusing of philosophical theology around the existential human situation, Moltmann's theology of hope, Pannenberg's theology of the future, and similarly, Dietrich Ritschl's "open system" approach, in which historical reality is contrasted with the old metaphysics. These men are examples of the mood of some theology today to see God's decisive activity in the events of our time. Whether existentialism is one of the executioners in the death of metaphysics or only one of the mourners picking up the pieces after the funeral, with its advent a more historical view has come to the center of the stage. Like it or not, what has happened to all of us is that we look for the ultimate meaning of life in what now is going on in our life. For us truth is concrete, not abstract. We do not turn to eternal structures which hover protectively but safely above the action and which offer us antiseptic verities in exchange for our appropriate notions of prefashioned thought and/or cultic faith. In this approach the center of theology is not in its reasoning operations which extrapolate universal truths from books written either by God or man, but it is in participatory observations and reflection in the places where people are caught in their unique everyday life-and-death struggles. The place where truth was once "applied," where the gospel was once "related to human need," is where we are to learn the truth itself. Thus, along with all the "relating" disciplines of theology, pastoral theology must move from the periphery to the center of theology. Obviously the old image of the pastor learning the truth from the theologian and then going to the layman to interpret it and apply it to his situation is obliterated. Now the picture must be that of truth coming alive, coming to be present, in the shared situation in which no one has the answer beforehand or is *the* minister. In the particularity of the historical situation and nowhere else, the basic insights into God and man occur, in con-

sistency with "the Word made flesh." Existentialism pushes pastoral theology toward its proper adventure, defined by Hiltner as that field of theological knowledge and inquiry which finds its data in the involvement and perspective of shepherding and which draws conclusions of a theological order from reflections on these data.[2]

In the involvements of the living of these days we are confronted with what Jaspers calls the "ciphers," the hints of something more which make us think and feel at a level of ultimate concern and perhaps of ultimate discovery. Those things which theology has hardly noticed existentialism takes seriously, i.e., human shocks, passions, joys, griefs, guilts, fidelities, decisions, moods and feelings of all kinds. It does not just notice them, it uses them as prime data for its highest meanings, its "concrete metaphysics," if you will. Marcel, Sartre, and Heidegger are obvious examples. However, Kierkegaard has not been outdone here. Much of his theologizing focuses around his personal crises with his father, his fiancé, and with the newspaper attack on him. After reading a few hundred pages of his theological-philosophical love story, some may dismiss Kierkegaard with a psychopathological diagnosis and "close the book" on him. It *is* boring, yet psychologist Kierkegaard must have had some insight into what he was doing. In a primitive, groping way he was telling us where the theological alternative to Hegel's logic had to be—in the daily trivia and glories in the experiences of a man, even if he is an oddball, even in the immature groanings of his love affairs. This is quite an alternative, still strange-sounding to us, just as present-day expressions of the historical alternative sound strange when they come forth from Bonhoeffer, Ebeling, Cox, Altizer, and others. Certainly there are huge distortions in Kierkegaard's experience and in the one-sided character of each of our lives. But the basic principle of existential truth is established, even *in* the distortion. Truth is truth-for-me. Subjectivity is truth. Only *in the distortions* of my peculiar life is the truth born for me. This is the strain and splendor of a thoroughly historical age. In this age only a theology pastoral enough lovingly to know real human beings can grow *as theology!*

3. This brings us another offering of existentialism, the phenomenological method or "the internal frame of reference." We think here of Pascal's "thinking reed," whose greatness consists in knowing that he is to be broken, and of Kierkegaard, who used "indirect communication" to awaken individuals to their own subjectivity, and of Sartre, for whom man's freedom is consciousness, understood as a "hole" of subjective nonbeing in the objective, materialistic fabric of being. They have the highest regard for the point of view of the living person before us—what *he* sees, feels, and makes of the world. What I think he should experience, what the "average" man feels, what "everybody" goes through does not count. Heidegger has pointed out this tyranny of *Das Man* and that Everybody is precisely Nobody real.

To be a person is to "have a world." Somehow, each man structures reality around his *one* point of view and thus gains for himself some order and unity in time and space. Man always turns his environment into a "situation," a "field" for action, a *Gestalt* within which he senses his own unique actuality in some precarious preconscious version of "I am." Existentialism contends that we do not even begin to know the person until we share his world of suffering and love. We do not know him when we diagnose and categorize him "from outside." The only accurate model is the person himself. In other words, meanings must be private meanings to be real meanings. As Luther said, each man must do his own believing as he does his own dying. Certainly, some existentialists seem to equate privacy with isolation. However, on the whole, existential phenomenalism refers to self-in-world. It is not navel- or mind-gazing. It is not an investigation of the internal relations in pure consciousness, separate from concrete experiencing, as is true in some versions of phenomenalism.

From Carl Rogers and others pastoral theology has been learning the internal frame of reference as a counseling method. Sometimes this learning has been somewhat unreflective. That it is *the way* to counsel, or that it works, may be as much as we think about it. Existentialism provides a reflectively responsible basis for the internal frame of reference not only as a counseling method but also as an approach to pastoral understanding of the whole human situation. For example, in its light we can be a little less frustrated with those parishioners who stubbornly hold an illogical (to us) position or focus their lives around some mythical physical ailment. We can begin to understand in the context of their life histories that this patterning of existence is essential to their achieving a selfhood of any kind. We get nowhere (as Kierkegaard saw) by merely ignoring a false self-world picture, or by hoping it will go away by itself, or by blindly attacking it in order to flush out the "real person" underneath. We meet the person as he is in the shape of his self-world. We take *him* seriously by accepting it as somehow true *for him*. When he finds that he does not have to defend his world against us, he may open it a little to let us in with our worlds, and in the communion we have ministry.

4. Existentialism implies a deep personal participation by the pastor in his relationships. It says that one does not help another by offering him detached insights from on high but by offering the healing participation of a self, an experience not an explanation. Research in psychotherapy has discovered that it is the relating to the clients regardless of, and often in spite of, the theories of what we are doing which is the healing agent. Kierkegaard said, "Freedom is constantly communicating." [3] Buber develops this insight and sees being as dialogic; life is in the "in-between" where people share themselves. In therapy or ministry, therefore, a decisive encounter is one in which change occurs in both participants, not just in the "patient." Only when a pastor shares and risks his own being enough to be changed himself will he be the catalyst for the person's growth. Research in existentialist approaches to schizophrenia demonstrates that acceptance of the person is not bland noninvolvement but is a matter of devotion to him, suffering with him, sharing his strange world enough so that one's presence will help release him from the categories which

bind him.[4] It is being open and defenseless enough to permit the person to let go of some of his defenses. This pastoral openness does not necessarily mean telling the person more about oneself, one's successes or troubles. It is more a matter of attitude, listening as a sinner to a sinner. It is trusting oneself as an instrument which resonates with the person's feelings and communicates without words that he is "received." Of course we cannot disregard the dangers of countertransference and of turning the direction of the therapy entirely toward the counselor. At times we have been so much warned about this danger that some of us have become overly detached. Yet personal involvement is vital in pastoral care. In a symposium on existentialism Carl Rogers comments that whenever his real self has been drawn into the counseling relationship the best therapy has occurred.[5]

5. Existentialism poignantly draws our attention to the meaning of time in the human experience. Pascal was frightened comparing his own span and the great reaches of time. Kierkegaard searches for "repetition." Heidegger "locks in" on death and experiences temporality constantly in the midst of life. In his *Introduction to Metaphysics* he sees time as the content of being. *Sein* is a verb, "to be." Being is present tense. Being "is" constantly![6] This is the existentialist "metaphysic" in which the locus of reality is not in the past or future in another realm but in this realm at this time in which a man is a process from past into future and vice versa. Man is always unfinished; he has no ready-made, substantial self which he is to realize. Man is possibility. He comes into being constantly in terms of his "projects."

Existentialists see the authentic life as being lived in this intense awareness of time. They do not attempt to flee the ravages of time as philosophers since Plato have done. For instance, Kierkegaard describes the knight of faith as one who gets back the temporal and lives fully the time he has.[7] In their sensitive appreciation of time, existentialists have sensed "subjective time"—that we experience time in terms of our internal frame of reference. In terms of our situation and our point in the life process we experience the same "objective" segment of time differently, as never ending, as nonexistent, as oppressive, or as delightful. To shepherd means to take account of a man's subjective time of life. As Hiltner has suggested, this means viewing young adults differently from middle-aged adults, etc.[8] In general, existentialism encourages us to utilize time in our pastoral care. We minister to the human condition in its inevitable processes and crises of time. We watch for the right time to speak and to be silent, to awaken people to the day of salvation, or to wait while the Spirit does his underground work in time.

6. Existentialism alerts us to conflicts and crises. Whereas some versions of pastoral care tend to opt for silver linings, existentialism finds teaching value in difficulties. Kierkegaard saw his vocation as helping people by making things difficult for them, throwing them into the ocean 70,000 fathoms deep, in contrast to many others who seek to make life easier. Pascal, of course, finds greatness and tragedy spawned at the same point. Jaspers sees our humanity refined in the crises of boundary situations. Heidegger sees authentic life as one long confrontation with death. Sartre entitles his major work *Being and Nothingness.* Existentialism holds that we develop and sense our being in conflict with our nonbeing, life's sweetness in contrast to death's bitterness, willing in the context of being opposed and predetermined, purpose in conflict with absurdity, fellowship against a background of solitude, intuition within negation, responsibility in the crisis of inner conflict and uncertainty, creativity within the dangers of distortion and loneliness, faith in the context of doubt. Thus it holds with psychoanalytic and developmental psychology that anxiety, conflict, and other negative experiences are not necessarily destructive. Thus while pastors have enough to do without gratuitously creating difficulty, they can learn from existentialism to confront human crises with the confidence that growth springs from them.

7. Thus existentialism renews the tradition which finds a sense of need salutary, even a sense of tragedy and sin. With scrupulous

sensitivity it takes the universe as a place of *real* injuries, ambiguities, bondage, and sinfulness. It sees that the world, including *Umwelt, Mitwelt* and *Eigenwelt,* can be too much with us. It finds our needs deep and intense. Camus struggled against the universe in which children suffer and die.[9] Existentialists see a normal human guilt which goes with living and which cannot be analyzed away. It accepts determinism as a prelude and context to its insistence on freedom and responsibility. It is our freedom that we see our bondage. This realistically pessimistic review of our situation is exemplified by Kierkegaard, who saw consciousness of sin as the *conditio sine qua non* of Christian faith.[10] But it is also exemplified by a man of different persuasion, Heidegger, whose description of "care" is a penetrating analysis of our idolatrous preoccupations designed to awaken us to our alienation from Being.[11] Several existentialists seek to awaken us to the pervasive power of "objectification" as the modern sin. The old exhortations about and descriptions of our needs and sins are out of date. So while men learn from some human scientists that they are "caused," they do not have the equipment to understand that they are ultimately dependent on their God and have sinned against him. Thus they discover themselves as unaccountably troubled, mysteriously uneasy, strangely psychosomatically ill, and covertly self-destructive. The precise and passionate examination equipment of existentialism helps us locate and clean the festering wounds so that the healing can begin. Existentialism helps pastors once again to see, in realistic terms, people as sinners and to see their task as the *cure* of souls.

8. However, existentialism calls into question healing, or some less than ultimate versions of it, as the central value of pastoral theology. It is suspicious of penultimate comfort, satisfaction, adjustment, and utilitarian morality. It questions the premature closure of satiety, finds men able to be genuinely joyful and open in suffering. It would rather that man be a dissatisfied *man* than a satisfied pig. It prefers neurotic conflicts developed in the real world to wholeness in a sheltered world. It is not as repelled by

personal burdens and guilts which are corollary to a dynamic identity as it is by sheer dullness. Alan Harrington writes of life in the contemporary crystal palace of a prosperous, decent, peaceful, remote, conformist suburban corporation and indicates that some versions of healing are, at least, boring.[12] He concludes with part of Dostoevski's objection to the crystal palace:

> And why are you so firmly, so triumphantly, convinced that only the normal and the positive—in other words, only what is conducive to welfare—is for the advantage of man? . . . Does not man, perhaps, love something beside well-being? Perhaps he is just as fond of suffering? Perhaps suffering is just as great a benefit to him as well-being? [13]

Of course Dostoevski develops this theme most fully in *The Brothers Karamazov*. In it the Grand Inquisitor wants to be a comforting pastor who protects his people from the tragic doubts and conflicts of existence. He wants to heal them. In order to do this he must banish the Christ who, according to Dostoevski, values dignity and freedom, even with tragedy, far more.

Yet some pastoral theology has fallen into the grip of culturally determined mental health values. Kierkegaard, Nietzsche, Kafka, etc., are dismissed because they were obviously sick, without its being seen that their distress came from a culture sicker than they were. We have not only learned the methods but also may have confined our values to the level of penultimate versions of cure and salvation.

9. Also, as an expression of a radically historical approach to being, existentialism would cross-examine Hiltner's definition of healing in terms of "rebecoming." [14] This term suggests that an ideal selfhood was given "back there" somewhere in a fully mature Garden-of-Eden existence and that we must repristinate it. Contrary to Hiltner's intention, I am sure, it sounds substantialistic. Healing, in an existentialistic sense, is profoundly in process and is open-ended. It is "man who is possibility" in dialogue with the "God of the future," becoming the wholeness he will be rather

than rebecoming what he was. Such healing celebrates change rather than covertly sabotaging it.

10. As we saw in Dostoevski, the greatest thing we can do for another is not to take away his discomfort but to allow him his freedom. Thus an existentialist pastoral theology will constantly clear the way for the person to make his own decisions. It will see him as someone who really needs and wants to be his own active center, either in obedience or disobedience. Existentialism is consistently voluntaristic. In fact, in a thoroughly historical view of being where unities are not given, the only way to unity and consistency is from "within" a man's decision and commitment. Kierkegaard's famous "willing one thing" is continued by Heidegger in his structuring of authentic existence around the "resolution" which keeps a man from being diffused by his drives, by the changes in his external circumstances, and by conflicting social pressures. It is a *dynamic* unity which replaces the old substantial unity of the soul.

Whether or not it has learned it from the existentialists, contemporary ego psychology is moving more in the direction of challenging patients to be responsible. Therapists attempt to move them beyond mere passivity in the face of the determinisms of their lives. Contemporary pastoral theology can do as well. Valuable as the insights into our helplessness have been to lead us to be less legalistic and blindly demanding in our care of souls, they have tended to sweep us along too far. We have not known if and when we could challenge men to be men, not mice. We certainly do not know all the answers about this yet. But existentialism at least awakens us to the great gift of self-mastery and responsibility. Certainly no one of us choses to be born, but one of the better moments of our lives was the time, short or long, in which we decided to take charge of this absurd accident of our being alive. The most satisfying events in a pastor's life often focus around people who demonstrate unexpected courage in living with impossible problems. They have become responsible even if, according to Camus' image, it means unceasingly pushing the same rock up the same mountain.

In this day of change and of the broken citadels of the old homogeneous ways of life and value, it is also impossible to do what the at least paternalistic *Herr Pastor* used to do, i.e., tell people how to live their lives. Existentialism does not bemoan this development but rather sees it as a great opportunity. This opportunity may be for a more intense humanism but also, à la Kierkegaard, for a more genuine faith in service of a God whose omnipotence is expressed precisely in his granting us freedom. In such faith a man finds the "Archimedian point" with which he is able to lift the world off its usual hinges. Whatever sort of existentialism he draws upon, he sees man as responsible and able to create a new situation. This responsibility may take various forms. Sartre represents the intensely self-creating-self variety. The later Heidegger points us in the direction of responsible openness toward Being; in fact, we are reverently to "shepherd being." Obviously, pastoral theology is here directed toward the priesthood of all believers. We are each to be responsible to God for ourselves and our neighbor. We are challenged to grow up together in Christ, to become capable and concerned human beings. At this point in this *Festschrift* I recall that Seward Hiltner once told a group of his students that dynamic nurturing of such responsibility was the focus of his vocation in his pastoral concern for them.

11. Existentialism has implications for our pastoral use of reason and language. Existentialism has little confidence in reason by itself and obviously rebels against the shaping and categorizing of relationships with it. We cannot objectify our pastoral care while we are involved in it. Yet we can use our powers of observation and analysis to look back at what happened. As Kierkegaard said, "life is lived forward," but "it is understood backwards." [15] Existentialism puts reason into its proper place; it does not attempt to destroy reason. It must use reason too. But the kind it uses is a "broken reason." It does not really seek to build airtight

cases. At best it points! It is a receiving, intuitive, submissive reason rather than a controlling reason. Heidegger uses it to be open to Being, as he listens with the poets. Such reason humbles itself to be united with passion and commitment. It is not afraid to see profundity in simplicity as does Dostoevski's Idiot when he cuts through the superficialities of sophisticated society to see the basic aches and joys of people. Such a type of reasoning seems quite suited to the theologizing which grows out of reflection on pastoral experience. Certainly there is a danger of becoming sentimental, soft, and amorphous. However, in our attempts at times to imitate hardheaded styles of scientific prediction and control in our pastoral work, we can miss the human, pastoral point altogether.

Similar points may be made about existentialism's use of language. Like Marshall McLuhan with the printed word, it uses a great number of words to tell us that words are not everything. Usually existentialism does violence to language in order to make language do its proper work of expressing reality in a union of symbol and experience. For example, Kierkegaard, Marcel, Heidegger, and Sartre all do odd things in their writing. They use "indirect communication," diaries, and drama, create new words, and are purposely disorganized and obscure. They want to break us out of our decrepit symbolic molds. The dramatists, like Beckett and Ionesco, have moved a step further, and in the theater of the absurd seek to shock people awake by cutting through the protective film of illusion which the theater implies. All existentialists dramatize the ordinary, finding the divine in the childlike or feeling nausea simply about our physical existence. All this is part of the extraordinary sensitivity that is existentialism. It intends to make speech existential too, i.e., honest, concrete, personally meaningful. It insists that speech need not be empty chatter which hides but is to be pregnant dialogue able to give birth, full of the possibility of revelation. Thus Heidegger is concerned with the false names of God and seeks to sweep them away and waits for new names to appear.[16]

Is not this attitude toward language that which pastoral theology must continue to develop both in its ministry and in its reflections? Do not our best pastoral conversations always involve a broken language? Both pastor and person struggle to say what they cannot quite say, but together in trying to say it do they not come to know it? Do not the silences become full of insight and meaning? Do we not clear away people's false names of God in our pastoral dialogues and reflections and thus break out to what God is? Often we are ashamed of our broken pastoral language, and we hide it because it does not measure up in elegance to other branches of theological study. From the existentialists we learn that our battle-scarred language is what it is because it still carries in it the sounds and smells of the action. We should properly treasure it as conveying the messages of God and man.

Conclusion

Existentialism would push pastoral theology in the direction of crisis, passion, involvement, and above all, uncompromising honesty and sensitivity about our lives individually and collectively. Without doubt, even those existentialists labeled religious feel more at home with unbelievers who know the right questions than with those who use religion to evade the truth of the human condition.[17] They too may yearn for God, but they refuse to attempt to retreat into the few broken puffs of low-hanging fog which remain after the break up of the all-enveloping centuries-long cloud of the union of metaphysics and theology. They will not permit themselves the luxury of the unexamined religious feelings which may be a pseudomagic security blanket. They prefer life in the open, without shelter, in the heat and light of the streets crowded at high noon with preoccupied people.

Existentialists admit much more to themselves than do the older rational men or the present machine-and-organization men. They confess they are shaken human beings. With them we confess that we are not on top of the situation as much as we would like to be. Our experiences grip us and make us fight for our lives. We lose control, act out, rationalize, deny, project, and in general, use all the defense mechanisms psychoanalysis describes. Underneath our surface coolness we live in not-so-quiet desperation which we would do well to admit, express, and examine more often. Existentialism says this not only to the sheep but also to the shepherds in the pastoral scene.

In this context existentialism is basically not a finished theory about existence, but rather it is a process of "working through" the human experience of existing. This working through is the essence of what existentialism offers to pastoral theology. To illustrate, the child works through the strange threats and possibilities involved in growing up in his "autocosmic" play. Play is the child's work. He is discovering the world and shaping his place in it in his play. There is an adult talk which is working through in a similar way. This type of talk occurs most often and intensely within relationships of trust and openness, e.g., between husband and wife. It is a rehearsal, either before or after the fact, of the significant events of our lives. It goes over the events, replaying them again and again so that the person can get on top of them, master them somewhat, emotionally as well as rationally. Certainly the grief situation intensely demonstrates this kind of talk, but any new thing, including delightful surprises, can set it off. This is existential talk. An ego-psychological interpretation of dreaming sees it as basically a working-through process. It replays the threats to our existence and satisfactions which the everyday brings, and we wake up refreshed, a little more ready to face them realistically. There is testimony beginning with Shakespeare that people need to sleep not only to rest but also to dream, while Humpty-Dumpty *is* put back together again. Working through in playing or talking or dreaming involves some withdrawal from the action. Thus all these activities have been called escapes, and, indeed, for people too frightened to go on, they must be used for escape. But essentially they involve withdrawal in order again to get the perspective which enables one to see reality for what it is and to leap into it again. For much of Western humanity existentialism has been the working through of the shock of the changed human situation. It offers its method of working through to pastoral theology. It implies that we must share in the working through that people today must do to go on as human beings. We cannot put their breaking worlds together for them, but we can enable them to do so themselves by sharing in their talk, their play, their dreams. We help them discover the meaning and continuity of one real story for their days as we share in the broken pieces of their life histories. We help by being sensitively with them and taking them seriously as they struggle. They tell us that this is so —our being with them in their distress means more than our solving their problems for them. This accepting a person on existential terms, as he is chagrined and passionately involved, is probably a good description of *agape* love. In such love we work through in the involvement of pastoral conversation, and we also work through in the pastoral theological reflection afterward. This is existential pastoral theology.

Our time, Heidegger suggests, is between "the No-more of the gods that have fled and the Not-yet of the god that is coming." [18] It is like waking up after a nightmare and finding that the nightmare woke us up to the way things really are. We shake a little but are glad to know what we are up against. We work through with people the dreadful experience of empty lives echoing the "Holy Emptiness." With Bonhoeffer, we help each other *live* in a world without God, and in this adventure we may bring God into being for us after all.

Notes

1. Jean-Paul Sartre, *No Exit* and *The Flies*, trans. Stuart Gilbert (New York: Knopf, 1954), p. 61.
2. Seward Hiltner, *Preface to Pastoral Theology* (Nashville: Abingdon Press, 1958), p. 20.
3. Søren Kierkegaard, *The Concept of Dread*, trans. Walter Lowrie (Princeton: Princeton University Press, 1957), p. 110.
4. Francis A. Macnab, *Estrangement and Relationship* (Bloomington: Indiana University Press, 1966), p. 170.
5. Rollo May, ed., *Existential Psychology* (New York: Random House, 1961), p. 88.
6. Martin Heidegger, *An Introduction to Metaphysics* (New Haven: Yale University Press, 1959), p. 70.

7. Søren Kierkegaard, *Fear and Trembling* and *The Sickness unto Death,* trans. Walter Lowrie (Anchor Books; Garden City, N.Y.: Doubleday, 1954), p. 51.
8. Seward Hiltner, *The Christian Shepherd* (Nashville: Abingdon Press, 1959), pp. 159-78.
9. Albert Camus, *Resistance, Rebellion, and Death,* trans. Justin O'Brien (New York: Modern Library, 1960), pp. 52-56.
10. Søren Kierkegaard, *Journals and Papers,* I, ed. and trans. Howard V. Hong and Edna H. Hong (Bloomington: Indiana University Press, 1967), 179.
11. Martin Heidegger, *Being and Time,* trans. John Macquarrie and Edward Robinson (New York: Harper, 1962), pp. 225-73.
12. Alan Harrington, "Life in the Crystal Palace," *Man Alone: Alienation in Modern Society,* ed. Eric and Mary Josephson (New York: Dell Books, 1967), pp. 133-43.
13. Fyodor Dostoevski, *Notes from Underground,* trans. Constance Garnett (New York: Dell Books, 1960), p. 53.
14. Hiltner, *Preface to Pastoral Theology,* p. 89.
15. Søren Kierkegaard, *Journals and Papers,* I, 450.
16. Stanley R. Hopper, "On the Naming of the Gods in Hölderlin and Rilke," *Christianity and the Existentialists,* ed. Carl Michalson (New York: Scribner's, 1956), pp. 148-90.
17. Eugene B. Borowitz, *A Layman's Introduction to Religious Existentialism* (Philadelphia: Westminster Press, 1965), p. 228.
18. Hopper, "Naming of the Gods," p. 169.

Pastoral Theology and a Theology of Discipline—A Next Step

James G. Emerson, Jr.

If the church of the future is to survive, it must recover the true meaning of discipline. Discipline has come to mean punishment, at worst, and strict order, at best. In Christian thought it is neither. Rather, discipline, for Paul, is a dynamic concept. Discipline is that which gives the freedom to live creatively.

We live in years when there is tension between views of freedom and order. Some understand modern education in terms of complete permissiveness. Modern ills are blamed on authoritarianism. Others react to the unrest of our decade with a call for complete regimentation. They blame modern ills on Dr. Spock. Whether one speaks of the life of the individual, the family, or the society, neither alternative is the answer. It is not freedom for freedom's sake that is needed, but the freedom to meet creatively the problem of any moment.

This essay seeks to suggest how the recent history of pastoral theology has brought us to the need for a next step and how a theology of discipline is that step.

I. The Place of Relatedness

In my personal experience it is pastoral theology that has shown that the Christian faith is genuinely related to life as it is. As a seminary graduate twenty years ago, I left the parish for graduate work to see if the Christian faith could indeed be relevant, for my experience in the church raised doubts. In work under Seward Hiltner at the University of Chicago, I found an approach which, when I returned to the parish, gave me an affirmative answer. It is an approach that sees the true importance of "relatedness." Since in my view discipline deals with creative relationships, we begin with the importance of "relatedness."

For many in and out of the church today the problem of relatedness keeps both the church and theology on trial. At various church meetings one often gets the impression that the church is talking to herself alone—and not often with clarity. The more one reads theological material, the more one is impressed that theologians are talking only to each other. Many of them, for example, would not have heard the death-of-God discussion had the mass media not been titilated by the idea itself.

Consider briefly what has happened to the idea of relatedness in this country. In his lectures on the philosophy of process, Alfred North Whitehead spoke of the importance of relatedness. He was speaking philosophically, to be sure, but the problem of relatedness has been the cornerstone of pastoral theology when that theology has been seen as a genuine theology and not just a matter of techniques.

Although Karl Barth sensed the need for relatedness, his later works have never seemed to discuss the theological side or relatedness itself. At the end of World War II he was caught by the awareness that he had nothing to say to his generation. The liberal theologies of the late nineteenth century, for all their virtues in trying to meet science, simply were not relevant. His *Römerbrief* and subsequent writings were monumental and helpful for many of us in finding a message that spoke to the day of post–World War I. Yet whereas the message made sense, the question as to why it made sense was never raised. Thus in the days after World War II many of us found ourselves confronted with precisely Barth's dilemma. In a time of population explosion, the ghetto, and atomic power, of space flight and sophisticated physics, we had nothing to say. Riesman told us that people had a problem of consumption, of absorbing all that zeroed in from our fast-moving age. In 1948 theologians of crisis were telling us what was needed to help men find meaning in lives that were void. Yet within five years the problem was to find meaning in a life that was filled with too much of everything—filled with both rags and riches.

Some people overlook the philosophical meaning of relatedness. Others reject the idea that belief must be relevant. I think of an excellent physician on the West Coast who is theologically conservative. He was quite disturbed when a university pastor said that faith must be relevant. "The ways of God are past understanding," argued the physician. His reply was based on the assumption that relevance was a synonym for understanding, but it is not. Electric power is not fully understood, but it is highly relevant. So also with faith.

Others think of something as relevant when it leaves them feeling happy or fulfilled or meaningful. Yet even the discovery of purpose in life is no proof of relevance. Despite the writings of Viktor Frankl, there are people who cannot see the meaning in life who yet continue as genuine human beings. A careful study of Anne Frank's diary suggests that the conviction that there is a purpose is what makes the difference, whether or not that purpose is known. "Despite it all," she wrote, "I still believe that the goodness is there."

What does it mean to speak of a faith that is related? It means simply that God is a part of everything that happens. When a person is aware of the presence of God in his life, he usually feels his faith is relevant. Relatedness, however, goes beyond that and suggests that all knowledge and all experience somehow are bound up with each other. It is the thought Paul tried to express when he spoke of Christ being in all and when he wrote: "In him all things hold together" (Col. 1:17).

In the early church this concern for relatedness grew from pastoral experience. To Athanasius, for example, the experience of the power of God in the individual was part of his total soteriology. Thus Hastings' *Encyclopedia of Religion and Ethics* states that Athanasius' quarrel with Arius grew not out of technical theology but out of pastoral concern. Because the individual was related to the total of God's cosmos, the Nicene controversy was not a debate on debatable issues but a battle for the integrity of life itself.

The same can be observed in the Reformation. There were those for whom the quarrel with Rome was as political as it was pious. For others such as Zwingli, Luther, Calvin, the issue was the relationship between an individual's oneness with God and his oneness with the fellowship.

This view of relatedness which understands relevance as finding the universal in the individual has been criticized severely. Some have seen it as a form of pantheism and others as a form of sheer subjectivism. Those who follow Rudolf Otto argue that the universal God must be understood as "wholly other" in order to avoid pantheism. Those who are concerned about psychologizing God read some of the modern books on pastoral theology and ask—as one reviewer asked me—"But do you really believe in an objective God?"

Pastoral theology insists on relevance or relatedness in its basic framework. Yet these are neither pantheistic nor subjective. What the critics need to see is that when they speak of an objective concept of God, they are usually speaking in terms of a three-dimensional world. Einstein has forced us to see that the world must be seen in four dimensions. When this is done, one goes back to the Bible and sees that Western thought has imposed a three-dimensional view of the world on a literature that did not always speak in three dimensions. Eastern language, whether in its Hebrew or Greek form, is not three-dimensional in the Western sense. To insist on relevance or relatedness is to insist on a view of objectivity that takes into account the "different way of thinking about space" and the "different way of thinking about time" (Karl Heim) that go beyond the three-dimensional formula.

II. The Life of the Person

On the basis of the problem of relatedness, then, pastoral theology asked the question, "How do you meet a person where he is?" The theologies of the 1700's and the 1800's were highly articulate. However, when someone was hurting, recitation of the shorter catechism solved nothing. Out of these centuries emerged a drive for a process that would meet the real needs. In the religious sphere Christian Science and the holiness groups emerged. These might be called groups that centered on the practice of the Holy Spirit. In the secular field the dynamic psychologies began to emerge—especially in the first half of the present century. These might be called groups that centered on the practice of human process.

During the Depression days there began a push for the integration of these parallel attempts in the sacred and secular worlds. The quest might even be typed as a call for a theology of the Holy Spirit in practice. Many times this effort has been trite, amounting to nothing more than a psychologizing of religion—even where the people involved are highly competent therapists. On the other side, there are those who have tried to develop a new theology that would allow for a truly practical pastorate—a pastorate genuinely practical because it had grasped the depth of Christianity, a pastorate genuinely Christian because it had expressed what was relevant to the practice of life.

Two factors caused the modern development of pastoral theology to center on the individual. One was the frustration ministers felt in dealing with personal problems. The other was the great body of information that came from the sciences of man, especially the work in psychoanalysis and personality psychology.

In the contest of these two factors, a small but growing group of individuals sought to relate theology to the study of the individual. Although Seward Hiltner was not the first of these, he has certainly been one of the leaders in this group. These people did not seek to substitute psychology for theology, as did the humanist, nor did they see psychology as just a footnote to man's condition of sin, as did the neo-orthodox. Rather, they sought to see the implied theology that formed the real if unrecognized presuppositions of science.

This group also tried to understand the refined ways the new sciences developed for understanding the processes of life. Thus as the prophets of the Old Testament had learned to see how God worked in nature and in history, so pastoral theology set about to learn anew how to see the processes of the life force and how to interpret them. Because these new insights generally grew from studies of man as an individual, it was inevitable that the cutting edge of pastoral theology should be centered on the individual.

This is not to say that there was no awareness of group process and group dynamics. However, the place of the individual in the group seemed to have been so dominated by the educators and the vacuum of the individual as a person was so great that the emphasis of pastoral theology was on the individual. At times this was an accidental differentiation—as in the rush of many to some form of clinical training because they want to "help people." At times it was a studied differentiation, as at the University of Chicago in the 1950's, where the desire was to see the emphasis on the individual and the emphasis on the group as two alternative areas in which people would concentrate for study.

This emphasis led almost inevitably to identifying the work of pastoral theology with the work of the minister. As Seward Hiltner has shown, there is good historical and theological precedent for this identification—especially in the area of the pastoral or shepherding perspective itself. In addition, this work, the theological and personal breakthroughs, and the nature of this emphasis have all been necessary in the search for theological relatedness. The steps could not have been bypassed.

Historically speaking, however, this emphasis has allowed those outside the field of pastoral theology to emasculate it. People from Schleiermacher to Barth and Tillich to the contemporary pastor have been so accustomed to reading pastoral theology as practical theology that they never noted the difference between the two. Even in our most forward-looking seminaries rare is the instance where pastoral theology is really understood as a theology that speaks to our time, much less to theology itself. Instead it is seen as a more refined means of learning techniques, of understanding them in depth, and of relating them to the theological enterprise that is conducted elsewhere. Pastoral theology has become an intellectually respectable discipline on the seminary campus more easily than psychoanalysis has become accepted in the medical school, but it has yet to be accepted as truly theological.

The result is that as one reads the death-of-God books, or the theology of hope, or the secular city literature, one would never know that there has been a pastoral theology. The writings in these different areas sometimes present as new, things that to pastoral theology are obvious; often this literature wrestles in areas that would be clarified by a knowledge of pastoral theology.

The emphasis on the individual has been of value. Yet something is still missing in the discussion about the church of today. As the approach of Schleiermacher was not relevant for Barth in the twenties and as the approach of neo-orthodoxy was not relevant for others of us in the fifties, so the pastoral theologies of the fifties and sixties may well not prove adequate in the decade that begins with a man's being placed on the moon. It is my thought that what now is needed is a next step.

There are current developments in studies of human relations that suggest a direction for the future. This direction is the need of pastoral theology to see itself in relation to the concept of discipline—properly understood. It must do this because the basic question of discipline is the question of relatedness.

III. The Meaning of Discipline

Historically it is the function of discipline to maintain things in a creative relationship. One might say that discipline is the science that deals with the relatedness of things (as discussed earlier).

Anyone with psychological background knows that "discipline," properly understood, does not mean punishment. The word is prostituted when reduced to the idea of disciplining a child. In its relation to the word disciple, discipline had to do with following a trusted teacher. In its relation to the Greek slave who taught, discipline had to do with service. Presbyterian Church polity speaks of an administrative discipline as well as a judicial discipline—which is no more than to speak of the way the church relates to itself and to others, not just to legal procedures.

The need to study discipline as a means of understanding relationships has already been caught by people in the "secular" world. It is symbolized in the shift of one such as Carl Rogers. Rogers began and made his name with his study of individuals. He developed a theory of counseling and a theory of personality. Over the past few years, however, he has done very little personal counseling and has shifted his attention primarily to groups.

Not only across America but in Europe as well, great attention is being given to administrative processes. The master of the Cunard Lines' new *Queen Elizabeth II* was sent to a management school, and literally hundreds of thousands of dollars are spent by corporations to give their executives "sensitivity training." Production problems are not as easy to meet as people problems, and the secular world is raising existential questions about discipline. As once there was a rush to the techniques of psychiatry, now there is a growing rush to group work. As once it was the "in" thing to be a pseudopsychiatrist, now it is the "in" thing to be a facilitator. It is to be hoped that the people of the church have learned sufficiently from previous experience that we do not simply substitute group process for personal psychology as personal psychology was often substituted for faith or theology.

As the study of that which allows for relatedness, discipline deals with structure in a two-fold way: (1) to speak of discipline is to speak of a structure which allows for relatedness, (2) to speak of discipline is to speak of a structure which expresses a relatedness that has already been experienced.

The arrangement of chairs in a room can be an example of both kinds of structure. Chairs in a row with a speaker's table in front create the condition for one type of relationship. It is a relationship where people have more in common with the speaker, who may be some distance from them, than with a neighbor who may be right next to them. If these chairs were suddenly put in a circle, however, the relationship is changed. The structure of the arrangement of the chairs now puts more and more people face to face and allows for relatedness among them. The discipline by which the structure was set up not only allowed for but determined the type of relationship that would exist.

During a lecture people are usually seated. At the end of the lecture they may applaud and stand. The applause and the standing show a new structure. Whereas before one person—the speaker—was standing and all others were sitting, now all are standing, facing the speaker and perhaps turning to one another in comment. If it were possible suddenly to lift all the people from their seats and see the floor plan, it would be clear that the seats were not in orderly rows. Some would be pushed back, others would be turned slightly to one side or the other. Of if one were to look at any room in which there have been group discussions, some groups of chairs will be close together; another group will show sections of rug matted down where people sat on the floor; elsewhere, a cigarette burn may indicate either nervousness or the absorption that let someone forget and thus mar the furniture. The structure now seen is an expression of the relationship experienced by the people in the group.

In both examples there has been a structure. In one instance the structure determined the relatedness. In the other instance the structure expressed the relatedness.

Both aspects of discipline are needed today. The population explosion is crowding people together. It is creating the necessity for solving a problem unknown in the days of the frontier. An emphasis on piety and the individual was needed in a day when people were alone on the farm. The aloneness of the city is a different aloneness. It is an aloneness that grows from the failure to find a structure that allows one to relate. It is not the problem of the cure of souls that now is basic, nor is it even the matter of shepherding. Now the crucial problem is discipline—that which studies relatedness.

IV. Discipline and Pastoral Theology

This discipline applies to the individual, to the group, and to the universe. Paul spoke of the church after the model of the relatedness of the parts of the body. He spoke of the "whole creation" groaning in travail.

This emphasis on discipline may lead to a redefinition of pastoral theology. It is my personal view that pastoral theology should be defined in terms of the work of the pastorate rather than of the pastor. However, that redefinition does not have to follow from the argument of this essay. What does follow is this: where pastoral theology is seen as shepherding—healing, sustaining, caring—that shepherding must be discussed within the reference of a specific question. The question is, What allows shepherding to take place? This question of structure is the question of discipline.

Such questions raise the issues of attitudes and types of organizations in areas like the ghetto, in the counseling room, in the yacht club community. Such questions also raise the problem of cosmology. What is the structure of the universe, and what is the process of the universe? Answers about the universe determine the matter of relatedness just as much as the arrangement of chairs in the room. Is God at the heart of the universe or not?

Thus questions that grow from a theology of discipline pull together views of God, of groups, and of individuals. These questions talk about processes—whether of the Holy Spirit or of human beings or of interpersonal relations. It is this approach that brings the divergent elements of theology together as one enterprise, but it also speaks to those questions that are the concerns raised in the secular world. For the secular world sees discipline in various ways. In one community a particular police chief is at odds with the power structure. The commissioner comes from the gang-buster days of Thomas Dewey. He has a hardline view of discipline. The police chief, by contrast, has lived for years in the area where he is responsible. He sees people as people far more than as criminals. He also sees "his" men as intelligent human beings whom he can trust to do the jobs that need to be done. The conflict between the two men and the two views is a live battle in their community. The conflict expresses two ways of seeing discipline.

In the business world community most experts see discipline in terms of the problems of administration. In Barnard's old but classic book *Functions of the Executive,* the executive function is described as one of communication. As one reads in the book, it becomes clear that communication is not such for its own sake but for the sake of relatedness. That is true whether the view of a good executive is authoritarian or not.

This view of discipline as the science of creative relatedness is the "new step" in pastoral theology.

V. Discipline and New Theology

A "new theology" will be able to withstand its modern trial when it speaks to those questions and this time. To do so, that theology will have to understand its own heritage, and then it will discover that this theology is not new at all. For as one moves through the experience of the early church, one finds that this problem of relatedness was central. Today we may feel far more comfortable with the solution of Peter, who dreamed that nothing created by God was unclean and thus that he could eat with those of a different culture, than with the ancient practice of excommunication. Today we may center more on Paul's view of the Christ who broke down the middle wall of partition than on the old anathemas. Yet when we read the problems of Gregory the Great, who was overcome with too much detail in his work, or Tertullian, who first felt the church needed more structure and then left it because it had too much structure, we discover that the "new" theology was discussed in the early church perhaps more insightfully than we have ever understood.

From a Christian standpoint, I have defined discipline as that which allows the freedom for a relationship of creativity. In Christ, Paul speaks of this relationship to God as being one of "a new creation." To other people, John speaks of this relationship as the fellowship of ministry to each other at the Lord's table. It is a relationship that leads to the needs of a people and the discovery of meaning.

The task of pastoral theology, therefore, in following its own tradition, is to do with modern tests what it previously has done with the Q sort and the TAT. Its task is now to find those devices that help us understand people in relationship. The Harry Levinsons and the Chris Argyrises have given us bold starts. In the field of pastoral theology the Seward Hiltners have shown us the method of perspective and the means of using the devices from the sciences of man. The need is to build on both. The result will be a "new theology." It will be new not because its discoveries of truth are different but because it has discovered the meaning of the new situation in which the eternal truth is now expressed.

Methods of Study in Pastoral Theology

Coval B. MacDonald

Over ten years ago Seward Hiltner said pastoral theology was a parvenu among the theological disciplines. It is still a parvenu. Roughly at the same time, a study on theological education by Niebuhr, Williams, and Gustafson reported "the development of pastoral theology as a theological discipline is still in process." [1] It is even now in process. While this field has generally been gaining recognition as a theological discipline, particularly in theological education, it has not yet developed a systematic theory of pastoral theology. Ten years ago Hiltner provided a substantive preface with the aim that it would lead to systematic theory.[2] The discipline, however, still remains at the preface level.

The current lack of theory-building in pastoral theology is somewhat parallel to a similar problem in another field, psychology of religion. For years psychology of religion has been deflected from the construction of systematic theory by narrow research studies and allied interests. It would appear that pastoral theology is suffering the same fate. Pastoral psychology deflects from a study of pastoral theology, as do the dialogical studies between theology and personality. These areas of inquiry are indeed necessary, but as Hiltner correctly points out, they are not to be confused with pastoral theology.[3] The former deals with psychological data related to pastoral work; the latter deals with psychology in a broader sense and is logic-centered in its study. In contrast, pastoral theology emerges from "the examination of pastoral operations." [4] While there is much overlap between pastoral psychology, theology and personality, and pastoral theology, pastoral theology is distinctive in its study of pastoral operations. It is here suggested that this field has not moved beyond the preface stage because, in part, attention has been directed to these related areas of inquiry. The fact that little theory-building has been done for a *systematic* pastoral theology since Hiltner's pioneering effort seems to reinforce this observation.

This essay will, then, return to Hiltner's contributions with particular attention to his method and supporting model. Its aim will be to grasp some of his essential points and to suggest relatively new resources for the development of a systematic pastoral theology. No attempt will be made here to give a historical survey of the methods of this discipline. Hiltner has done that already. This will rather be an attempt to build on what Hiltner has established.

A basic assumption of this paper is that scientific and technological models shape theological construction. If there is substance to the charge—and there usually is—that theology is not up to date, it is so because theology is slow in using models provided by science and technology. The continued strength of existential thought in theological formulations simply indicates this point, for basically existentialism is a reaction to the scientific models of the early nineteenth century. In contrast, within the theological enterprise Hiltner drew upon a powerful scientific model of this century, the field theory model, and created both meaningful and relevant theological construction. Whether rejected or accepted, whether unconsciously or consciously employed, scientific models shape theological construction.

Following this assumption, the thesis of this essay is that a systematic pastoral theology can be developed by (1) building on Hiltner's contributions in conjunction with (2) the methods and models of general systems theory. Hiltner wisely grasped the significance of field theory as a model for pastoral theology. In fact, he at points seems to be reaching beyond field theory when he deals with concepts very closely associated with systems theory. While not ignoring field theory, general systems theory goes beyond it in its explanation of data. Pastoral theology—and theology in general—needs now to address itself to these critical contributions to knowledge. In this brief essay no attempt will be made to delineate in specific terms the use of systems theory in pastoral theology as a support of this thesis. All that can be done is to raise this thesis as a viable resource for pastoral theology.

I. Hiltner's Method and Model

Any discussion on the method of pastoral theology must begin with Hiltner's *Preface to Pastoral Theology*. This statement is not prejudicial; it is factual. One must remember, however, the scope of Hiltner's effort. It makes no claim to be a systematic pastoral theology. It is rather "only an introduction to such a statement of systematic pastoral theology," or in other words, it is a "constructive preface to pastoral theology." His work is also primarily concerned with method: "Above all else, what I have sought to demonstrate is the *method* by which a systematic pastoral theology can be constructed." [5] Consequently, it is the beginning and not the end of a theory which undergirds pastoral theology. Moreover, in speaking of the healing aspect of the shepherding perspective, he states that this aspect is "not spelled out in detail," although guidelines are clearly laid down. In addressing himself generally to his work he reminds us that the *Preface* is an attempt at system, "but not to the extent desired or needed." His use of data, related almost entirely to one-to-one relationships, is explained on the grounds of "analytical simplicity" rather than comprehensiveness. All in all, there is unfinished business at hand, and Hiltner's contributions are only starting points for the development of a systematic pastoral theology. It is a preface, aptly described by its title. One can build from this foundation, however, and hopefully the methods and models of general systems theory can assist in this task.

Although the limits of the field theory model used by Hiltner need to be reviewed in light of the current models in systems theory, his basic method is foundational for pastoral theology. It first of all "proceeds from and through revelation."[6] It must "emerge from the faith, examine with all possible intellectual tools some basic aspect or dimension of our faith, and return to the faith with a creative and systematic account of its fallible but illuminating findings."[7] Without this starting point in the method itself, the task would be something other than theological inquiry. But the method also includes the organization of data, the assessment of the significance and relationships of these data, and the drawing of implications from these data. Method is more than practice and techniques of operations. Using these criteria, one finds that the method underlying pastoral theology involves bringing theological questions to bear on pastoral operations from a particular perspective, namely the shepherding perspective. Hiltner presses this point strongly when he asserts that "by no other method of theological examination is it possible to get answers to questions of this order," that is, of the order of pastoral theology.[8] Other disciplines do in fact study shepherding even as he defines it, but the method he claims for pastoral theology is "not necessarily inherent in their discipline as such." Other theological disciplines might also deal with similar theological questions, but by not employing this method they miss the answers peculiar to pastoral theology. The method, therefore, is critical to the development of pastoral theology. Perhaps one of the clearest and best examples of the productivity of this method is found in an article by James N. Lapsley entitled "Reconciliation, Forgiveness, Lost Contracts."[9]

Theological questions emerging from faith are brought to the data. As stated earlier, these data are not found in psychological data per se, either narrowly or broadly defined. They are found in pastoral operations, in "data secured from inquiry according to the shepherding perspective." Concrete, living "human documents" are basic data (a phrase attributed to Anton Boisen but to be found in a fascinating introduction to pastoral theology by Clement Rogers some twenty-four years before Boisen).[10] For

Hiltner's *Preface* these concrete data are limited to one-to-one relationships, but he makes it clear that "the data are more diverse than our discussion, if read uncritically, might suggest." All data within the shepherding perspective are to be studied by means of his method of correlation. Granted his right to select certain data for the *Preface*, we must use other data as well in the development of pastoral theology. He encourages their use, although it is not always clear what they are or how they are related to the system.

The method and data Hiltner employs are closely related to the model underlying his theoretical framework. That model does not at all dominate his discussions; it does permeate them however, influencing both his method and data. In referring to the lack of methodological concerns in the previous writers in this field, Hiltner absolves them in part by saying they did not have available "certain intellectual tools and models that have emerged in this century." The point to note here is that methods and models are integrally related. The model helps shape the method, and the method reflects the model. While Hiltner's perspectival approach is philosophically based in process philosophy, his model is clearly found in field theory, a theory developed during his lifetime. The field theory model is often referred to as a means of explaining his method. Although it is used primarily in speaking of communicating and organizing, he also uses it with the shepherding perspective.[11] If models influence method and if the field theory model is less explanatory of data than systems theory models, then without rejecting Hiltner's basic method, it might be that this method can be more productively employed *and expanded* with the use of the currently emerging models in systems theory. The point here is that Hiltner's method has been productive with his use of a field model; it might be more productive with models that can explain more of the data, namely systems models. As will be noted later, one almost gets the feeling that Hiltner searches for just such models, being somewhat dissatisfied with the limits of field theory.

II. Emerging Issues in Hiltner's Theory

A characteristic of a good hypothesis is that it generates other hypotheses. This is also true of a good theory; it generates further theorizing. Hiltner's perspectival approach to systematic pastoral theology is not only substantive, but it also produces further theorizing. Granting its substantial and potential contributions and granting its introductory character, certain basic issues emerge which must be considered as this field builds on Hiltner's significant foundation. These considerations are related to questions of data and models rather than method, but it is clear that a more rigorous definition of data and more viable models would contribute to methodological precision as well.

First, Hiltner constantly reminds us that pastoral theology is an operation-centered discipline. This key concept is described in functional terms and also in terms of focus and field, the latter description being derivative of field theory. Operation is basically understood, then, to involve two characteristics: function and force. However, operation also involves *linkage* of functions as well as *systems* of force. It is here suggested that a more total examination of the meaning of "operation" itself will provide critical clues for a methodological analysis of the shepherding perspective, namely an examination of *how* the functions are *linked* up and *what systems* are giving shape to force. It would seem that Hiltner's insistence on the operation-centered character of pastoral theology is a distinction that must be made and maintained, but this very distinction involves more data than he in fact handles. The data related to linkage and to systems of force are relevant to a study of the shepherding perspective and hence to systematic pastoral theology.

To be more specific, Hiltner's position is stated in brief form as follows: "The content of pastoral theology is, then, the theological theory resulting from study of the operations of pastor and church approached from the shepherding perspective and studied under the headings of healing, sustaining, and guiding." [12] He also describes these subheadings as "aspects of the shepherding perspective." [13] Feeling a bit uncomfortable with the lack of clarity in the word aspect, he appeals to the analogy of a prism in which a beam of light is broken into different colors.[14] However, in spite of the analogy, healing and sustaining and guiding are neither aspects nor even perspectives. They are *systems* organized around particular functions and *linked* to a major system which is shepherding. One need not stop with the rather vague notion of aspect, but one can go on and examine healing, sustaining, and guiding as subsystems of an overall system. Such an examination could well provide new data which themselves would give clues to a more rigorous methodology and a definitive systematic pastoral theology. It seems Hiltner's method is rigorous up to a point, but because of his basic model the method fails to deal with such data as systems of force and linkage of functions, leaving us with the imprecision of "aspects of a perspective."

A second issue which emerges for consideration is related to a definition of data and in particular of their scope. As already stated, the data go beyond simply one-to-one relationships. They will also include other data. But in precise terms what are they? The social context in which the pastoral operations occur? If a shift from healing to sustaining or guiding occurs because of the "need" of the person involved, is "need" to include the cultural and ethnic needs as well as the social and psychological needs of the person? If so, do these become data for the shepherding perspective? How are these data to be organized? Moreover, if a shepherd "is and has and feels more than this perspective," do these factors become significant data for the shepherding perspective itself? [15] When one considers, then, the *scope* of data related to shepherding, it would seem Hiltner's viable method needs the supplementation of methods capable of dealing with such diverse data, and his hitherto useful model needs to be supplanted by a model also capable of handling this diversity. The results of both his method and model are indeed solid. Real gains have been made. But like a good theory, they push beyond themselves to new territory, requiring more precise methods and more viable models.

A final consideration involves shepherding in relation to communicating and organizing. Hiltner says, "It is peculiarly important for the specialist in pastoral theology to know something about the other branches of theology that are focused on operations and functions." [16] Those branches are communicating and organizing. As he develops the relation between these operation-centered disciplines, he emphasizes the structure and content of these operations, but little attention is given to how these are linked with the shepherding operation. Indeed it was not his task to do this, but it is suggested that a major part of that "something" a pastoral theologian must know in this regard is the nature of linkage between these operations. Clarification of perspectives, delimiting data, and suggesting relationships are important; but there is more too.

III. Emerging Methods and Models for Pastoral Theology

While general systems theory is itself in the process of definition, the advances over the older equilibrium, organismic, and field models are unmistaken. This is noted not only in the biological sciences, but it is also noted in such diverse disciplines as systems engineering and social work. The methods and models of modern systems theory emerge from three primary sources: general systems research, cybernetics, and information theory. It is here suggested that just as Hiltner laid a foundation for the development of pastoral theology with the use of field theory, so can that foundation be built upon with the use of systems theory, in particular, using the data from the three primary sources just noted. The manner in which this is to be done is not clearly evident, but the kinds of issues Hiltner leads us to consider involve the analysis of systems.

We are now in a new technological revolution, a revolution prompted not by the processing of energy but by the processing of information. As Anatol Rapoport puts it, "The discovery that information is actually coded on the genes of a living organism in the form of 'information' on how the organism is to be put together during gestation provided further evidence that the understanding of a living process is intimately bound up with an understanding of information processing." [17] Halstead's work on memory is further evidence of this fascinating process.[18] Consequently, a vitalistic position which maintains that living organisms and processes are not governed by the same laws as nonliving organisms and processes because living beings are governed by goals and purposes is now under severe criticism. There now appears to be a profound teleology operant in living and nonliving processes, manifest in their systems, feedback controls, and information flow. General systems theory, then, goes beyond the analytic method of traditional science and without foregoing scientific discipline examines the holistic character of extremely complex life processes. In the sense that the shepherding perspective involves extremely complex life processes, it would appear that it could be examined profitably in the light of general systems theory.

Anatol Rapoport succinctly defines what is involved in such a theory:

> A whole which functions as a whole by virtue of the interdependence of its parts is called a *system*, and the method which aims at discovering how this is brought about in the widest variety of systems has been called general system theory. General systems theory seeks to classify systems by the way their components are *organized* (interrelated) and to derive the "laws," or typical patterns of behavior, for the different classes of systems singled out by the taxonomy.[19]

This method includes three basic resources: the structure of the system (how it receives, stores, processes, and recalls information), the functioning of the system (the way this structure responds to its environment), and the evolution of the system type. In other words, being and acting and becoming are "fundamental aspects of all organized systems." [20] In this sense general systems theory is concerned with the nature of wholes, believing that the nature of the parts alone is not basic but rather the way they are interrelated, and believing, furthermore, that the parts take on properties that "they owe specifically to being components of a larger whole." [21] Systems are perspectival in nature, to use Hiltner's word.

General systems theory finds much "benefit deriving from a focus on the detailed nature of the interrelation or organization per se of components, regardless of whether the focus is considered to be physical, psychological, sociocultural, or even electromechanical." [22] Dare we add "pastoral theological"? We dare. We dare because pastoral theology does deal with the operations of complex life processes and also because "the system approach to the study of man can be appreciated as an effort to restore meaning (in terms of intuitively grasped understanding of wholes) while adhering to the principles of *disciplined* generalizations and rigorous deduction. It is, in short, an attempt to make the study of man both scientific and meaningful." [23] The "whole" of the shepherding perspective, together with its "parts," can be understood in greater depth through such an analysis because to a major degree the shepherding perspective utilizes data involving life processes and behavioral patterns.

The methods and models of general systems theory not only include Hiltner's perspectival approach; they also focus on the very concepts Hiltner employs in one form or another. As Bertalanffy says, perhaps the most important concepts in general systems theory are wholeness, organization, teleology, and directiveness—which today are "amenable to scientific analysis." [24] Hiltner's appreciation of timing also indicates his sensitivity to the sequential nature of a system's hierarchical structure, a concept which is also central for systems theory. Moreover, Hiltner presses for principles which emerge from the analysis of concrete data. It may prove worthwhile to examine the data within the shepherding perspective from the already established principles of Bertalanffy: wholeness, sum, centralization. differentiation, leading part, closed and open system, finality, equifinality, growth in time, relative growth, competition.[25] Exactly what these principles, established by the methods and models of general systems theory, mean for the shepherding perspective remains to be seen. But the current impasse in the development of a systematic pastoral theology warrants such reflection. From a strictly theological point of view the rejection of mechanistic thinking by general systems theory and its emphasis on autonomous systems preceding structured systems, together with its emphasis on the independence of systems from their starting conditions, all warrant attentive theological ears.

As stated earlier, Hiltner appears to search beyond the basic model he in fact uses and to reach for concepts associated with general systems theory. This is not done in any systematic fashion, but it is still there. In speaking of the function-centered disciplines in theology, he sees them as either tied to practice without moving to theory or developing theory without reference to practice. He then states, "It would be desirable if a key methodological concept could be found that would guard against these prevalent distortions. . . . A word has been sought, so far in vain, that would connote movement back and forth, acknowledging agreement or contribution when real, retaining tension when real." [26] Note the words considered in the context from which the preceding quote comes: interconnect, interpenetrating, interrelated, interinvolve, nexus—words leading in the direction of general systems theory! Methodologically, he appears to search for systems methods and models. Moreover, he constantly refers to pastoral theology as a "system" whose primary organizing principle is shepherding.[27] In extensive discourse he defines "system" in such a way that he invites the findings of general systems theory into the shepherd's tent! [28] His concern for holistic phenomena, his description of the automatisms involved in the problem of overweight, his references to the stages of sustaining,[29] all reveal an implicit but undeveloped systems theory peering through the shepherding perspective. It is more formally presented when he says, "As an inquiry what pastoral theology is systematic about is the actual process by which shepherding—healing, sustaining, or guiding—is brought about. When this knowledge is put together into a system, although an open one, clarifying the common currency of the faith, we have a systematic pastoral theology."[30] Both formally and informally, Hiltner goes beyond the limits of the field model. Advances toward a systematic pastoral theology will occur when we take seriously Hiltner's pointers toward systems theory and in a disciplined fashion analyze the shepherding perspective in all its component parts from the point of view of general systems research, cybernetics, and information flow. This must not be done in a dilettante manner; it must be done responsibly and with discipline.

The general thesis of this essay, therefore, simply states explicitly what is already implicit in Hiltner's search for a theory of pastoral theology. This explicit statement is both gross and imprecise. No specific knowledge is given which advances this field, and no specific methodological contributions are offered. The thesis is a hunch, but a realistic hunch. The point is: tools are now available to explore that thesis. Without rejecting Hiltner's method it is possible to expand the implications of that method and thereby move on toward a systematic pastoral theology.

Notes

1. H. Richard Niebuhr, Daniel Day Williams, and James M. Gustafson, *The Advancement of Theological Education* (New York: Harper, 1957), p. 122.
2. Seward Hiltner, *Preface to Pastoral Theology* (New York: Abingdon Press, 1958).
3. *Ibid.*, pp. 23, 36-37.
4. *Ibid.*, p. 115.
5. *Ibid.*
6. *Ibid.*, p. 22.
7. *Ibid.*, p. 217.
8. *Ibid.*, p. 115.
9. James N. Lapsley, "Reconciliation, Forgiveness, Lost Contracts," *Theology Today*, April, 1966, pp. 44-59.
10. Clement F. Rogers, *An Introduction to the Study of Pastoral Theology* (Oxford: Clarendon Press, 1912), p. 96. In speaking of the four capacities in which a minister works, Rogers says, "But he must also be a student of human documents, learning to discern the needs of men and to read their characters, observing the phenomena of spiritual life, testing them and experimenting as far as can be done with reverence for the souls of his fellow creatures." Indeed, this is an interesting statement on the ethics of scientific research, which Rogers calls for in pastoral theology. One wonders if Boisen, during his theological

training, came across Rogers' book and was caught by this unusual phrase, "human documents."

11. *Preface to Pastoral Theology*, pp. 57-59, 61, 99-100, 101, 111.
12. *Ibid.*, p. 69.
13. *Ibid.*, p. 113.
14. *Ibid.*, p. 117. It can be noted, however, that even the spectrum is a range of subsystems.
15. For a thorough review of all the research dealing with the therapist as a major piece of data in helping relationships, as well as other dimensions of helping relationships, see the Spring, 1969, issue of the *International Journal of Psychiatry*. The entire issue covers these results to date.
16. Hiltner, *Preface to Pastoral Theology*, p. 35.
17. Anatol Rapoport in Walter Buckley, ed., *Modern Systems Research for the Behavioral Scientist* (Chicago: Aldine Publishing Co., 1968), p. xvii.
18. Ward C. Halstead and William B. Rucker, "Memory: A Molecular Maze," *Psychology Today*, June, 1968, pp. 38 ff.
19. Rapoport in Buckley, *Modern Systems Research*, p. xvii.
20. *Ibid.*, p. xx.
21. Buckley, *Modern Systems Research*, p. xxiv.
22. *Ibid.*, p. xxv.
23. Rapoport in Buckley, *Modern Systems Research*, p. xxii.
24. Ludwig von Bertalanffy, "General System Theory—A Critical Review," in Buckley, *Modern Systems Research*, p. 14.
25. *Ibid.*, p. 15.
26. Hiltner, *Preface to Pastoral Theology*, p. 223.
27. *Ibid.*, pp. 219-20.
28. *Ibid.*
29. *Ibid.*, pp. 94, 95, 123.
30. *Ibid.*, p. 220.

II. Pastoral Theology and Theological Education

Dialogue in the Religious Academy

Leighton M. McCutchen

Dialogue is the subject of this essay. Although it is a well-worn idea, perhaps its place in the religious academy can still intrigue us.[1] To "have dialogue" is the goal of many teachers of religion. Whether or not we can "have it" as a possession, we must continue to shape curriculum and methodology in order to evoke it.

As readers of this volume know, Seward Hiltner conceived a field of investigation at the Ph.D. level called religion and personality.[2] Indebted as we are, we all can celebrate the wisdom of that conception. Similar efforts of the future will continue to pay attention to R.P. Although R.P. has matured, some of its deepest passion and insight remain as elusive as ever, lures for fresh investigation. Unless we reexplore these depths, the field could empty itself in concern with smaller ideas which only seem more timely to educators concerned with future doctoral programs.

R.P. grasps one exciting side of human experiencing. This essay tries to point to that with the construct "dialogue." The real force of this idea comes only after its more conventional interpersonal features have been taken for granted.

Dialogue is not simply duologue. It is more than two persons talking, listening, and accepting each other. Dialogue is a working through of the structure, the logos, of persons. We can only use a structural framework and analysis to understand it, one that is not bound to the idea of persons only but can in fact illuminate human dynamics.

I. Religion and Personality in Dialogue

Without giving direct reference to the dialogic idea, Hiltner established a passionate concern for it, moving from its conversational form to a critical investigation of the many facets of personality within the religious perspective, and vice versa, of religion from the viewpoint of personality. A quote from the 1959 *Announcements* of the Divinity School of the University of Chicago will remind many of the clarity of focus Hiltner provided.

It is the purpose of the Field of Religion and Personality to explore from the point of view of religion those sciences of man that converge on an understanding of human personality and to explore religion from the point of view of those sciences. That distinctive nature of the field within the theological curriculum may be thought of as a study of man viewed developmentally and existentially. In this context "developmentally" refers to lawful sequences, factors of continuity and objective understanding. "Existentially" refers to the decisive and critical points and factors in development, to transformations and reversals, inward understanding, and the element of concern.

The statement cannot be improved upon as an expression of dialogue within the religious academy. Implied within it are concerns that lend themselves to a pedagogy of staged examinations, the rigorous interrelation of distinct perspectives, and the possibility of a self-consciousness about method heretofore somewhat lacking in certain doctoral programs.

Of the many details of the Hiltner program the field examinations stand in the center. They cover a manageable range of problems without losing the field's integrity. Religion is put in dialogue with such partners as the sciences of man, theology, methodology, church concerns, and the operational principles of individual students. An oral examination based on a constructive position within the field is conducted by the field's faculty and others from the faculties of the Divinity School and the university.

These details enfold the more general concern for dialogue.

Furthermore, they give us a context for plumbing some of the depths of dialogue. A brief review of the central methodology developed in the field and one of its best dialogical images can set the stage for reevaluation.

For several reasons Hiltner moved toward clarification of method under the heading of pastoral theology. Although the method secures dialogue, the fact that it focuses on theology and not religion leaves some interesting loose ends. Brief passages from his *Preface to Pastoral Theology,* dealt with more fully elsewhere in this volume, will suffice.

The central effort of the pastoral theologian is "the activity of beginning with theological questions, bringing them to the shepherding material, and returning either with theological answers or with new theological questions." [3] The "system" of pastoral theology is "bifocal," embracing both the body of divinity and human knowledge in general as these fasten onto the meaning of shepherding. The focus on shepherding means at least that the unique caring of the church for its members and mission is central. But the commerce between theological language and any relevant insight is free and open, as long as it explicates shepherding.

Man's assimilation and understanding of revelation, regardless of the finality of revelation itself (which Hiltner nowhere seriously questions), is never final in appropriation. We continually have to receive revelation. Contrasting his thought with Tillich, Hiltner denies that distinctions between ultimate and preliminary concerns can protect theology from new questions and even new answers. The continual activity of assimilation evinces novelty on both sides.

> We believe that a full two-way street is necessary in order to describe theological method. If we hold that theology is always assimilation of the faith, not just the abstract idea of the faith apart from its reception, then it becomes necessary to say that culture may find answers to questions raised by faith as well as to assert that faith has answers to questions raised by culture.[4]

Supplementing this formal method, students of Hiltner remember the "village green" metaphor. Somewhere there was a green, a village common, around which was built a church, a school, the offices of doctors and lawyers, and the town hall. No one had exclusive rights to the green. All could enjoy walking on it and caring for it, though each had access to it from special concerns and each carried out his general responsibility beginning with his own concerns.

For the sake of method, one had to recognize when he was on the village common and when he was in his own establishment. Furthermore, he had to note what difference it made to any conversations held on the common that each person came out with special cares. Finally, the fact that one's own establishment was a more direct neighbor to some and a more distant one to others had its effect.

In this image there lies a complex methodology of dialogue. When it is added to the formal statement, the cause of dialogue is advanced. But some potentials for dialogue, often actualized in specific studies, are left unstirred and unnoticed by both statement and image. There are three related questions that need to be asked. First, is it fair to the "religion" side of the dialogue to use the construct "theology" as the primary representative of its passions? Second, does the emphasis upon church and ministry, that whole professional side of the pastoral, abstract from *concrete experiencing* which is *the basis* for official professional acts and which is *the phenomenon* needing understanding? Finally, does the term personality make explicit the impersonal, nonpersonal, and structural aspects of human existence which inevitably influence dialogue? These questions guide the remaining thoughts in an effort to further the tradition of R.P.

First, as to the ability of theology properly to represent religion, the difficulty arises when the method of pastoral theology (P.T.) is used as the only method in R.P. When theology is construed broadly enough to attempt to cover the full range of phenomena that are religious, it becomes somewhat unsure of itself, sometimes pretentious, and more often than not condescending to its offspring psychology. To begin always with theological questions shades imperceptibly toward always beginning with the "old queen's" (theology's) words before the response of the common people is sought.

Religion as a construct points to more holistic and concrete processes than either "theos" or "faith" in themselves allow. Its interest in cult and ritual, taboos and myths, and the repetitions of healing and ecstasy have only distant relations with "God" or "faith." R.P. must continue to wrestle with a constructive position on religion and not settle for a constructive theology only. Somewhere in between the generality of the field of history of religions and the idiosyncracy of the field of religion and literature, the dialogue must come to terms with the extent of reach within religion itself.

Second, as to the emphasis on church and ministry as an abstraction, one may move away too easily from the essence of religious practices per se, those phenomenologically present to man. A simple translation of P.T. methods into R.P. suffers the temptation of making the official religious activity a kind of possessive mother looking with seductive interest at her son, psychology. No one properly engaged in R.P. needs more than a chance to spot the foolishness perpetrated in the name of applications of the eternal gospel by means of modern psychology. This devil, banished from the front door, comes in stronger through the rear, however, unless the pastoral is construed as an *example* of events, occasions, and operations important to both sides of the dialogue. With P.T. we are properly limited to church and ministry. But this neatness cannot be left unsmudged.

Hiltner saw even in pastoral theology the necessity to construct "middle principles" for clarifying the discussion between the events of church and ministry on the one side and theology on the other. These perspectives, called shepherding, communicating, and organizing, are exciting still for pastoral theology. But can they function as middle terms between concrete human experiencing and the bifocal relation of religion and the man sciences? Even if they can, they have yet to be argued to that end.

Finally, the third question about the adequacy of the construct "personality" must be addressed. As a guide for relevancy of contact between psychology and religion it has proved very helpful. Whether it can still function as an organizing principle for students confronted with the vast differences, increased methodological wisdom, and enormous challenges of the field of psychology, itself almost a secular religion, is another question. Psychology is at least a smart young adult and no longer a child, though it may not yet be fully grown. It does seem ready to "marry" with a number of partners and has already, without benefit of clergy, produced a number of offspring from such unions.[5]

In these several ways it seems that the method of P.T., while clearly dialogical, is not exhaustive of the meaning of dialogue in R.P. As for the metaphor about the village green, a criticism of it comes down to realizing that while it allows for complexity, it is still too cozy. There are now hippies camped on the commons. A great deal of unofficial, unprofessional, hard-to-pigeonhole cultural life must be that which R.P. tries to understand. This is no argument for the field to become the domain of pop culture exclusively, but it *is* able to respond creatively to that data.

Dialogue looks like duologue when only two factors are brought together. Our questions suggest a third, basic to the two which must be recognized. Allowing for the temptation for any duologue to be a repeat performance of the idealized mother-child symbiosis, we might draw an analogy: what bothers us about R.P. is that the mother-child symbiosis keeps creeping back. We project duological dynamics as we are in actuality growing up into a more complicated mother-child-father dialogue.

Duologues in R.P. mean that religion, the mother, is too interested in having a good boy, a "little man" who will support her. In other words, we can too easily fudge over the chaos that is the perspective of psychology and use only the compatible ideas. For his part, psychology feels a little like a bastard at the family reunion, trying to show off to religion that he does not need her and can do it better himself. This refers to the problem of data mentioned above and to the challenge for religion to recognize herself in the child's eyes.

II. Projecting the Father in Dialogue

In terms of the language of projection, what we need to do is to move toward dialogue that includes the father with the child and the mother. This would give the child status enough to make him more secure and genuinely independent, and it would give the mother prime satisfaction, instead of leaving her to frustrate herself at the child's expense.

How can this image, common as a goal of clinical treatment, be translated to curricular structure and methodology? The answer is obscure; only a direction can we suggest. Part of the unclarity comes from the difficulty in finding a father image in the academy. The current emphasis upon colleagueship, democratic participation, and a general rebellion against monarchical forms in theory and practice (as presidents and trustees have been noting) is part of the reason. The passing of settled hierarchies, if not of monarchies, has had long-range ramifications.[6] But in any event, monarchical forms do not automatically shed light on the function and form of fathering.

Perhaps we are on firmer ground if we approach the problem within the context of projection as a means of coping with death-in-life. This would suggest that the father is an image not only defined by any given "daddy"; it is also a synthetic image produced by the projective copings of mothers and their sons. The father is an opportunity to the extent that he is a late emergent within the context of mother-child symbiosis and is partially evoked as a means of coping with the more destructive features of that "binding."[7] He is the opportunity for duologue to become dialogue; he makes it possible for the child's ego to live through the structure of his origin. The father is a jetting forth of the life of the child ego, releasing itself at the proper time from duologue with the mother's life.

The father, seen in this way, is a sign of indirect potency to the child. His strength to enhance life and protect against death is not so obvious as is that of the mother, but it can be actual. When threatened by desires to return to the womb and its annihilation prebirth or when tempted by desires to escape the mother altogether, the father is the projecting of a middle way. He is the one who can continually risk alienation but through it find a rhythm of leaving and returning. He need not succumb to strangeness as he experiences it. The child ego learns there is a pleasure associated with the delay inherent in the father's schedule; after the waiting the satisfaction is more intense. Without the father the son is left with the certainty of the symbiotic relationship or with anxiety and nihilism due to its absence.

The father's function is to introduce ambiguity and ambivalence as a desideratum. Threats of death are warded off by bringing on the feelings of threat and uncertainty, by testing risk and experiencing resistance, by mixing the trivial and the profound. For the ego, dialogue differentiates into a threefold movement with moments of certainty, ambiguity, and a between state which can be a kind of resting in neutral or a piecemeal patterning that may or may not go anywhere.

How is all this to be present in the academy's dialogue in R.P.? It already is of course. The search for certainty of union between religion and personality is often overturned in favor of more than one kind of interchange. We look to those times in dialogical method when there is a phasic movement for the ego; it concentrates on coping by exposing itself to ambiguity; it allows itself the luxury of certainty, those enthusiastic moments of knowing and being known by the data; it encourages the discipline of patient search, a slow, bit-by-bit pattern formation; it rests easy when nothing particularly is being learned or worked on.

It is not that we need to do something different in R.P. but that there is the need to articulate what dialogue is at its best within the field. Hiltner's insight in using "religion" and not theology and "personality" and not psychology is still sound.

What we need is some reminder of the richness of these constructs, avoiding duologue and taking cognizance of the complexity introduced by the projection of the mother-child-father pattern.

My thinking has gone no further at the moment than to suggest two constructs which point in the needed direction, though each has definite limits. They are attempts to explicate a "third" for R.P. Granting for the moment that God and person are attractive to students as assumptive agents of dialogue, what is the character of the third—the father—which is not subsumed under either, but broadens the discussion?

1. *Body,* or "love's body," is a point of view celebrated by many, particularly in the writing of Norman O. Brown.[8] In the special meaning of his vocabulary it refers to the "polymorphous perverse" body of the infant. In its more general meaning—the playful union of all alienated individuals undertaken immediately—Brown escapes some of the problems of appealing to Freud's phrase.[9]

The art of Bosch, the thought of apocalypticists and utopians, and the expression of the romanticists are used by Brown to suggest that all intended work can be discarded in favor of direct, playful union. Immediate satisfaction is for him a distinct possibility, one that man has continually denied in his hostile preoccupations with delay, thought, calculation, and possessiveness. Man's fearfulness of death-in-life has, according to Brown, precluded him from enjoying the fullness that is nevertheless present in life.

Without underwriting his claims, Brown has posed for R.P. a set of issues that must be faced. His radical challenge to that acquisitiveness which is based on a kind of cultural "anality" cannot be overlooked. Especially when one thinks of educators who try to predict and control dialogue by structure, who see ideas as possessions of authors, and who take their programs and productions so seriously, one cannot but hope for some of Brown's challenge to succeed.

It is not just a matter of reassessing boundaries between fields or of becoming more tolerant to new specialization or more reminded of past wholenesses; it is a matter of the quality of discussion and the goal of pedagogy and the kinds of data which methods address. How is it possible, for instance, to take account of the playfulness in the academy without becoming downright sloppy or even anti-intellectual? How can the body be celebrated not just in a bloodless way with discussions of "need" but intensely as a phase within the academy's reflective processes?

Perhaps it cannot be done. But "body" should point in the direction of carrying on the kind of dialogue in R.P. in which a concern for play, direct satisfaction, and regression can be paramount. Again, projection as a function of the ego reminds us of the inescapable way in which all intellectual discussion serves a particular ego at some point or other, and this is always an ego which is first and foremost a body ego. What this does to the problem of truth is to insist upon the inclusion of idiosyncracy in any epistemology. The ego projections of the humans who manage their quest for truth take on equal importance with the process of projection grasped as such.

2. The "communal" as one of the two modes of existence, along with the agentic, is a construct Bakan has ably defended.[10] He insists that the preoccupation with agency—with power, initiative, change, technology, prediction and control, hard fact—has robbed man of the actuality of his heritage rooted in communal existence. We can intuit directly the bonds between men. We can note, without guilt to our scientific superegos, the celebrations of union which come preveniently into the human scene.[11]

Further clarifications of Bakan's meaning can be readily gained elsewhere. Of all the terms suggested this one comes closest to being that third, more or less transcendent transformation of God and person, one that has genuine connections with both religion and personality without being subsumable under either one. Its usefulness for dialogue is limited by two considerations. First, the communal is frequently confused with the institutional. Second, the communal lacks the power to seize upon those differentiations of the ego as it projects its own individuation, and Bakan's other term, "agency," is not much better for those purposes.

The first limitation is best illustrated in that fact that R.P. grew out of a dissertation, in part, in the field of ethics; it is continually tempted to be drawn into the strictly ethical perspective. This would be well and good if the ethos of ethics were not itself lured constantly into the orbit of institutional life and analysis. The institutional is, however, only one explicit form of the communal, with the ecological being an important and distinct form.

III. Toward a Solution

We began with a search for a third term as an answer to the question, Where is the father function in the religious academy? To answer now that this function is carried by the "third" of body-community misses the crucial point about the father metaphor in projection. To project the father, from the view point of the mother and child, is not to fashion a single and unified function; it is rather to have one's singleness of mind loosened. Phenomenologically, the impression on the child is one of mystery that sometimes functions cohere in the father and sometimes in the mother.[12]

What this means for the academy is that *God* and *self* cannot be left alone in duologue. In order to escape the symbiotic problem, a third must be introduced which sets the dialogue spinning without locating the father at any of the three points. God is not the father only. Such linkage has been a commonplace assumption. Before the ego "comes of age" and when it is not regressing, the father-God keeps the lure of the father projection clearly in the forefront. But now such a position amounts to a nervous and regressive recapitulation, authentic only under limited conditions.

Nor is the ego itself its own father. Bakan has argued that it is time for man to throw himself into the fathering role heretofore reserved for the gods.[13] We can join in the spirit of that venture. And yet if "I-experiencing" is burdened with the lonely struggle of finding a partner only with itself, no matter how extended this "itself" is throughout all of humanity, the burden will prove too much to bear. To press in this direction is to move the ego toward a kind of mania all too obvious in individual pathology.

The ego cannot father itself; that is the work of the superego, the strange amalgam of *das es*—the id—and the real environment represented by parents. And yet this even says more than is legitimate, for father projects itself from the limitations, largely unconscious but not totally so, imposed by cultural evolution. Some taboos, some types of taboos at least, will have to reinstate themselves as "natural," "endemic," or even "revealed" within the human condition for true fathering once again to become unequivocal in our Western culture. The ego, no matter how broadly conceived, still needs to meet its limitations in order for the father projection to emerge.

Nor can what I have called the "third"—some combination of body and the communal—be construed as itself the father. This side is too nonspecific, mysterious, and mythological. Until we learn to use and play with our dreams without obeisance or indifference, there can be little direct dependency on this side. I speak against nativism, the hawking of regressive principles out of context with progressive ones, and the purely romantic appeal to impulse.

The "third" of dialogue in R.P. is the concreteness of man in this culture, experiencing himself through his projections. In this light the method most likely to work is one which is even more circular than the question-answer-question of Hiltner's P.T. One need not begin at the theological side to make a legitimate start; one can begin anywhere and carry on the dialogue with a phasic appreciation for the logical rigor and for playful, more or less free associations of ideas. The church and ministry can be approached without the professions of seriousness usually made and with a sense of irony and humor. The safety of the revealed truth need not be undone, nor should it be a preoccupation any longer.

Summary

The essay has spent itself in exploring the meaning of dialogue in R.P. at the doctoral level of study. "Dialogue" connotes the interweaving of perspectives that are religious and personal only when these concerns open themselves to the structural, implicit, and impersonal factors also present. Methodologies that are strictly theological or those inattentive to the need for new academic language and form probably will be transformed by those that begin bifocally: on the one hand these perspectives will use a new vision about the nature of religion as such; on the other hand they will face the task of articulating the fathering function within our culture in terms appropriate to the academy.

Notes

1. Mallary Fitzpatrick ("Footnotes on Theological Education," *Hartford Quarterly*, VIII [1968], 7-28) has influenced my thinking in this essay. The term "religious academy" is one with which I try to escape problems involved in using "theological education" as if that were something monolithic. Fitzpatrick suggests the need for such a term, e.g.: "Today, the needed reform of the seminary curriculum must be undertaken by a discrete faculty of a given school, and when so undertaken becomes an instance of confession of faith."
2. In this essay the shorter form of "Religion and Personality," namely R.P., will be used to designate a structure of doctrinal study. Though initiated at the University of Chicago Divinity School, R.P. is to be understood as a form of education. When I refer to it, I do not mean to denote the actual program of R.P. now being undertaken at Chicago.
3. Seward Hiltner, *Preface to Pastoral Theology* (New York: Abingdon Press, 1958), p. 220.
4. *Ibid.*, p. 223.
5. E.g., E. Marcuse's work in *Eros and Civilization* (Boston: Beacon Press, 1955) represents a union of psychology and politico-economics; Norman O. Brown's work in *Life Against Death* (Middletown, Conn.: Wesleyan University Press, 1959) brings us a symbiosis of psychoanalysis and classical (utopian) humanism.
6. Not the least of these ramifications has been the current controversy over the "death of God." The loss of nonarchical forms is hailed as necessarily the loss of God by one side and as the shucking off of obscurities from apprehension of the living God by the other side.
7. The discussion of fathering here is severely limited by two assumptions: first, that the Western form of the family is in focus; second, that it is legitimate to expand from the pathology of infantile symbiosis to a description of the usual processes of development during that stage.
8. Norman O. Brown, *Love's Body* (Chicago: Rand McNally, 1966).

9. Brown's logical problem in invoking the regressive principle with a phrase Freud intended to display developmental and potentially progressive principles has never been overcome in his thought. To go beyond this and make a commission out of an analysis designed to provide understanding is an even more difficult problem.
10. David Bakan, *The Duality of Human Existence* (New York: Random House, 1966), pp. 14-15.
11. "I have adopted the terms 'agency' and 'communion' to characterize two fundamental modalities in the existence of living forms, agency for the existence of an organism as an individual, and communion for the participation of the individual in some larger organism of which the individual is a part. Agency manifests itself in self-protection, self-assertion, and self-expansion; communion manifests itself in the sense of being at one with other organisms. Agency manifests itself in the formation of separations; communion in the lack of separations. Agency manifests itself in isolation, alienation, and aloneness; communion in contact, openness, and union. Agency manifests itself in the urge to master; communion in non-contractual cooperation. Agency manifests itself in the repression of thought, feeling, and impulse; communion in the lack and removal of repression." (*Ibid.*, pp. 14-15.)
12. Usually the father function is construed as introducing directionality and focal pointedness for the child. I am suggesting that this is a result of an earlier dynamic which structurally means that the overly unified field of reference for the child is broken and diffused; out of this introduction of mystery the child then can locate diffuseness with the mother and directionality with the father.
13. Bakan, *Duality of Human Existence*, pp. 200-201.

The Practical Fields and Theological Education

Paul E. Irion

The practical fields have found a new place in the pattern of theological education in the past quarter-century. It is my purpose to assess their progress from the vantage point of the present and to delineate some of the important issues which have been posed by these developments for theological education as a whole.

I. Background

The beginnings of the concept "practical theology" in the theological curriculum are found primarily in the nineteenth century. Schleiermacher in *Die Praktische Theologie nach den Grundsäzen der Evangelischen Kirche* in 1850 laid the foundation stones for the present meaning of practical theology. He indicated the possibility for understanding such traditional elements as teaching, preaching, and the care of souls not merely as the application of theological knowledge. Rather he saw the potentiality of reflecting theologically on the functions necessary for the maintaining and perfecting of the church.

But Schleiermacher's insight was eclipsed for nearly a century as continental theological education maintained a fixed orientation on classical, academic theologizing and American seminaries gradually developed training programs in pastoral skills based on the offices of the minister: catechetics (Christian education), homiletics (preaching), poimenics (shepherding), halieutics (missions), and liturgics (worship).

For many decades courses in practical theology proliferated in American theological curricula. For the most part they appear to have been constructed on a model that assumed the teacher as professional exemplar and the student as imitator. Heavy emphasis was placed on the "how to" dimension, skill training. Functional competence was often understood not in terms of mastery of a theory upon which the pastor operated and of the capacity to reflect upon one's operations in the light of that theoretical understanding. Rather competence was seen to rest in the person of the minister—his zeal, his piety, his evangelical fervor.

Then in the second quarter of the twentieth century the practical fields gradually began to note developments in the behavioral sciences and to see their relationship to the operation of the church and its ministry. Christian education found important insights emerging from educational psychology. The literature and practice of psychotherapy and developmental psychology began informing the pastoral counselors. Homiletics found that new scientific studies of communication and behavioral change needed to be considered. Work in missions and church and community turned to emerging insights from the social sciences. In the early stages of this new awakening to scientific exploration of human behavior the practical fields used the findings of science to apply more effectively theological insights received from the traditional fields of Bible, church history, and systematic theology. Secular science became in a sense a facilitator of theological transmission.

Nearly twenty years ago a group of teachers of practical theology, in response to a workshop on theological education in the practical fields sponsored jointly by the Conference of Seminary Administrators and the Department of Pastoral Services of the Federal Council of Churches, of which Seward Hiltner was executive secretary, formed the Association of Seminary Professors in the Practical Fields. Practical men that they were, they recorded the situation which brought forth this effort to associate. They pointed to four needs which moved them to affiliate.

1. The need for a learned society to formulate the body of knowledge distinctive to the practical fields.

2. The need for a way of collecting data, developing and testing hypotheses in the study of what happens to people religiously.

3. The need for integrating relationships within the various branches of the practical fields which may have been associated historically out of expediency or accident.

4. The need for relating the practical fields to the other fields in an effort to develop a truly integrated and comprehensive curriculum for theological education.

To one who was not among the founding fathers and who approaches the text of this statement of needs with more detachment, there appears an implicit mood of defensiveness in these propositions. One finds such statements as: "We do not pull sufficient weight in the theoretical end of seminary teaching. We have been too much just practitioners," or "We have to go too exclusively to secular sources for methods, data, hypotheses," or "We must be able to cooperate with other fields of seminary education out of strength, not from weakness."

So the association was formed with five clearly enunciated purposes:

1. To serve as a symbol of the unity of the practical fields.
2. To promote fellowship among men who teach in the practical fields.
3. To provide a continuing means of defining the nature and meaning of the integrity of the field; and to promote the kind of relationships which follow from appreciation of that integrity and unity.
4. To discover the principles which can integrate the practical fields with other fields of theological study.
5. To stimulate both research and scholarship in the practical fields.[1]

These goals represent emergence of a new focus for work in the practical fields, a focus upon which the scholarship of the practical theologians has centered down.

During the period since 1950 numerous studies have been undertaken which have been influential in the development of the practical fields. Landmarks among them are: the Niebuhr, Williams, Gustafson study of theological education; Blizzard's descriptive study of the minister and his role; and the Feilding study, *Education for Ministry*.[2] Each of these studies in its own way focused on professional education for ministry.

The Niebuhr, Williams, Gustafson report challenged theological education to clarify its goals, pointing to the debilitating uncertainty about the nature and task of the ministry, particularly as it relates to the preparation for ministry. The study was critical of the pattern of fragmentary transmission of knowledge and skills which characterized seminary education. The emphasis rather should be on developing the capacity for independent thought and study in the student, preparing him to grow constantly as a lifelong inquirer, *learning as he ministers*. The study made an analysis of issues in the theological curriculum. It expressed unhappiness with the distinction between "practical" and "theoretical," preferring to see all elements of the curriculum interrelated as parts of an organism are related. Ideally, a faculty should be living and working as a collegium, rather than each professor working in his own compound completely oblivious to what is being done in other fields. The study encouraged a broader relationship between theological education and the secular sciences.

Also in the mid-1950's the research of Samuel Blizzard pointed to the need for extensive attention to the operational aspects of the ministry. He found a vast and distressing disparity between the minister's theological understanding of what ministry is and his operational understanding of what the minister does. Lack of a clear understanding of how ministry is to be understood, together with sizable role conflict, was raising the level of frustration for many ministers. Many pastors found that they were devoting most time and energy to those very duties which they enjoyed least and for which they could formulate the least theological justification. In its own way this study pointed to the consequences of the divorce of theory and practice in theological education and called for another careful look at the way in which the theological curriculum provided preparation for ministry.

The American Association of Theological Schools' study headed by Charles Feilding pointed to the same problem lifted up by the previous surveys. Careful observation of theological curricula and teaching methods in the mid-1960's showed that there was still a damaging discontinuity between preparation for ministry and the work of ministry. Too often even the fields that are to teach the practice of ministry teach by talking about practice rather than engaging in ministry. Feilding concluded that theological education should be based on the model of a professional school rather than the model of a graduate school in the humanities with some added opportunities for practice.

From these studies we see that there is a continuing ambivalence in American theological education i.e., struggling hard to be effective in providing professional education while torn between the extremes of the trade school and the university graduate school. Solution of this difficult problem is one of the most crucial problems encountering theological education today.

That this should be true in spite of the very real advances which have been made in the practical fields in recent decades is surprising. The methodologies taught in many of the practical fields have profited from major advances in various behavioral sciences: Christian education has utilized new insights emerging from the study of group process, the developmental understanding of the person, and learning theory; pastoral care and counseling have found that the self-understanding of the minister and his grasp of the individual human situation are deepened through insights received from psychotherapy, particularly when channeled through clinical pastoral education; preaching is taught not only with a new emphasis on exegesis but also with new knowledge about the communication of meaning; cultural anthropology has contributed to the teaching of missions by pointing to a new way of encountering world religions in a context of rising new nationalism; the teaching of the work of the church in the community is informed by new sociological understandings of man as a political creature; the teaching of worship is carried on in the light of new forms of ministry which do not have access to all the traditional symbols of the church; field education lays new emphasis on adequate supervision, learning not by imitation but by critical reflection upon one's own operations. Either contributions of this order are not yet widely enough utilized, or they have not yet been integrated into any significant patterns of professional education. Since no massive rebuttal of Feilding's critique has been registered, it must "tell it like it is."

II. The Issues

With this background in mind it appears that there are really three central issues to be considered as one assesses the practical fields in theological education. These are issues described nearly twenty years ago in the founding of the Association of Seminary Professors in the Practical Fields and implicit, at the very least, in the studies indicated. They are:

1. The nature of the practical fields: Are they an integrated whole, or are they diverse elements haphazardly joined?
2. The relation of the practical fields to the rest of the theological curriculum—the traditional or classical fields.
3. The nature of the contribution (either actual or potential) of the practical fields to the whole of theological understanding.

Perspectives on these issues will of necessity vary from school to school, reflecting the dynamics of particular faculties and institutional traditions. But still some generalizations can be made.

Unity of the Practical Fields

As one explores the nature of the practical fields, it is legitimate to inquire whether they constitute a single field or several closely related fields. There is support for using the plural designation. The ASPPF in its name specifically acknowledges fields. In its programs it has repeatedly held "cross-field discussion" (e.g., Christian education with field education, preaching, pastoral care, etc.). Furthermore, in addition to this organization most of the practical fields have also organized independently. A sizable list of field organizations could be compiled, organizations resulting from the need each group has felt for fellowship and professional discussion.

There are two possible ways for understanding this emergence of separate field organizations. It may be that there is really not enough in common among the practical fields to hold them in a meaningful unity. Perhaps it could be argued that the practical fields have in common only that they represent a collection of things that did not fit elsewhere in the theological curriculum. In this case, reference to a unity of the practical fields is just a matter of defensive expediency.

This suggests another possible understanding of the movement from a common field to separate fields. Perhaps only as the practical fields did not feel so threatened and took a less defensive stand were the several fields able to operate on their own. This is not unlike the emergence of identity and independence in the adolescent after a period of strong peer-clustering for protection. It does not mean that the adolescent no longer has anything to do with his peers, but he does move forward with the capacity for individual action.

Nevertheless such reflection on the reasons, however valid, behind separate organizations in the practical fields offers no really theoretical basis for affirming or denying that there is an integrity in the practical fields. These fields can be seen as distinct entities and yet unified. It can be argued that they are not united for expediency but because of an underlying common ground. The task then is to define that unity.

It is a unity based upon a common and distinctive understanding of the educational task, a common and distinctive educational method, a common interest and concern with secular science, a basic understanding of the possibility of doing theology on the foundation of functional ministry. The unity, then, is in the investment which the practical fields make in the totality of theological education.

The presence of both unity and diversity would suggest that the practical fields are related to each other like members of a family. They are discrete individuals, yet very similar in language, life-style, loyalty, objectives. We shall return to this theme later when we discuss the contribution of the practical fields to theological education as a whole.

Integrated Theological Curriculum

One of the significant concerns of the practical fields as they sought their own identity has involved their relationship to the rest of the theological disciplines—the biblical, historical, and systematic theology fields.

Terminology poses problems here. To speak of some fields as practical implies that others are impractical. To refer to some as theoretical or content fields causes one to infer that others are devoid of theory or solid content. It is not uncommon at present for professors of systematic theology or church history or Bible to decry the outmoded differentiation between "content" and "practical," usually by prefixing the word "so-called." Although the distinction persists in the minds and mouths of a few whom we choose to think of as academically conservative or professionally insecure, it is increasingly accepted that while there are legitimate differentiations between all the fields in the theological curriculum, there is no hierarchical arrangement, no implication of superiority or inferiority.

The theological curriculum is divided into fields on an arbitrary basis to provide the possibility of a comprehensive and systematic approach to the study of theology. No field is really more theological than another; none is in actuality more basic to theological education than the others. We are burdened with an inadequate terminology which must somehow be revised to describe more accurately the individual function of the various fields of the curriculum and their relationship. The terminological inadequacy and the pejorative connotations of past decades do not truly describe the way in which the practical fields, per se, have found acceptance in the community of theological education.

Support for this acceptance has come from a number of developments of the past several decades. First of all, some new perspectives for understanding the theological curriculum have emerged. We can illustrate this with Seward Hiltner's thoughtful distinction between logic-centered and operation-centered disciplines, as related in his *Preface to Pastoral Theology*, providing both academic and theological legitimacy for the practical fields. Hiltner's attention was on pastoral theology, but the model he constructed was fitted for all the practical fields. Although his intention was only to write the preface for theological reflection on the basis of pastoral operation, he provided a methodological warrant that made it clear that the practical fields, those concerned with the operation of the minister, were contributors to as well as beneficiaries of a body of theological understanding. The theme which was developed in this work has borne fruit in some of the scholarship emerging in recent years from the practical fields. By taking very seriously the dialogical relationship of Christian faith and Christian life, it has been possible to develop a new perspective for understanding the relationship of the component parts of the theological curriculum.

We can also point to increasing strength of faculties in the practical fields. Prior to the present generation it has been difficult to do advanced graduate study in the practical fields. Most of those who taught in these fields were autodidacts, schooled in the richness of their own experience and in the classical disciplines. Acceptance of the practical fields has grown with stronger academic and broader experiential preparation of professors in those fields and by strengths manifest in more clearly defined educational goals in the practical fields. Rather than the example-imitation pattern of instruction, it is now more common to develop theoretical knowledge based on generalizations arrived at by reflection upon operational experience.

Mention can be made of the more general acceptance in theological education of what had been some of the distinctive concerns and methodologies of the practical fields. Learning through involvement and reflection on experience as a basis for developing and testing theory was no longer limited to the practical fields. New and often strident demands for relevance in an age of encounter made contact with every facet of theological education. The impact upon the entire course of theological education of such programs as Metropolitan Urban Service Training, the Yale in-Parish Pastoral Studies Program, Clinical Pastoral Education, and many others like them bred dissatisfaction with learning isolated from experience. An abiding concern in many theological schools for courses of study that are relevant to the effective ministries required in a changing world has helped to blur the distinction between the classical and functional disciplines. Relevance is the concern of the total enterprise, not just of a "practical" portion of the curriculum.

Progress has been made, but there is ample evidence that the task of integrating the theological curriculum is not yet finished. The Feilding study reports that too often when the division of theory and practice exists, it causes a student to have two theological understandings which do not in any sense become integrated—each remains irrelevant to the other.

Further evidence of deficiency in integration of the theological curriculum is seen in the proposal of the Resources Planning Commission of the American Association of Theological Schools for a theological curriculum of the 1970's[3] which, in spite of some extremely creative and promising features, runs the grave risk of patterning theological education after a continental model of university followed by *Predigerseminar* (theory followed by practical application). Although some aspects of this proposal, e.g., instruction in small integrated groups centered on the task of thinking theologically about contemporary life, are welcome promises of things to come, others appear to move backward toward a renewed separation of theory and practice. Although the intention of the authors of this curriculum was integration, the clear-cut geographical and structural separation of the centers for theological reflection and the centers for training for ministry would undoubtedly widen the very gap they were seeking to bridge.

There is little question that some gains have been made in overcoming the partition between elements of the theological curriculum. However until a completely new perspective for formulating the curriculum is developed, it is unlikely that a totally integrated curriculum will emerge.

The Contribution of the Practical Fields

If one thinks of the curriculum as an organism, it becomes apparent that each part must make a contribution not merely for its own survival but for the support and growth of the entire organism. The practical fields have such a function in the total curriculum. They have a unique contribution to make to theological education as a whole.

It has been pointed out that the practical fields ordinarily provide the point where contact is established between theological education and secular disciplines, particularly the behavioral sciences. Leaders of the practical fields in 1950, as noted in their description of the situation leading to the founding of their professional association, took the position that the practical fields had not developed their own constructive theories but had been too dependent upon secular sources. The practical fields have been uncomfortable with this liaison role for two reasons. First, they do not feel that this is a *unique* function of the practical fields but see possibilities for more active and relevant dialogue between the secular sciences and all the theological fields. Ecclesiology is not only a subject for systematic theology but involves sociological observations as well. Biblical studies can be enriched by probing inquiry into the psychological understanding of man. A second reason for the discomfort of the practical fields with the role of sole liaison between theology and secular science is that such an exclusive role may deprive the practical fields of the possibility of making a constructive contribution to theological understanding. There is good reason to be dissatisfied with the passive role of providing a channel between classical theological education and science. A more active role is more appropriate for a fully participating member of the organism. As Hiltner argued in *Preface to Pastoral Theology*, is it possible to undertake theological reflection on a base of operational experience.

In the present situation, then, it would appear that the contribution which the practical fields would want to make to the whole of theological education is a demonstration that conversation between the secular sciences and *any* dimension of the theological curriculum is productive. Such dialogue, which must be genuine dialogue and not merely apologetic or eristical confrontation, must become a part of the total enterprise. The practical fields offer testimony to the value of such encounter, functioning not merely as the sole connecting link but as a forerunner for widening dialogue.

Another contribution of the practical fields, at least in their normative manifestations if not always in actuality, is the way in which they have pressed for acceptance of a learning theory that is based upon experience, involvement, participation, induction. Laboratory and clinical models have been widely employed. Careful supervision of both performance and reflection on performance has been sought. It has been hoped that the model composed solely of transmitted knowledge could be replaced by the more flexible process of learning to think theologically about concrete existential situations. A mark of this contribution may be seen in the development of aspects of level II of the theological curriculum of the 1970's. Here small groups of students and faculty members representing both theological and behavioral disciplines investigate immediate situations involving contemporary human problems in an effort to learn to think theologically about them. Study would not be isolated but would require involvement and participation by students and faculty in such things, for example, as poverty programs, mental health clinics, etc. Their experience would be reflected upon in the light of the church's theological heritage. This experiential and inductive approach provides a mode of theological education that has for some time been a part of the educational method of the practical fields. In this innovative curriculum it is projected for all theological disciplines.

A third contribution of the practical fields is an intense concern for the personal development of the student. This is not to imply that teachers in other disciplines are coldly indifferent to the student as a person. Rather it is to say that the personal involvement of the student is more obviously a part of his work in the practical fields. Because so much of the work of ministry, in its many forms, is focused on change factors in personal relationship, it is quite natural that considerable attention be given to the potential for effective relationship in the person of the minister. This kind of attention has broadened seminaries' concern for the student beyond the more familiar dimensions of intelligence and piety. The willingness of the student to understand himself as a person and the demonstration of his capacity to enter creatively into relationship with those whom he seeks to serve become additional significant focuses in his theological education.

As these contributions are enumerated, there must also be an awareness of some liabilities involved. There is always the danger that the emphasis on experience will stop with the experience itself rather than affording an occasion for sufficient reflection on experience to develop and communicate a theoretical structure. In order to achieve maximum learning from experience, several factors must be present. The experience itself must be significant and immediate, not superficial. Experience must really involve the student in ministering, that is, serving, catching him up in responsible action. This is vastly superior to observation, even participant observation. Supervision must do more than guide his performance; it must help him to an awareness of the strengths and weaknesses of his involvement as a person in ministry. Supervision should not be limited to a particular experience but should lead the student to formulate a theoretical basis to guide his learning from continuing experience. It must be admitted that at times the experience-oriented learning fostered in the practical fields has not been as productive as it should have been because of a lack of a proper supervision in the reflective assessment of it and because of the failure to develop general principles on the basis of that experience.

Another liability grows out of failure of the practical fields to be sufficiently flexible in responding to the development of new forms of ministry. One notes how much of the work in the practical fields is explicitly oriented toward the parish ministry. Without suggesting that the parochial ministry should be ignored, some realistic provision should also be made for experience-oriented learning for those who seek new and sometimes strange ministries. The Feilding report urges development of a self-educating professional who will be able to continue to learn from the unfolding of unfamiliar experience in new forms of ministry. This is certainly one way for removing the factor of unplanned obsolesence in the production of ministers.

Conclusion

Theological education in this decade is in a very fluid state. New institutional alignments provide opportunities for profound self-examination and for emergence of innovative curricula. Changing forms of ministry as well as a "new breed" of theological students demand a kind of relevance that is hard to pour from old wineskins. Theological education is challenged to develop truly professional education at the graduate level.

As one seeks to understand the state of the practical fields, a portion of Erik Erikson's model for understanding personal development seems applicable. Like the late adolescent person, the practical fields are beginning to consolidate the gains that have been made in the identity struggle. No longer is there need for defensiveness. The shift is being made from feelings of inferiority in the educational system to the sense of being able to contribute meaningfully and effectively to theological education as a whole. It still remains for these contributions to be more fully articulated and for the emergence of these disciplines to full parity in the educational community. This is the task of the next decade.

Notes

1. "Report of the Association of Seminary Professors in the Practical Fields," June, 1950, p. 3.
2. H. Richard Niebuhr, Daniel Day Williams, James M. Gustafson, *The Purpose of the Church and Its Ministry: Reflections on the Aims of Theological Education* (New York: Harper, 1956); H. Richard Niebuhr *et al.*, *The Advancement of Theological Education* (New York: Harper, 1957); the study of the ministry by Samuel Blizzard was not published as a whole but is contained in reports to various organizations; Charles R. Feilding *et al.*, *Education for Ministry* (Dayton, Ohio: American Association of Theological Schools, 1966).
3. *Theological Education,* Spring, 1968.

The Place of Field Experience in Theological Education: Clues from Pastoral Theology

James E. Spicer

It is startling from one point of view to realize that pastoral theology as a discipline has had such little influence and in some instances practically no application in the process of theological education. This judgment must be tempered by the major exception of the acceptance of the idea of supervision as being a significant dimension of ministerial training. But even the notion of supervision, which in its early days held the promise of being the long-sought elixir which would resolve the conflicts between the academic and the professional, has proved less valuable than originally hoped. Where it has been used at all, the theory of supervision has been diverse and its application uneven.

It would seem clear that the ancient liberal arts image of the minister as the learned man or the scholar-saint has now broken down beyond repair. So have most of the other images and roles which we have used to guide the training of ministers. They have for the most part been agrarian, and our increasingly urbanized society has simply transcended them. What the modern day calls for is not only learning but also skills—*competency*. In fact, the much discussed identity crisis of the clergy seems to me to represent a cluster of issues which are most clearly defined in terms of professional competence.

The major issues of theological education, if allowed to surface at all, come neatly to focus in the problems of field education. The relationship between work and/or experience and the formal academic structures has been dealt with by assumption rather than analysis. The consequence is that schools continue to train men to be good students rather than competent professional men.

It does not seem amiss for an educational institution, a divinity school, to have some direct, formal, high-order concern for educational process. Effective teaching is a legitimate goal. In fact, this concern seems most often to be expressed in the almost perpetual round of curriculum redesign and change. Perhaps there are other levels where this concern might be appropriately focused.

I. A Partial Educational Model

To begin with the obvious, the old tried-and-true methods *do* teach. Many generations of ministers have gotten along tolerably well with a training that consisted largely of three years of lectures. Moreover, while some of the "new" models of education, such as clinical training, have offered a new dimension to theological education—often helpful—they have shown no promise in any comprehensive way of dealing with the whole of professional education. The "new" methods to some degree presuppose that some of the old education has in fact taken place.

This then suggests the necessity of coming to an educational model which will see, recognize, and retain the values of tried-and-true procedures, while at the same time moving toward the inclusion of other approaches which will offer both precision and flexibility. Let us take a point of view which is essentially Freudian, enhanced by ego psychology and contemporary behavioralist research.

If one accepts the view that we learn both from experience and through formal educational procedures, our proposed model will have to account for both factors and show how they relate. This we will contend is feasible on the basis of sound, empirically validated learning theory and equally well-accepted psychological principles.

The first question is, What is an experience? For present purposes we will use the term to refer to the fact of the human organism's immersion in an environment which is external to it but with which it has contact and over which it has some degree of control. From this point of view "experience," or responsive contact with one's environment, is not a singular, discrete event which can be isolated for study but, to use the term of William James, "a flowing stream" that begins with life and ends with death, interrupted only by severe pathological conditions. Even in sleep, then, the human is in contact with his environment, though at a lower threshold of responsiveness. Because it is continuous, the only way we can study or discuss experience is to take a kind of Bergsonian "slice" of experience, an artificial interruption of the stream, which will allow us to dissect an "occurrence" or to examine a "moment of experience."

Any moment of experience has an immense "givenness" about it. The elements which are brought to the experience are ranged about two poles: the individual and the situation. The variables involved in the givenness of the situation are indefinite in number and valence. From the perspective of the individual they involve his genetic heritage; his previous learning and/or experience; his fundamental perceptual and intellectual abilities; his current, momentary state of health; etc. The givenness of the situation may be relatively simple but is usually infinitely complex. Together these poles comprise the base of potentialities upon which the experience rests.

The first thing which "happens" in a human experience is obviously *perception*. Through the use of the perceptual apparatus—the five senses with their capacity for overtone, undertone, and degree of awareness—the individual comes into contact with his environment. The first stage of perception is by no means a conscious awareness. Perception—staying in contact with the environment—goes on all the time, twenty-four hours a day, from birth to death. In sleep some aspects of perception are dulled, but one can be wakened. Thus one is never completely out of touch with the environment.

Following perception there is a complicated but relatively complete physical or *visceral response*. The nervous system accepts the information provided by the perceptual system and files it appropriately in relation to the previously established response patterns of the organism.

Closely following the physical intake of the perceptual information there occurs a very low-level, diffuse, preconscious awareness which we shall term the level of *feeling.*

To illustrate the meaning of experience up to this point let us take a very common experiential phenomenon and examine it. Imagine for example that you are at this moment seated in a room. The temperature in the room is reasonably comfortable although obviously in a constant state of fluctuation. If the temperature should happen to climb, say five degrees, the perceptual system of your body, its heat-sensing apparatus, would communicate this change in the environment to the neural structure. As a consequence of this there would be a highly complex chain of events set off in your body directed toward maintaining homeostasis, or a relative balance in your temperature. All this occurs below the level of consciousness. If the temperature variance becomes too great, say up to six or seven degrees, the experience begins to rise to the "feeling" level, and you may begin to shift about in the chair or make other random movements with only a vague feeling that something is wrong.

Should the temperature continue to climb, the experience moves to the next level, the first level of consciousness or that of *meaning.* That is, the capacity of the physical organism to make the necessary adjustments automatically, or without the intervention of the conscious intellectual system, has been exceeded. The "meaning" first comes to awareness as a feeling. This feeling is then referred to the memory traces for like or similar experiences. Thus memory is the second level of conscious activity. Once the proper neural trace has been located (there can be mistakes in this process, and this is usually what we mean when we talk of misperceiving something), there emerges in consciousness a concept. In the case of our illustration the concept "I am hot" moves into the center of your conscious awareness.

At this point *intellectualization,* or what is commonly referred to as "thinking," is required. Having become aware that you are hot, you must now determine what course of action, if any, you will take to relieve the perceived imbalance. In this process there is a constant interplay between reference to memory and the projection of fantasy. That is, we "as if" ourselves into a variety of trial situations. Ultimately, we must select among the various alternatives which fantasy has provided and at this point make a decision. To refer again to our illustration, having recognized that you are hot, you then recall other times when you were hot and fantasize the alternatives (such as removing your coat, opening the window, resetting the thermostat, etc.), ultimately moving to a decision, which is in large part based upon other aspects of the experiential situation which must also be thought through (will your action interrupt the speaker, is the window stuck, is there a thermostat in the room, etc.).

Finally, this experience, if it is sufficiently vivid, may become *symbolized.* That is, the entire experience with all its complexity is summarized and can be recalled simply by the lifting up of some symbolic aspect of the experience. Again to use our example, if you become too hot in a meeting where it was inconvenient to remove your coat, where you could not adjust the room temperature, and the only alternative was to sit and swelter, the next time you go by the room just looking at the door may cause you to think of being too hot. That is, instead of remembering the content and action of the meeting, you remember the room because it has now become a symbol of the experience of being too hot. This has been the primary experience of the meeting. Or to use the example of a religious symbol, a cross held up in a worship service will symbolize many different things to those present. To the Jew who is visiting it may cause him to recall and reflect upon experiences of horror, denial, isolation, etc. To one of rural background it may recall pacific and delightful periods of childhood. For the clergy present it may remind them of their vocational problems and thus set off a momentary anxiety. This view gives substance to the wisdom of the Roman use of Latin in the Mass and is suggestive in its implication about the confusion and difficulties involved in the Protestant use of symbols where often they are supposed to have discrete, common points of reference for everyone present.

This model of experience can be visualized in the following way:

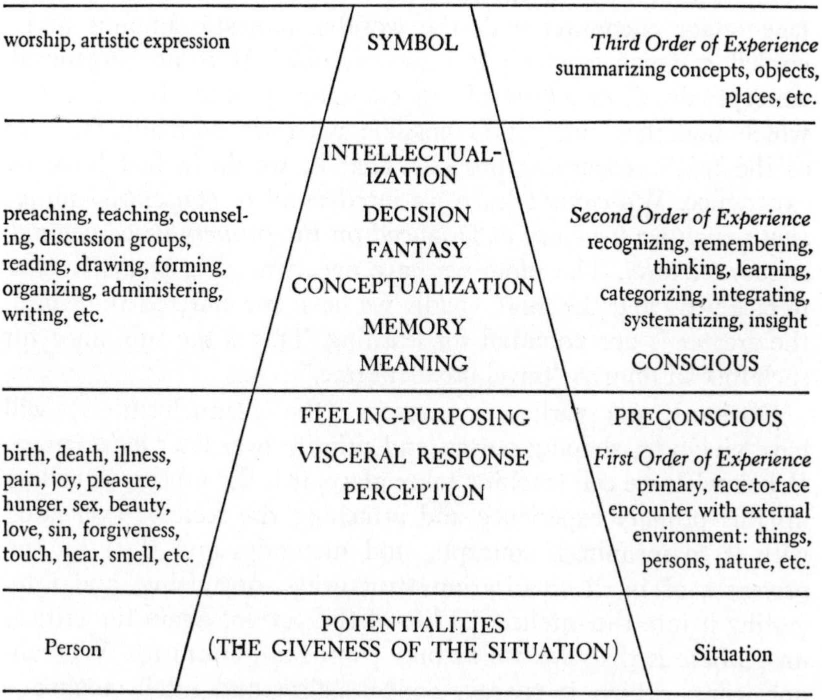

Notice that in the figure we have divided experience into levels. The first level, or primary experience, is preconscious. Since the source of this level of experience is the direct encounter of the perceptual system with the environment, there is from birth to death a constant inflow. We have potentially in the storage cells of our brains a record of every second of our existence. Obviously, most of this experience is routine and is dealt with by the automatic responses of our body with no need to go through the process of conceptualization and intellectualization or integration and structuring in our thought systems. Thus most of our primary experience remains as diffuse, disorganized, and only potentially available. At times some critical primary experiences can be left at this level (for reason of stress or neglect), and should they be needed in terms of the development of our life, they become the object of therapeutic search and recovery. The critical point is that there is in this reservoir of primary experience or face-to-face encounter with the world a fantastic amount of recorded experience which is only *potential.* It is not organized, conceptualized, or a part of our conscious process. It is this fact which underlies and makes possible what we normally think of as the teaching-learning process. That is, we do in fact learn by experience. *We cannot learn, in intellectual or conceptual terms, that which we have not experienced on the primary or perceptual-encounter level.* The more we have experienced in primary, face-to-face ways and the more vividly we have encountered the world, the greater is our potential for learning. This is the substance for such folk wisdom as "travel broadens one."

Obviously our earlier experiences (the channelizations) will have vividness, shaping power, and priority over later experiences. When what we call teaching takes place, it is the process of calling up this primary experience and attaching the feelings associated with it to meanings, concepts, and memories and then by the processes of intellectualization structuring, organizing, and integrating it into the intellectual life of the person. Again the critical image here is that *this works only from the bottom up.* We cannot learn—which is to say, conceptualize and intellectualize—without the underlying primary experience.

Such a statement seems to raise many problems and objections. When one reflects on how one has learned some kinds of things, this approach would seem to have validity. But there are other kinds of learning that it does not seem to cover. For example, one can "learn" about Germany even though one has never been in that country. But if one traces the learning process carefully, it turns out that one learns about Germany by the process of analogy, based upon one's experience with other countries. The differences between knowing Germany as an abstraction, which is to say, as an analogue, and knowing Germany through primary experience is profound. Or to take other illustrations, how can one learn abstractions such as mathematics or foreign languages? Mathematics, even in its highest, most abstract forms, can be learned because one has primary experience with that to which mathematics points, namely the relationships between objects in time and space. One can learn a foreign language because one has had previous primary experience with one's native language. This basic knowledge can then be extended to primary experience with other language forms and the rules of grammar, etc., reconceptualized, reorganized to cover the additional circumstances.

Thus primary, face-to-face experience is a critical ingredient for learning. But it is equally important to see that *no learning takes place until this primary experience has been conceptualized, organized, and made a part of the intellectual tools of the individual.*

The most significant defense of this view of the educational process can be seen in the problems we face with the so-called culturally deprived child. The term cultural deprivation points precisely to a lack of primary experience. One cannot teach such children about friendly policemen, firemen, etc., in the way characteristic of most of our early public educational procedures if the child has in fact never seen a friendly policeman, fireman, etc. Therefore the first educational task is to provide the child with that reservoir of experience which can then be utilized by the teacher in the conceptualizing process. The teaching process in this situation is further complicated by the fact that the ghetto child has learned a separate language or symbolic-conceptual scheme by which he understands most of the world. Thus the average middle class teacher has difficulty making contact with such pupils because he does not speak their language nor they his. The conceptualization-intellectualization process is difficult —a difficulty frequently no less profound in theological seminaries and churches.

From this point of view there is also a key to the master teacher. All of us have known those teachers who were able to make things extremely clear for us and to facilitate our learning process so that over and over again we were swept with the "Aha, now I see" experience. The secret of this is the teacher's ability to recognize and attach meanings and concepts to the primary experience of the student. This is why in teaching, as well as in preaching, the illustration becomes so central to the learning process. It is the illustration which enables the student to identify his primary experience, to attach previously unsuspected meaning to it and to conceptualize it. The master teacher is one who is able to do this consistently.

This process of conceptualizing and organizing the primary experience is normally identified as the teaching task. It is the process by which a lecture, sermon, discussion group, bull session or any other kind of learning-teaching situation works or fails to work. To understand this process and to be able to use it with precision is the key to being an effective teacher or communicator.

One of the prime difficulties in most educational settings is that little or no attention is paid to either the problem of the necessary base of primary experience or the problem of precision in attaching concepts and intellectualization to those experiences. Thus courses, lectures, or data are offered almost at random and the actual learning process reduced in some instances to almost the level of the accidental. *The value of this model is that it shows us that in relation to what we intend to teach, certain experiences must be provided, and that if learning is to take place, these experiences must be accurately interpreted.*

Symbolization, the third order of the experience, must also be taken seriously if the full learning situation is to be exploited. Usually symbolization is left completely to the realm of the accidental. Thus students tend to symbolize their learning by picking up the affectations of their professors, wearing unique garb, smoking pipes or the like. A theological seminary should be particularly aware of this problem especially as it relates to worship and the liturgical activities of the church. The major point about symbolization which needs to be made is that one symbol can stand for a tremendous amount of primary and secondary experience. A whole year's hard academic work may be symbolized by one slogan, one paper, or some object which is related to that work in the mind of the individual student. We have few symbols which are generally accepted, have the imprimatur of the whole community, and stand for levels of accomplishment. The high school student, for example, may wear a sweater which symbolizes the activities in which he has participated, the honors he has received, and the amount of time he has devoted to the matter. In the typical theological school there are only covert symbols, the pipe, the look of confidence, etc., or at best, a few overt symbols of success such as a carrel in the library.

II. Experience and the Training of the Minister

This kind of view of the meaning of experience in education will, I contend, shed light upon both the appropriate character of traditional academic procedures and the significance of field experience in theological education.

If the model we have suggested is at all correct, it would imply that the student can never be expected to know or to learn in the sense of integration and functionality that which he has never experienced. Thus if the subject matter under consideration is grace and the student has never had the experience of abject judgment and forgiveness, the best he will be able to do with grace is to deal with it as an analogue. Here one of the traditional and fundamental differences between Protestant and Roman Catholic theological education can be seen. The Roman Catholic experiences judgment and grace as a daily part of his training. He is judged, charged, and forgiven. The Protestant student from a fundamentalist background has usually encountered something like this in his early church experience. He was judged, frequently in public by a fire-eating sermon which called attention to some of his human frailties, and then he experienced an equally public but also private sense of forgiveness often in the conversion experience. To this student the categories of sin, judgment, and grace will have a vivid and often shaping power. However, to the average contemporary Protestant student, reared in middle and upper middle class America, judgment and forgiveness are essentially strangers. One suspects this to be the source of the powerful impact of the racial confrontation of our time among theological students. This is the first time direct judgment has been drawn down upon them, and they have been named the sinners. The flailing about caused by this issue—which has occurred in most seminaries—often seems to be a quest for an equally direct forgiveness. Perhaps it is well for clergy in training if this absolution does not come easily or too soon.

But to move beyond the level of the personal-experiential it is not hard to see why most young clergymen, after a few years of experience in the parish, feel that they have been either mistrained or untrained for their task. It is not irrelevant that three to five years after seminary is high point for dropouts from the ministry. Whatever else happens to him, the Protestant minister is constantly immersed in two realms, people and institution. Neither human beings nor contemporary institutions are simple monads or mere verbal constructs. Each is a highly complex organism. Yet it is perfectly possible for a student to wander through the full spate of educational structures training him for the ministry and to have very limited, warped, flat-sided experiences with both. It is extraordinary if the student is able to encounter even adequate analogues to the kinds of experiences, expectations, and requirements which will be laid upon him once he begins professional activity.

Therefore, from my point of view, *if field education is to be meaningful at all, it should provide with precision and clarity those fundamental experiences which are necessary for the student to grasp the import of the Christian faith and the fundamental operations of the ministry as a profession.* When I say fundamental experiences, I mean primary, face-to-face encounters with feelings, persons, and institutions. Until this base is laid, no real teaching can take place.

The second lesson to be learned from our small model is that traditional forms of teaching—lectures, seminars, etc.—miss their potential power unless they are expositions of the primary or direct experience of the student. Now of course most graduate-school teachers think of themselves as being in the role of expositing subject matter rather than students' experience. Perhaps this is an adequate and graphic description of the failure of many faculty to be teachers. Specifically, this suggests to me that there should be a live, direct, and ongoing corellation between what the student experiences in the field (that is, beyond the classroom in direct face-to-face encounters) and the content and nature of intellectualization or rationalization in formal structures. If the Bible is meaningful for contemporary man, it should be possible to find some situation where the student can experience its meaningfulness to modern man. From this point of view perhaps the easiest fields in which to teach today are ethics and pastoral care, where the student's own live involvement in situations can become the occasion for his classroom learning. Please notice that I said that *teaching* was easiest here, not knowing *what* to teach. That is, the procedure which our learning model would suggest does not relieve the scholar from the obligation of adequate and proper interpretation of materials. Nor does it mean that the materials to be introduced in the classroom are limited to the experience which the divinity school has supplied the student. The student brings to the classroom a vast amount of diffuse, undifferentiated experience forming a reservoir upon which the teacher can call. If he has had the basic experience necessary to undergird the subject area, the teacher can elaborate upon this, refine it, and make it understandable. If not, it should be supplied. Moreover, where a void exists, the teacher should have the freedom and resources to enable the student to engage in additional experiences in the area of concern. This is the essense of good teaching.

My contention here is the obvious. Field experience and the academic structures in theological education should not be held apart at all; rather, precise coordination and interpenetration should be the goal. But further, it is my contention that the wisdom of pastoral theology has much more to offer in the design of a theological curriculum. For example, few if any schools today make any real effort to view the student developmentally and to take seriously what this means to the possibilities of learning. Field experience is precisely the place where a kind of coordinated relationship between the student's maturity and his professional opportunity and degree of responsibility could take place. Paying attention to these conditions is necessary if the learning situation is to be maximized.

Again, few faculties have considered the cost to the church and the ministry involved in the process of personal and intellectual intimidation which inheres in traditional academic structures. How can a man learn to minister, to be the shepherd extending "tender solicitous care," to use Hiltner's phrase, without some direct experience of this from his mentors? The student's problem with authority is met head on by the faculty's problem with authority and then is directly translated into ministerial practice in the church.

None of the suggestions for maximizing the learning situation which I have put forward are complete, detailed, or fully experimentally validated. But they are possible, long overdue, and essential if theological education is to catch up with the needs of the church in the present world.

Pastoral Theology and Clinical Training

Lowell G. Colston

For almost half a century clinical pastoral education has had a growing, decisive, and formative influence upon pastoral theology. The movement grew out of a concern for a dynamic understanding of persons, social institutions created for the health and welfare of persons, and theology. The clinical setting was observed by the early charismatic leaders of the movement, such as Anton Boisen, Richard Cabot, and William Bryan, to provide the structured context within which these personal, social, and institutional dynamics could be related to theological study. Furthermore, the understanding and comprehension of these dynamics promised greatly to enhance not only the pastor's self-understanding but also his effectiveness in his ministry to persons and groups.

Anton Boisen, for example, described clinical pastoral education as demanding careful study of "living human documents." He insisted above all that theology "should be living," thus "related to the most dramatic, existential, and critical experiences of living; and that it could never, at its peril, neglect the method of studying what was really going on." [1] He emphasized the need for disciplined study of immediate experiencing and for continuous effort to derive theological data from such experiencing. This has been the hallmark of clinical pastoral education.

How then was the minister to identify himself in the clinical setting? What model was to be adopted? Seward Hiltner has contended that the ancient model based upon the shepherding metaphor continues to offer the best interpretation of the pastor's true function. In his classic demarcation of the parameters of pastoral theology, *Preface to Pastoral Theology*, Hiltner states: "Every minister must serve as shepherd; and therefore, among other things, he must be a pastoral theologian." The latter phrase summarizes the implicitly understood, if not always explicitly articulated, primary goal of the clinical pastoral educator. He strives to help the minister or the ministerial student, as the case may be, in his ongoing process of *becoming a pastoral theologian*. His fundamental task is to assist the minister in developing his critical functions as he struggles to bring his pastoral image, his shepherding activities, and his theological understanding together.

Clinical pastoral education, therefore, is an important enterprise in which the minister is presumably engaged in "doing theology" under the critical gaze of those who are mutually involved with him in the learning process. "Doing theology" occurs as the minister confronts each existential situation imaginatively and creatively, giving himself fully to what is being addressed to him in and through the situation and, as he grasps what is being communicated, responding, seeking clarification of his understanding, and testing the validity of his analysis.

Thus every new existential situation presents a fresh demand upon him and a further opportunity for sharpening his theological discernment. He risks what he has inferred from previous engagement and what he holds as true in each subsequent encounter. His openness to this process, however, distinguishes him as pastoral theologian. He more adequately serves people as he freely consents to the rigorous discipline inherent to the enterprise of "doing theology" in this manner. Anything less than this leaves the total theological task unfulfilled.

Clinical pastoral education proceeds from this basic premise of doing theology in the concrete existential situation and includes the concern for developing pastoral competence in meeting such situations. Thus the fundamental goal is to vitalize the polarity between pastor and theologian in the minister and to assist him in actualizing this dialectic in his pastoral operations.

I. The Pastorhood of Believers

The call to become pastoral theologian extends to the layman as well as the minister. To put this in the framework of our discussion, I would presume to rephrase Hiltner's statement to read, "*every layman*, along with the minister, must serve as shepherd; . . . he must be a pastoral theologian." In fact, it may be argued historically from a biblical theological point of view that the minister's essential vocation is to equip the layman for that task. That the layman is responsive to the call is demonstrated in the growing number of well-attended lay schools of theology across the country.

Clinical pastoral educators are involved in the layman's becoming pastoral theologian, both directly and indirectly. Some offer programs which are particularly designed for laymen; thus they have opportunities to become engaged directly with persons in crisis situations. The layman is, of course, affected indirectly by the clinical pastoral education of his pastor in that the training process is usually and understandably extended into his relationship with the people he serves. The pastor becomes a provocator and an enabler of laymen, urging and supporting the layman's emerging theological consciousness.

II. Person and Pastor

The clinical pastoral educator understands one important part of his task to be that of calling out and reinforcing the student's personal and pastoral *authority* and provoking him to become aware of the crucial relationship between his personal existence and his professional functioning. As the student confronts the authority of the clinical supervision and that of his peer group, he begins to appropriate his own.

The personal dimension of the minister's emerging authority has to do with developing modes of prehending reality. His reliance upon one mode, whether it be intuitive, cognitive, affective, or sensitive, obviously tends to make him one-sided and closed to important aspects of his existence. In his struggle toward wholeness he is prompted to give attention to undeveloped modes of prehension. In this sense he becomes aware of his personal dynamics, and his ego capacity is strengthened. He is less controlled by a previous mode of functioning and more free to interact with his environment.

Ideally, clinical training provides the context for and employs methods designed to stimulate cognitive, affective, and conative processes within the minister. The clinical pastoral educators, which designation, I am inferring throughout, includes fellow students of the trainee, confront the student as person, especially to impel him toward a rapprochement between his conceptualizations and his feelings. The student thus becomes more discerning of events in which he participates, less crippled by anxieties and defensiveness, and consequently more able to give himself to decisive action.

These assumptions are predicated upon the conviction that the "being" of the pastor—that is, his being and becoming as a person—is of central significance. What he says and what he does flow from what he essentially is. This is not to suggest a chronology because of course his being is continually informed by dialogue and action. Critical encounter between person and function is at the heart of the becoming process.

Specifically the student's professional functioning is affected by the clinical pastoral educator in ways which Seward Hiltner has outlined as follows: "From supervised analysis of his own work with persons at particular times, the student learns several things: the potential strengths and wesknesses of the other; the degree to which his own intention and his performance are in harmony; and whether his attempt at ministry is consistent with the message and the church he represents." [2] Thus the student is confronted with the need to understand his own and the other's personal dynamics, to be responsible in his pastoral functions, and to be consistent in his representation of the kerygma in particular existential situations.

In all his experiencing in clinical training, the student is establishing his authority, which arises out of his fulfillment of personal and professional responsibility. Such responsibility is integral to what is being called "spiritual formation." The spirit of a man is decisive in his ministry. Robert S. Paul has expressed the gist of the matter: "Undoubtedly professional competence, historical continuity, and doctrinal orthodoxy are important, and in some measure necessary to a minister in fulfillment of his vocation, but his authority as a minister can come only from the stamp of Christ's character. A minister's authority must be judged by its fruits, and the fruits are the fruits of the spirit." [3]

The fruits of the spirit are the responsible and creative expressions of authority in his parishioners, called out by the inspired and informed spirit-filled leadership of the pastor. This I have long been calling an *incarnational* theology—the word becoming flesh and dwelling among men. The guiding image of Christ is precisely shown in these terms, as Robert Paul has shown; thus to bear the stamp of Christ is to embody his spirit in the world by emptying oneself and taking on the form of a servant.

III. Distinctive Characteristics of Clinical Pastoral Education

In clinical pastoral education the term clinical once referred largely to an institutional setting which provided the structure for the educational process. The word has undergone a considerable shift in meaning within the understanding of clinical pastoral educators themselves. For example, Thomas Klink notes that the shift has moved toward a methodological rather than a purely situational interpretation. He observes that case method constitutes the central methodology of clinical pastoral education. However, it is not just case study; it is *case work,* for there is "a specific relation of responsibility and involvement in which the person studied and the person studying are bound together in a process within a social system." [4]

Case work, therefore, is not interpreted primarily as doing something for a person; rather it is being involved with him in his struggle to cope with his situation. The "humanization" of the pastor is required, especially the act of becoming aware of his common humanity—his relatedness to those who come under his shepherding care—and acknowledging it in all his relationships.

A dictionary definition of "clinic" tends to support an expanded view and to permit the degree of flexibility in usage which I am suggesting. *Webster's Third New International Dictionary* defines it as "a class, session, or group meeting devoted to the presentation, analysis and treatment or solution of actual cases and concrete problems in some special field or discipline." Rollin Fairbanks has shown the breadth of interpretation given to the term clinic within clinical pastoral education. He asserts that the performance of pastoral work under competent supervision, case work, and work being recorded and submitted for evaluation and criticism comprise what is normally regarded as the effort of clinical pastoral education.[5]

From these definitions the essential elements of clinical pastoral education become apparent. They are: context, content, method, and supervision. Context, or setting, is one in which lines of responsibility and communication are sufficiently defined to enable the student to comprehend organizational structures. The context must be conducive to the application of clinical methods in the study of concrete situations. The student thus is thrust into actual arenas of life while he is challenged to gain a perspective upon them.

The clinical setting, thus broadly interpreted, provides for an extension of education into the community, which in that sense becomes the clinic, or the context in which special problems are studied by concrete examples. The trainee is given the opportunity to perform a bona fide service to the persons with whom he works while sharpening his comprehension of their situation and learning to act in ways relevant to their needs. He is trained to be what he should be: a leader of the people who helps them to attain dignity and fulfill their responsibility as children of God.

Thus "clinic" is coming to be regarded as *any* setting in which special problems may be studied by concrete examples. This includes settings which have been traditional to clinical pastoral education—such as hospitals, correctional institutions, parishes

—and new forms of organized efforts in behalf of persons. Although the new forms cannot be strictly termed clinical, they are equally concerned with the dynamics of persons and groups and the structures which affect them.

Another distinctive characteristic of clinical pastoral education is method, which I have already noted may be described best as case work. Surely no one can deny the validity of the effort of the student to reach competence by wrestling out the dynamic factors in operation in any person and his existential situation. His discernment in seeing what is required in helping the person to help himself and his capacity to act wisely, justly, and decisively are brought to the test in his work with particular cases.

The method of training is perhaps best indicated in the terms developmental, existential, and phenomenological. It is developmental in that the focus is on process-learning rather than upon the impartation of content. Existentially the student is involved in present experiencing, in which not only his self-consciousness is expanded and enhanced, but also his pastoral skills are developed. The method is phenomenological in the sense that the respective uniqueness of the person being served, the context, and the pastor performing the service are studied each in its particularity. Any effort to reduce any of these to one or several descriptive categories does a grave injustice to that uniqueness.

Supervision is also a key concept in clinical pastoral education. The practice of clustering several students around a supervisor who gives immediate and direct attention to their case work and helps them to fuse personal and professional identity has been at the heart of clinical training.

i) Supervision is a unique and identifiable educational procedure;
ii) it requires as supervisor one who is both engaged in the practice of his profession and duly qualified to supervise;
iii) it assumes as student a candidate seeking fuller qualification in the practice of his (intended) profession;
iv) it requires for its setting an institution within whose activities there are functional roles in which student and supervisor can negotiate a "contract for learning";

v) the roles of both supervisor and student must be appropriate to their particular professional identity (in this case the Christian ministry);

vi) lastly supervision requires for its environment a wider community of professional peers associated in a common task.[6]

Supervision, thus, is an activity of considerable responsibility because even the supervision itself is under the scrutiny of professional peers.

If the student is to be prompted to develop as a pastor-theologian, the supervisor must maintain the polarity within himself. Although he is sharply aware of the language, issues, and concerns of other professionals within the context in which he serves, if he is to be a qualified supervisor of a pastor-theologian, he will affirm that identity and engage actively in the dialogue it represents.

IV. Critiques of Clinical Training

Criticisms of clinical pastoral education have centered on assumptions regarding supervision. Those who mistakenly view the institutional chaplain as a kind of spiritual caretaker do not appreciate how socially active are most of the chaplain supervisors in the various institutions. If such critics are not in contemporary dialogue with such supervisors, they are reacting to clinical training on the basis of false premises. To say this is not to be defensive but to portray what is demonstrably true. However, openness to appropriate and responsible criticism is in order.

One charge is: clinical training accentuates the *professional* functioning of the clergyman at the same time the man in the street is reacting against professionalism. The clerical image is already a barrier to be overcome, such critics say, yet clinical training fosters that image or at least does nothing specific to enable the student to move through it. These critics recognize that the student tends to pattern himself after his clinical supervisor, whose professional character he may strive to emulate. Supervision should be reinterpreted, these critics insist, to be a confrontation of person with person in a training group without regard to the professional functioning of either. A professional, then, becomes one who is precisely competent to help all people become responsible participants in society. He is an enabler because he has the specific knowledge of power structures required to be effective in his relationship to those structures.

The recommended pattern of supervision arising from the concern to overcome the irrelevancies of professionalism is suggested in three parts: students are encouraged to participate in encounters as sensitively reflective observers; then they move toward mutual analysis and reflection through peer relationships; finally, they are engaged in a specialized task under supervision. The assumption is that the student begins clinical training at the point to which the above described pattern of supervision finally leads. Critics of clinical training who support this view actually feel that the clinical educators are premature in introducing the student to the supervised professional experience. Humanizing experiences prior to that level are prerequisites and are preparing the student to fit his person to his professional role.

This recommended pattern of supervision emphasizes the student's need to discover his and others' essential humanity. The clinical setting, it is argued, is so structured that the ministerial student may take refuge in the professional role and thus avoid the raw, human-to-human encounter which strongly tests his courage and ingenuity. While this criticism is reasonably convincing, it argues less for the superiority of one mode of supervision over another and more for various coordinated patterns of supervision.

Another critique of supervision as currently practiced in clinical pastoral education has been written by Henry Babcock Adams in an article entitled "Consultation: An Alternative to Supervision." Adams argues that the medical model of supervision has "limited use for wide scale education of pastors." He makes his assertion on three grounds: (1) limitations of time and money in the face of costly and lengthy programs in a central place of training exclude many pastors; (2) "stereotyped circumstances imposed by nearness to a center for supervision" make the transfer of learning difficult; (3) the training is in institutions where therapy is the primary focus, but this may not be the only form of ministry in which the minister engages.[7]

Adams suggests consultation as an alternative to supervision and recommends that a consultative team of specialists, peers, and both involved and detached laymen be formed to offer critical and supportive relationships to the minister.

Adam's critique is appropriate to my basic thesis that our goal in the training of ministers is to reinforce the dialogue between *pastor* and *theologian* which goes on within them. However, several of his assumptions regarding clinical pastoral education are subject to serious question. First, he states that the medical model of supervision has been adopted almost exclusively, requiring concentration of students around a supervisor in a central place. This is indeed its strength. Responsible educational centers tend to move in that direction. Better control of standards and more efficient and economic operations ensue. Furthermore, in the clinical situation the minister in training is less able to set up consultations which are less of a threat to him and which thereby enable him to avoid confrontation by his peers, from whence comes some of his most valued learning.

Second, although the medical model may be influential, the pastoral model is emphasized, and the minister's pastoral work in a particular community, the hospital "parish," is observed. In many respects the hospital parish bears strong resemblance to the minister's own parish; in addition it offers the minister controlled conditions where he can test his total functioning in a relatively brief period of time.

Perhaps the clinching argument for clinical supervision has always been readily acknowledged by students who have responded positively to it; that is, the student is enabled to retreat sufficiently from the immediate arena of his involvement to get a perspective upon himself and his functioning. The personal enhancement and enrichment gained from viewing his pastoral operations in a community other than the one he regularly serves have been affirmed and demonstrated by the student. The setting for supervised education is important, as I have shown, but not as critical as the process itself. The student is presumably developing his capacity for transferring his learning from one situation to another. Consultation does not really eliminate that need.

Many other important responses could be made to the type of criticism represented by Adam's views. Suffice it to say, I cannot accept the implication of his title: "Consultation: An *Alternative* to Supervision." Both seem valid to me. I would accept, "Consultation: A *Supplement* to Supervision" more readily. However, I am willing to rest the controversy on whatever well-documented research studies may reveal as to the validity of either.

V. New Directions in Clinical Pastoral Education

A developing concern of clinical pastoral educators is how to view newly emerging patterns of supervision. What are viable patterns of supervision of training in a parish setting? How is a student prompted to evaluate his experiences in training in the inner city? How do clinical pastoral training centers fit into the proposed clusters of institutions for theological education?

Joint planning for the creation of new patterns of supervision by clinical pastoral educators and by leaders in urban training programs is imperative to the continued relevance of both to the education of ministers. If the former are to break through the barriers of professionalism which tend to separate them sharply from segments of society and if the latter are to develop qualified professionals to equip indigenous leadership, they will do well to work together to effect revised modes of supervision.

What I have said regarding relationships with urban centers applies as critically to the parish. Patterns of supervision in which the minister learns to become a leader of his laymen, calling them into renewed vitality in their shared responsibility for a ministry of reconciliation to alienated persons and groups in our society, are required. The minister's task as mobilizer and enabler is thus reinforced and supported.

Clinical pastoral education, which actually began as a seminary-generated movement, became independent of seminaries and is now closely relating to seminaries throughout the country. It is potentially a creative force in the developing clusters of institutions for theological education. The aim of coordinated learning experiences is to enable the student to gain "first rate theology firsthand,"[8] to answer the charge given by Charles R. Feilding in his report on contemporary education for the ministry. This requires programs of clinical pastoral education which are integrated with other theological studies.

Conclusion

Clinical pastoral education is a mode of pastoral theology. The fundamental aim of the clinical pastoral educator is to call out the authority of the student as pastor-theologian, which in Seward Hiltner's terms represents the appropriate dialectic for the minister. The clinical pastoral educator's setting, method, and supervision provide the unique resources to mobilize and enable the student's authority to emerge. He is confronted as person and as pastor and is challenged effectively to relate his being and his function. Processes are set in motion which help him, in turn, to educe the authority of his laymen and thus to mobilize and enable them to fulfill their ministry.

Whatever can be developed in new patterns of supervision in combined efforts among clinical pastoral educators and leaders of other training centers for ministers, and which will contribute provocatively and supportively to the integration of the pastor-theologian, is greatly needed. A first-rate theology from firsthand experience is the first line of defense against spiritual disintegration in a tension-fraught world.

Notes

1. Seward Hiltner, "The Debt of Clinical Pastoral Education to Anton T. Boisen," *Concerns: Clinical and Theological Education* (a report on the proceedings of the Joint Fall Conference of Chaplain Supervisors, Miami, 1965), p. 6.
2. From an unpublished paper of Seward Hiltner presented as an address to the

Ecumenical Institute, Chateau de Bossey, Switzerland, February, 1967, p. 20.
3. Robert S. Paul, *Ministry* (Grand Rapids: Eerdmans, 1965), p. 190.
4. Thomas W. Klink, *Depth Perspectives in Pastoral Work* (Englewood Cliffs, N.J.: Prentice-Hall, 1965), pp. 65-67.
5. See the article by Rollin Fairbanks, "On Clinical Training," *The Christian Century*, April 24, 1963, pp. 556-59.
6. Thomas W. Klink, "Supervision," in Charles R. Feilding *et al.*, *Education for Ministry* (Dayton, Ohio: American Association of Theological Schools, 1966), p. 177.
7. Henry Babcock Adams, "Consultation: An Alternative to Supervision," *Developments* (a bulletin of the Department of Ministry, National Council of Churches), June, 1968.
8. Feilding, *Education for Ministry*, pp. 33-34.

A Theological Interpretation of Pastoral Supervision

John H. Patton

The primary focus of pastoral supervision is the becoming minister's quest for unity between action and being—between his action as a minister and his emerging professional self. Paul Tillich's theology can give us a valuable clue in thinking theologically about this quest and in understanding why we who are pastoral supervisors so often shift the focus of our supervision from the dialogue between action and being to the teaching of a particular action. In this essay I shall first discuss some of my understanding of the process of pastoral supervision. Then I shall move to a presentation of one of the themes in Paul Tillich's Christology which, I believe, can be helpful in interpreting supervision theologically. Finally, I shall interpret a brief clinical incident in pastoral supervision within the framework I have proposed and suggest some implications of this interpretation.

My concern with pastoral supervision grows out of the process of becoming a pastor as I have experienced it during the past decade and a half. This process has become exciting for me at exactly those points at which my action as a minister or the action of my students has been brought into dialogue with an emerging personal and professional identity. Although the greater portion of my experience as a pastor and a supervisor has occurred within the context of a health institution and in supervising theological students in a ministry of pastoral care, a small but significant portion has occurred in a parish and in supervising laity in other tasks of ministry. My intention is to say something about pastoral supervision which has relevance for a variety of *contexts for* and *types of* ministry.

For a number of years a growing literature on pastoral care, group work, and psychotherapy has been developing out of the experience of chaplain supervisors and related professionals involved in clinical pastoral education. Surprisingly, there has been only a limited amount written and published about what seems to me to be the major contribution of clinical pastoral education, namely the theory and practice of pastoral supervision. One of the most valuable articles is that of Thomas Klink, who defines supervision as follows:

> i) Supervision is a unique and identifiable educational procedure;
> ii) it requires as supervisor one who is both engaged in the practice of his profession and duly qualified to supervise;
> iii) it assumes as student a candidate seeking fuller qualification in the practice of his (intended) profession;
> iv) it requires for its setting an institution within whose activities there are functional roles in which student and supervisor can negotiate a "contract for learning";
> v) the roles of both supervisor and student must be appropriate to their particular professional identity (in this case the Christian ministry);
> vi) lastly supervision requires for its environment a wider community of professional peers associated in a common task.[1]

I have no disagreement with Klink's definition of supervision. In fact, I have been very much influenced by it. My differences come simply as a result of the purposes for which and the context within which I write. Klink's purpose, as I understand it, is to define a recognizable educational procedure within the context of theological education in order that the procedure may find its legitimate place in the process of educating persons as clergymen. My purpose is to view pastoral supervision as a part of the task of every minister whatever his context for ministry and for whatever category of ministers he has pastoral responsibility. It is an educational procedure, as Klink insists, but it *may* take place in relationship with persons, laity or clergy, whose conscious focus is more upon the task of ministry than upon the process of becoming ministers. In such cases the "contract for learning" is more implicit than explicit, but it does exist and should gradually emerge and become more focused during the process of supervision. If it does not emerge and the persons being supervised manage to avoid looking at their own identity as ministers, then the task of ministry suffers as well as the person, who fails to grow in his capacity to minister.

I use the term pastoral to describe this dimension of ministry because it conveys the idea of the supervisor's responsibility for the growth of the ministers, theological students, or laity who are within his care. The actual tasks of ministry in which both supervisee and supervisor are involved may or may not be specifically pastoral. "Pastoral," as applied to supervision, refers not to the type of ministry being supervised but to the fact that a pastoral supervisor oversees the ministry of whole persons, not simply their actions. In order to go further in describing this broader context in which, I believe, pastoral supervision should occur, I shall attempt to give my own brief description of the necessary and sufficient conditions under which adequate pastoral supervision may occur.

First, there must be one or more persons in quest of a more adequate professional identity. I am using the term profession in the broad sense of vocation or calling, inclusive of but not limited to the learned professions, such as law, medicine, or divinity. In this sense the Christian layman who has even in a limited sense committed himself to Christian ministry may be said to have an emerging professional identity as a minister. Another way I have thought of this condition for supervision is to say that the persons being supervised must at least in some degree be experiencing the conflicts of *professional adolescence*. Professional adolescence, like its physical and social counterparts, involves being and at the same time not being that toward which one is moving. The adolescent experiences the conflict between being a man and being a boy because he is both at the same time. The "becoming minister," whether layman or clergyman, experiences his identity as a minister in the same way. He is and is not a minister, and he feels the conflict between these two modes of being. It is this conflict which provides the point of contact between student and supervisor. The supervisee needs the supervisor in order to move through conflict toward the kind of sturdy professional identity which the supervisor conveys in his pastoral relationship.

I have come to feel that the movement through professional adolescence toward a recognizable and usable identity as a minister is the one thing we can expect from the pastoral internship for clergymen in clinical pastoral education. One of my present tasks is evaluating the readiness of students who have completed this required internship for our graduate program in supervised pastoral counseling. Because my responsibility is both to the prospective student and to the person who may be assigned to him for counseling, the first thing I must determine in the evaluation is whether or not the man being evaluated is recognizable as a minister to himself and to the potential counselee. If he is, and if his professional identity, though incomplete, is sturdy enough to stand up through the kind of anxiety that any good counseling must produce, I have little reason to worry about the acquisition of counseling techniques. The student will learn all the techniques he can effectively use. If the identity is not there, the techniques will be of little value to him or to the counselee.

Second, pastoral supervision requires that those seeking a more adequate professional identity be immersed in the human situation so completely that they cannot fail to experience it as a predicament rather than a problem. Theoretically the student in a hospital or the layman in a parish may have little difficulty in viewing life in this way. In actuality, however, part of his own predicament is that he tends to distort his view of life so that it is broken down into problems he feels he can or cannot solve. He fools himself into thinking that all he has to do is find the right combination of words and actions or secure the services of another person who does have the right combination. If he is in a setting where ministry can be identified with problem-solving, then adequate pastoral supervision is difficult if not impossible.

In contrast to this, immersion in the human situation, as I have experienced it, means to experience responsibilities for ministry which are more than one can possibly succeed in carrying out. A good training situation is one in which the student must stop fooling himself. Human need and one's inadequacy to meet it are so evident that they cannot but be noticed. Nevertheless, in spite of the insoluble predicament, persons in the clinical situation need the student enough to respond to his inadequate ministry and apparently benefit from it. He is immersed in failure and success that he cannot completely control. His techniques are proved inadequate, but to his surprise he discovers he is offering something to persons in spite of the failure of his techniques. The ambiguity of this situation provides the anxiety needed for the becoming minister to enter into a contract for learning ministry with his supervisor. Ministry to the human situation is a burden too great to bear alone; therefore the becoming minister must use his relationship to the supervisor in order to cope with his aloneness. A good training situation, then, is one in which this quickly becomes evident to the student. He cannot simply copy what the supervisor knows. He needs him as a pastor. Thus *pastoral* supervision becomes possible.

Third, adequate pastoral supervision requires a situation in which recognition is given to the fact that the supervisee needs to receive from persons as well as give to them. Built into the structure of the supervisory situation must be an opportunity to share with and be supported by peers in the ministry as well as a dependable continuing relationship to the supervising minister. Whatever type of ministry the becoming minister performs, it is important that there be some balance and flexibility among three basic types of interpersonal relationships: (1) relationships in which he is the minister, where he is the authority figure and where he is giving more than receiving; (2) relationships in which he shares a common situation with others, where he is a peer and where there is a relative balance between giving and receiving;

and (3) relationships in which another has responsibility for him, where he receives more than he gives and where he learns to deal with the authority of another person. I am suggesting here that one develops a professional identity in a way that parallels the development of a personal identity, namely through satisfactory experience in being a son, a brother, and a father. The satisfactions of all these relationships are needed throughout life, the amount of each type being dependent upon the person's stage of emotional development. I am convinced that growth in the ability to minister is dependent upon a similar balance of supporting and giving relationships within the situation in which ministry takes place.

Having stated some of my understanding of pastoral supervision and what seem to me to be the three necessary conditions under which adequate pastoral supervision can take place, I move now to a theological interpretation of the supervision I have described. This is not to suggest that what has been said before has not been theological. To say that pastoral supervision can best occur in a context in which the human situation cannot but be seen as a predicament and not a problem is obviously a theological statement which needs a much more adequate presentation than has been attempted here. To state that ministry requires certain types of supportive relationships in which the minister receives as well as gives is also a theological statement deserving a more adequate argument. I have chosen in this essay, however, to give attention to the first condition for pastoral supervision, the person in quest of a more adequate professional identity. Without this condition there is no need to be concerned with the others. Unfortunately, the clinical training movement, of which I am a part, has too often focused upon situation and relationship analysis without dealing with the primary focus of supervision, the becoming minister's search for professional identity or more specifically his quest for unity between his action and being as a minister. It is at this point that one of the themes from Paul Tillich's Christology can assist us in thinking theologically about pastoral supervision.

Tillich holds that every human being is asked to "take the form of the Christ" but that this can never mean copying concrete traits from the biblical picture. The characteristics of Jesus, he says, point beyond their contingent character to New Being. If they are imitated, they lose their power to point beyond themselves and become ritualistic prescriptions or laws. Nevertheless we are asked to participate in the New Being and to be transformed by it within the specific contingencies of our lives.[2]

Tillich rejects "the separation of the words of Jesus from his being, the pietistic separation of his deeds from his being, and the orthodox separation of the suffering of Jesus from his being."[3] These are, for Tillich, expressions of the New Being which cannot be viewed apart from their revelation of Jesus as the Christ. The biblical records do not psychologize or fragment. "They show only the presence of the New Being in him under the conditions of existence."[4] Jesus' actions are in all cases the encounter of the New Being with the forces of estrangement, not some specific psychological behavior.

In this aspect of his Christology, then, Tillich is insisting that Jesus as the Christ must be viewed holistically. He "is the bearer of the New Being in the totality of his being, not in any special expressions of it."[5] His actions express his wholeness. He is normative as man in that although he is fully personal and able to participate without limits in the world he maintains unity with God under the conditions of existence. That Jesus was able to resist the temptation to claim ultimacy for any aspect of his finite nature is one of two outstanding characteristics of the Christ which Tillich finds in the New Testament.

Tillich's picture of Jesus as the Christ is one in which there is an essential unity between his action and his being. No one action can be analyzed in its details as fully revelatory of his being, but every action of the Christ is an encounter of New Being with specific dimensions of estrangement. He is fully personal and participates completely in human existence but at the same time maintains unity within himself and with the divine ground of being. Moreover, because he maintains a unity between his action and his being, his actions are a full expression of his wholeness in the midst of the conditions of human existence. The Christ is one who correctly perceives the world as it is and acts appropriately in relation to it.

In contrast to this normative picture, all men other than the Christ experience estrangement from each other and within themselves. Their actions do not appropriately express their being. Insofar as they are representatives of the Christ, however, they participate in the New Being, the norm for ministry, receiving and mediating this new reality to the world.[6] Their ministry is, consciously or unconsciously, a taking of the form of Christ. This, however, as Tillich has implied, can never be a copying of concrete traits as revealed in the New Testament or their inferred behavioral characteristics. These traits and their accompanying actions, assuming they can be isolated, are not significant in themselves. They simply point to the New Being in Jesus and his transparency to the divine. If imitated, they lose all transparency and become barren legalisms.

What, then, can be the meaning of taking the form of the Christ? In the light of the theme from Tillich's Christology presented above, taking the form of the Christ can best be understood as *a quest for the kind of unity which the Christ exemplifies*. Although Tillich's theology rules out an "imitation of Christ" understood as the copying of particular actions, the form of Christ is, in actuality, his unity. Whereas the Christ was able to resist the temptation to claim ultimacy for any aspect of his finite nature, such as his ideas, his words, his action, other persons, in contrast, are estranged from the divine and consequently seek to make their actions, or other aspects of their being, ultimate. Whereas in persons other than the Christ perceptions of reality are distorted and actions are inappropriately related to the persons performing the actions, in the Christ there is unity between action and being, between theory and practice.

The form of the Christ which the Christian minister takes, whatever the specific expressions of that form in particular concrete situations, is a never completed quest for unity. Except for the Christ, "under the conditions of existence"—the human situation in which we attempt to minister—this unity can only be fragmentarily and temporarily achieved. Nevertheless, this quest for unity is an integral part of ministry which is representative of the Christ. Christian ministry, then, must involve both as appropriate as possible response to a specific exemplification of the human predicament *and* the minister's quest for unity between his response and his identity as minister. The term quest implies a continuing search for a difficult if not impossible goal and an attitude toward one's action which gives purpose and satisfaction to events in life which might otherwise seem unrelated and relatively meaningless. Although there are certainly unconscious elements involved, a quest is a conscious venture of the person involved. It is therefore an available focus for pastoral supervision.

With the theme "quest for unity" in mind as the theological focus for pastoral supervision, I shall interpret a brief clinical incident drawn from a recording of a clinical training seminar. I have chosen this particular incident for two reasons. First, it comes from group supervision, and this is the type of pastoral supervision most applicable to situations other than traditional clinical pastoral education. Second, it demonstrates some of the issues we have been discussing without extensive explanation of the situation. The particular theological students involved were participating in their first full-time quarter of clinical pastoral education in a general hospital setting. One of the students, Bob, began the group session by reading a selection from John Calvin as the devotional for the morning. His reading was illustrative of the kind of theological theory all the students had brought with them to training. After a few moments another student responded to Bob with a question which had been stirred up by the early weeks of his experience in ministry and the supervision of that ministry.

Doug: What does the reading you just read from Calvin mean? Let me see [the book] can I? I mean—I've heard crap like that all my life, and I have never been able to figure what they are talking about. [There is a pause while Doug finds the place, and then he begins to read from the Calvin passage.] "Let this be the first step—abandon ourselves and devote the whole energy of our mind to the service of God." Abandoning yourself—what does that mean? I mean it seems to me in these weeks I'm learning to understand myself and to know myself, and a lot of things I am finding out aren't pretty, but I am learning how to express my feeling. I'm trying to get over my reluctance to show my anger, and these are the kind of things I hear Calvin saying are bad—are sinful.

The first response of the group to Doug's quest for unity between the ideas he had heard all his life and his new awareness of his feelings was an attempt to reinterpret the ideas involved in the passage from Calvin. Bob, the student who had read the passage, responded to Doug's feelings by ignoring them and the struggle they represented. He used his intellectual ability to interpret the material read in its larger context and to discuss a similar idea as it appears in Thomas à Kempis' *Imitation of Christ*. Then a member of the group who was more practically than historically oriented spoke up.

Bill: What was that book that made such a big hit along the same line?
Supervisor: *In His Steps?*
Bill: I was real impressed with that to begin with, but then I began to start thinking about acting as Christ would act in every situation that I found, and that's a hell of a way to live. (*pause*)
Joe: What's the difference, sandals?
Bill: I just don't think that we are called to imitate anybody. I'm trying to find out who I am, you know, this business. I want to be me, and me may not be like Jesus.
Doug: How would you preach a sermon on "Let this mind be in you which is in Christ Jesus," the *kenosis* passage?
Bill: I've never preached on that.

The supervisor at this point stayed out of this discussion except to provide information and waited to see whether Doug's quest would be ignored or picked up by some of the others. Bill did move in quickly to express his feelings of frustration and failure in attempting an imitative taking of the form of Christ. What Tillich calls a way of barren legalism in which acts once imitated lose their power to point beyond themselves Bill emotionally referred to as "a hell of a way to live." Joe, flippantly but with some of his own conflict showing, suggested that it would be simpler if the conflict could be resolved by putting on something external like sandals. Bill responded by characterizing the predicament of the Christian minister, "Me may not be like Jesus." Doug refocused the question by bringing a biblical statement of the same problem, and Bill gave up the struggle of dealing with the question, at least for awhile, by saying, "I've never preached on that." Without relationship to a supervisor and peers in the ministry to keep the question before him, Bill would probably move on to his next situation of ministry carrying only the anger or guilt about having been neither like Jesus nor like himself.

Fortunately, Joe has not let his quip about the sandals rest with its cleverness but continues to feel the conflict and begins to relate it to his actual experience of ministry in the hospital. Here for the first time in his life he has found situations for which he does not have appropriate words or actions.

Joe: A guy who really gets involved with people has got to risk getting hurt. You know a boxer who gets in the ring can't be too proud of his nose. I've always been proud of mine.

Supervisor: Maybe that's what *kenosis* means for you—giving up pride in your nose.

Joe: Getting it busted!

Supervisor: Maybe so.

Joe: One of the feelings I have here in the hospital is that I would be a whole lot better off if I were completely armor-plated or didn't have to wear any armor at all. This business of being somewhere in the middle—allowing for yourself and your own reactions. . . .

With the support of the supervisor and the group, Joe, in contrast to Bill, stays with the tension he is experiencing between his action and being. The broken nose is a symbol of the kind of total involvement of himself with others that because of his skill with words has not thus far been necessary in his experience in ministry. The tension or conflict in his being a minister is symbolized further by the fact that he is always "somewhere in the middle." The minister must wear the role and express himself through it even though he often wishes he were free of the tradition he represents. The becoming minister feels awkward in the inherited "armor" of his profession, and there is in him something of the young David who wishes to junk it all and choose his own five smooth stones. But to continue with our illustration:

Joe: Aren't there some ways around this dilemma?
Doug: Lead with your nose.
Joe: Right! (*talking excitedly to the supervisor*) And like you said two sessions ago, you have to go back to Mr. Walters' room for him to die. [Joe is referring to the fact that the supervisor had insisted that he return to visit a dying patient in spite of the fact that he felt very anxious and could think of nothing to say.] I tell you before then the possibility had never occurred to me—in other situations in my life to go back when I was going to fail.

Joe's peer in ministry, Doug, tells him that the way to deal with the tension he is experiencing is further involvement and risk, not an abstract search for answers. Go *be* with Mr. Walters when you have nothing to say in the face of his death, and some of the tension between action and being, between the person and the role, will be resolved.

The supervisor underscores this point with a symbol used earlier in the session and indicates that the kind of "emptying" or giving up pride in one's nose, or in Tillich's terms, claiming ultimacy for any aspect of one's finite nature, is a process, not an accomplishment.

Supervisor: It sounds like more *kenosis* to me.
Joe: It's taken awhile for this to get to be an option.
Supervisor: It may take awhile longer too.
Doug: This kind of emptying I like! It's genuine, it's real. Now maybe there's a level that you can get to after you've led with your nose

> for awhile—been pounded. This other type of self-denial, I just feel like I'm wrapped in cords—bound—and I'm experiencing from that—I mean I'm experiencing freedom coming from Joe. This is a type of emptying I like.

This illustration of the pastoral supervision of becoming ministers in their quest for unity comes out of a context in which the primary ministry is pastoral care. It has been my contention, however, that pastoral supervision is as appropriate and necessary for a ministry of worship, community organization, or teaching as it is for a ministry of pastoral care. Without such supervision with its focus on persons rather than simply on action or theory, ministry is reduced to problem-solving, or a particular type of action is viewed as ultimate or at least in itself is identified with ministry. A prayer by a patient's bedside or the organization of a community for a particular worthy purpose can too easily be called ministry long after it has become barren of any expression of New Being.

Man's condition, however, is such that he tends to see the human situation as a problem to be solved with an idea, word, or action. As a pastoral supervisor, I have continually been tempted to teach a particular type of psychological analysis or method of interpersonal relationship, rather than involving myself with the student in a continual quest for unity between action and being. It is all too easy to forget Tillich's reminder that the minister, the professional adolescent, or the pastoral supervisor, to the extent that he does express New Being does so in the totality of his being, not any special expression of it.

In summary, then, I have argued that the primary focus of pastoral supervision is the becoming minister's quest for unity between action and being—between his action as a minister and his emerging professional self. I have made use of a theme from Paul Tillich's theology to deepen my theological understanding of this quest as well as the means by which I attempt to supervise those becoming ministers who, with me, are experiencing it. Christian ministry, whatever its form, must involve both an appropriate response to the human situation *and* a quest for unity between the minister's action and being.

Hopefully, Doug is right. Perhaps there is a level of being a minister "that you can get to after you've led with your nose for awhile—been pounded." Certainly this is the purpose of pastoral supervision—helping the becoming minister experience the pounding which is necessarily involved in his immersion in the human situation as an opportunity for discovering the unity which is the form of the Christ.

Notes

1. Thomas W. Klink, "Supervision," in Charles R. Feilding *et al., Education for Ministry* (Dayton, Ohio: American Association of Theological Schools, 1966), p. 177.
2. Paul Tillich, *Systematic Theology,* II (Chicago: University of Chicago Press, 1957), 122-23.
3. *Ibid.*, p. 124.
4. *Ibid.*
5. *Ibid.*, p. 121.
6. *Ibid.*, III, 189-90.

III. Pastoral Theology and Pastoral Care

Christs to One Another: An Essay in Group Pastoral Care

Joseph Havens

Small groups have hit the church. A spate of articles and books has documented this event and given it impetus. This essay focuses primarily on the pastoral care dimension of small groups, but it takes its direction partly from the insistence of Seward Hiltner that pastoral work and theological affirmations ought to inform and enrich each other. This is best done, he suggests, by a reflective moving back and forth between the concrete experiences of pastoral care and the creative rethinking of Christian theology. Thus I shall examine the workings of small groups by viewing them through the lenses of three Christian affirmations which grew out of the experience of the early church. But equally I hope that the contemporary and evident vitality of small-group interaction may bring a new aliveness and contemporaneity to the ancient doctrines.

Specifically we shall be dealing with the pastoral care of groups under three headings: (1) "the priesthood of all believers," i.e., a realization of the ways in which, through small groups, persons may minister to one another; (2) "members of one body," i.e., the growing awareness through group experience of the many levels of human interconnectedness; (3) "the winds of the Spirit," i.e., the emergence of insights and new directions as the group begins to trust its own unfolding life.

By small groups I refer to units of six to fifteen people who meet together regularly over a period of time (usually a minimum of ten meetings) to share deeply with one another what is going on in their lives. Part of my experience with such groups has been in what are called "search groups" within the Society of Friends. In these the topics of interaction have covered a wide variety of pastoral problems: difficulties with teen-agers, "other-woman" problems in marriage, loss of job, funeral arrangements and facing one's own death, religious education of children, evaluation of social action projects, racial tensions, personal religious experience, and fears of psychiatric illness. In the sections which follow I suggest some of the sources of power, ways of functioning, and possible results of these and similar groups.

I. The Priesthood of All Believers

Here we shall be concerned with two related matters: (1) the way in which a *group* of persons within a religious community may assume some pastoral functions usually carried by individual pastors and (2) the discovery that the least likely person often has the greatest gift of facilitating communication, understanding, and forgiveness.

An example of the latter point is given by psychologist Carl Rogers in a recent paper on basic encounter groups—perhaps all the more convincing because it occurs in a "secular" setting.[1] A man in charge of maintenance in an industrial plant, looked down upon by the higher-level executives in the encounter group, eventually came forth as the most psychologically sensitive member of the group, as one who "was alert to things which had not yet been expressed but which were just below the surface." Rogers concludes, "This kind of ability shows up so commonly in groups that it has led me to feel that the ability to be healing or therapeutic is far more common in human life than we might suppose." In the Church of the Saviour in Washington, D. C.—where small groups constitute the heart of the church life—a former prostitute was found to be the Christian most able to mediate forgiveness to others!

To return to point (1), the assumption of pastoral functions by a group is illustrated in the following account of a session of a Quaker search group.

After a period of silent meditation Trudy opened with a remark based on pre-meeting chitchat. She commented on Florence's unnecessary worrying about the possibility that the graduation exercises of two of her children might fall on the same day. The group then undertook to probe into Florence's tendency to worry and to set things up in such a way that conflicts were likely to occur. This was particularly evident as she talked about her inner demand that a Christmas party she had planned would be a glorious success for *everyone* involved. Her tendency always to see the failure side of her enterprises was finally linked to her guilt over abandoning her Lutheran upbringing and her consequent need to feel chastized. These connections seemed to clarify things for her. They led us to the theme of self-forgiveness and to Natasha's telling us that she had finally forgiven her sister—for the first time in her life. This conflict was one the group had been "working on" with Natasha so we all felt involved in this victory. Joel then wondered if he had ever forgiven anyone where real giving-up was necessary. After Ted said that he felt he forgave every day in the sense of no longer being angry with someone, Joel mused that perhaps he himself was looking for some great spiritual event to happen to him. Liz shared this same "irrational hope," as she called it. Then she went on quietly to describe her almost constant feeling of "living over an abyss" ever since her mental breakdown several years ago. But this very precariousness heightened the intensity of life and made vivid and precious the delights of her life, especially evenings with her friends. Both the "thin crust" and the "joys of oneness" were important in her life. Joel thanked Liz for letting us into her inner life in this way. Ted then raised a precariousness-of-life problem for him as a physician, i.e., having to tell patients or their relatives that the patient will soon die. We discussed at some length the connection between helping others to face death and coming to terms with our own mortality. Liz found facing her own death much easier than the threat of meaninglessness in her day-to-day existence. Trudy tried to convey to us how unbearable would be the loss of her husband, how much she wanted to "go first." There was a resistance to any formulas or easy answers, theological or otherwise. But the sharing of our radically different inner feelings about death was illuminating and even reassuring.

This particular discussion occurred after the group had been meeting fortnightly for about a year. Gradually we had learned how to move our discussion from the absent "theys" or the hypothetical "wouldn't-it-be-nice-ifs" to the immediacy of our here-and-now interactions. And we found it bearable to refrain from retreating into silence or a change of subject if a painful topic or an aggressive confrontation erupted. At the beginning there were two or three of us who clearly wanted this kind of encounter and pushed for it, but eventually nearly all the group came to want it. Most of us at one time or another interfered with "surfacing" and brought us back to the deeper matters we really wanted to work on. Thus the loci of control, the guiding norms, were more and more lodged in the group as a whole and not in particular individuals.

This establishing of a group climate of openness and honesty is hard work. It usually entails moving through valleys of anxiousness and anger and sometimes despair. But out of it comes not only a fuller knowledge of one another but also a concern for the other which goes far deeper than the "oughts" of our conventional lives.

This last statement raises implicitly a weighty issue which can only be touched upon here: To what extent do preexisting pictures of human nature and norms of behavior determine the emergence of genuine caring within a group? In some groups where there is an optimistic image of man and the norms are those of kindness and concern (many Protestant Church groups?) a pseudo or "ought" kind of caring is expressed in the group life. Sometimes it is extremely difficult to break through this prescribed behavior into more honest reactions. On the other hand, I have seen psychoanalytic therapy groups dominated by a pessimistic view of personality and by the expectation that everyone, driven by his sexual and aggressive urges, always is out for himself. Here tenderness and concern are suspect because they are assumed to be defensive against deeper impulses. My hypothesis is that preexisting norms set outside limits within which group experience can occur. Thus joy, self-giving love, and mystical experiences are unlikely to be reported in many therapy groups even if they are experienced, while murderous impulses and sexual desires and perversions are never recognized, much less voiced, in some church groups because members are incapable of knowing them in themselves. But even though these unconscious assumptions remain and limit what happens in particular groups, the range of potential human experience still is very wide indeed. An important function of groups is, as Léon Bloy says of suffering, "to bring into being corners of the heart which do not yet exist."

The pastorhood of all members of a religious community has implications for the leadership of small groups. As has been suggested, the crucial function of leadership is the establishment of the group norms we have described. A group leader especially trained to embody these norms in his own behavior and to teach them to the group can make a great difference in the group life. But if, as in our Quaker group, the values of searching honesty and the importance of feelings preexist in some group members, they can gradually be picked up by the whole group. Leadership is thus more a *function* in a group than a particular *person*. Of course it will always take the initiative of one or two persons to start a group and to carry it successfully through the first difficult meetings. There is available an extensive literature on the organization and leadership of small groups similar to the ones described here.[2]

II. Members of One Body

Seldom do we realize how revolutionary is Paul's vision: "If the whole body were an eye, where would be the hearing? If the whole body were an ear, where would be the sense of smell? . . . If one member suffers, all suffer together; if one member is honored, all rejoice together." (I Cor. 12:17, 26.) Yet it is precisely this radical interconnectedness which is discovered in groups which allow depths of feeling to emerge. Let me give an example drawn from the fourth session of a gathering concerned with the religious possibilities of group life.

Incidental to a veiled attack on my leadership, one member of the group remarked that he had lost his wife only a few weeks ago. No one picked this up; we talked about other things he had mentioned. But after fifteen minutes a member who had so far said little pointed out our failure to respond to this important statement. The bereaved man did not take up this cue to express his feelings (later it became evident how touchy the whole matter was for him), but two others did. One talked of the child she had lost and another of a friend who she felt had fully understood and accepted her. We were all moved by her honest sharing of this past grief. Then I noticed one person who had been silent crying quietly to herself. She confessed later that she had been weeping for her dog, who had died recently after thirteen years as a beloved and fiercely loyal family companion. The discussion and her crying helped her to realize how deeply she mourned Jip. She felt she was mourning also for the previous speaker who had lost her dear friend "who loved and understood you—just as I felt only my dog fully accepted me just as I was." But beneath all this there was, as I would formulate it, a kind of inner crying in us all for the grieving which the first speaker could not allow himself. In some way which we never expressed, we were carrying for him the grief which was so full of guilt and anger and anguish he could not bear to experience it directly.

Note the levels of interconnectedness here. First of all we were dependent on the bereaved man's testing our hearing, as it were, and the sensitivity of the person who noted that we had ignored his first mention of his loss. Second, the person who mourned her dog needed the deeper sharing of the one who *did* express her bereavement to feel how much the pet had meant to her and in fact *what* the dog had meant in terms of love and acceptance. And finally, of course, was the deepest and unexpressed level of our carrying silently the grief of one who could not yet bear it consciously himself. This is the level at which we affect one another by that which is felt but not verbalized; it is the level of unconsciously shared emotion. I remember once in another group being told that one tearful person was "crying for us all," and that all of us were "crying inside." I was skeptical, but when I finally really listened to my inner feelings, these phrases caught very well what was going on in me.

The fierce individualism of present culture veils our radical psychological and spiritual interconnectedness. We see our interdependence economically, but not otherwise. But light is beginning to dawn. Further research on marriage, the family, and small-group life will, I am convinced, demonstrate empirically the wider truth of Paul's compelling view of the church as "one body." [3]

Parenthetically it should be noted that this bearing of one another's burdens can occur not only within a small group but even *among* groups within a congregation or a conference. This is explicitly recognized and documented in a report on an intergroup exercise, part of a larger Group Relations Training Conference.[4] One group, Z, was seen as responsible for precipitating a sudden and irrational break-up into small groups which led to considerable confusion and difficulty in starting on the assigned task. Fighting the organizers or flight from the task were the dangers. The conference also had to contain the continuing temptation to flight throughout the task. It did this by creating in Z group a part of itself that carried the emotional burden for the whole. Z continued in flight from the task. It remained disturbed and unable to work because of its preoccupation with the results of the guilt that had arisen from the first flight, which it had absorbed on behalf of the whole conference. Thus it can be said that all three groups took an equal share of the work of the conference as a whole, of which they were all part and for which the task was being done.

The conference members did not consciously create this solution. It emerged in the ebb and flow of feelings and action as the exercise proceeded. It could be understood as a scapegoating whereby the guilt and inner conflict within the other groups were projected onto the more visible culprits, thus allowing the former to proceed without too much inner disturbance. More positively the solution may be seen as a sharing of tasks which has implications for the interrelation of groups within a single congregation or even for differing roles of churches within the ecumenical movement.

The subtle and frequently unrecognized interrelations of persons in a group, or even of several groups, may be the basis for an enlarged definition of pastoral care. Too frequently this function is understood only as a conscious, premeditated going out to the other in his time of need. It should also include the encouraging or catalyzing of individual encounters or group situations in which burdens can be carried and interconnectedness experienced, whether or not this is made explicit to the givers and receivers. One of the possible liabilities of the influence of psychiatry on pastoral counseling is overstructuring "the helping relationship" (i.e., a specified time/place and a specified helper and helped). In a period of growing democraticization of the church, the question of who gives and who receives should recede, and the problem of how to set up giving/receiving situations should receive more attention.

III. The Winds of the Spirit

There is rich historical precedent for associating the Spirit with the unexpected, unplanned, and exuberant outpourings of power in a small circle of disciples, where no one plans ahead how he is going to witness. Since openness to an unforeseen outcome requires radical trust in a guidance which transcends conscious, rational thought, it may be more possible in a religious context than in a rational-analytic-humanistic one.

In my own Society of Friends it is assumed—though not always practiced—that solutions do not result from individuals thinking out answers but rather emerge spontaneously when members of a disciplined group set aside preconceived programs and open themselves to what happens.

A dramatic instance of this occurred in the history of a small group set up to study the future of the Society of Friends. The two of us who initiated it had in mind a study group for which individuals, most of whom were in academic life, would write papers about the relevance of currents of modern thought—Teilhard de Chardin, Einsteinian physics, existentialist literature, the civil rights and peace movements—for Quakerism. But from the first session it became evident that the group was heading in another direction. We began with autobiographies, which set the stage for deeper personal encounter than the writing of papers would have fostered. Although we continued to explore at length the metaphors of contemporary religion, we also spent a good deal of time sharing and responding to one another's personal pilgrimages—evoking one anothers' *Daemons,* as we called it. Gradually it dawned that the dialogue among us as persons was more fundamental to our task of renewal than the content of our ideas. In one sense we had become a pastoral care group. Worship became more integral to our life together. On occasion we had to deal with blocks to the free flow of ideas and feelings, and that became a significant part of our work. The final chapter is not yet written, but most of us feel that we have been led into an experience and an exploration far removed from our original stated purpose, yet perhaps more germane to it than we had been aware. The critical determinant of this change, from the human side, has been our capacity, faltering occasionally, to trust the group life as it has unfolded.

Trusting the leadings of the Spirit may also bear fruit in the course of a single meeting. Our search group sessions are totally without agenda and begin with a period of quiet worship. Concerns arise out of the silence. In one group which had been meeting for about a year, only three of the four regular couples turned up one evening. The opening silence was broken by one of the women, Grace, who said she was troubled by the tension she felt between the other two women. Both were on the governing board of a local Human Relations Council. One of them, Sarah, had been complaining to Grace about the "holding back" and "over-concern for reputation" of the other leader, Rachel. When Grace said she felt concerned to discuss it further, Rachel said she was reluctant to bring up "outside" business in the group, but she was persuaded to discuss it when it was pointed that all three couples were to some extent involved in the tension, that no other agenda was impending, and that the group was "neutral ground" as far as the council's tasks were concerned. Gradually it emerged that Sarah's husband was "conservative" in a way similar to Rachel and that Rachel's husband played a "radical" role in her life parallel to that played by Sarah! Thus we worked for a good part of the evening on the way in which the marital tensions spilled over into community action. The differences of view were not eliminated, but the meetings of the Human Relations Council grew less tense, and business proceeded more easily.

Here is an instance of group pastoral care which deals not primarily with individual hang-ups but with the organizational tensions which they aid and abet. Many pastors spend a good deal of time trying to unravel such personality battles. I am convinced that pastoral groups can help to free communication, even in the wider community, and thereby drain some of the venom which frequently poisons institutional life. Such groups introduce new tensions as well—that between the "groupers" and the "non-groupers" for example. But this I believe is a healthier and more resolvable kind of conflict. And surely any kind of Christian ministry which reaches to the central vortex of personal frustrations and longings will not always smooth the surface waters.

It is difficult to specify what constitutes an openness to the leadings of the Spirit in group life. An open agenda and times of silence are important. But in the instance just related it was also Grace's courage in raising in the group a problem which seemed at first to lie outside its scope. The key here was Grace's *sensing* in the silence that the tension originating outside was present at that moment in the group. This combination of psychological sensitivity and insistence on an honest facing of what is going on is one of the critical leadership functions for a trusting of the Spirit. Our experience is that significant feelings or problems almost invariably emerge if the silence is worshipful and members are open to whatever may be pressing for expression.

I have suggested above that such openness to the new should be more familiar and more possible in church groups than in therapeutic or secular ones. In the present religious situation I am not sure how true this is. In spite of the great interest in small groups in church circles, there has been too little free experimentation with the possibilities—especially the spiritual possibilities—of groups. Secular research and practice (group dynamics, psychotherapy, organizational research) have been the major determinants of contemporary use of small groups in the church. By and large church people have not been as receptive to a workings-of-the-Spirit interpretation of what occurs in small groups today as their forebears were to such a view of prayer meetings, Bible study groups, etc.—perhaps because the spiritual dimension was more explicitly "programmed in." A more radical openness might lead to a thorough revision of church structure and polity. A prevision of this can be seen in Washington's Church of the Saviour, where, as mentioned above, the locus of authority and activity is small groups.

Conclusion

I have tried to spell out some characteristics of small groups which have a power to transform and heal. In secular terms they are shared leadership function, a sense of interconnectedness, and trust of the group process. By correlating each of these with a spiritual affirmation—priesthood of all believers, members of one body, the winds of the Spirit—I intend to suggest two things: that a religious frame of reference can potentially add breadth and power to group life and that vigorous small groups can bring new experiential meaning to "outmoded" theological statements.

I am mindful of my secularized, almost casual approach to weighty theological matters. It is audacious to apply Paul's members-of-one-body image to groups outside the church, where the cement of faith in Christ is lacking. And it is a skirting of subtle questions not to specify more clearly the "leadings of the Spirit" in the life of groups. But greater specificity, I believe, will have to await a clearer inward knowing. A developed and affirmative theology can grow only out of an immediate experiencing of spiritual realities. The popular appeal of Bishop John A. T. Robinson and the death-of-God theologians arose not from their theological adequacy but from the fact that they were witnessing to their own convincing experience of God's absence. I believe that the minimal religious affirmations of this essay are theological enough to guide us toward fresh personal encounters with the realities upon which the biblical writers drew. As these encounters occur, we can proceed to formulate and connect them with the Christian tradition and with the newer currents of thought which we daily breathe. The idiom of that formulation will be that of our own time.

Notes

1. Carl R. Rogers, "The Process of the Basic Encounter Group," *The Challenge of Humanistic Psychology*, ed. J. F. T. Bugental (New York: McGraw-Hill, 1968).
2. E.g., John L. Casteel, ed., *Spiritual Renewal Through Personal Groups* (New York: Association Press, 1957); the entire issue of *Pastoral Psychology*, June, 1964; L. P. Bradford, J. R. Gibb, and K. D. Beene, eds., *T-Group Theory and Laboratory Method* (New York: Wiley, 1964); articles by Carl R. Rogers and James V. Clark in Bugenthal, *Challenge of Humanistic Psychology;* William Schutz, *Joy: Expanding Human Awareness* (New York: Grove Press, 1968).
3. For a careful and intriguing study of the unconscious interconnectedness which exists in marriage, see Henry V. Dicks, *Marital Tensions: Clinical Studies Towards a Psychological Theory of Interaction* (New York: Basic Books, 1967).
4. G. Higgin and H. Bridger, *The Psychodynamics of an Inter-group Experience* (New York: Barnes & Noble, 1965).

Rogerian Therapy and Optimal Pastoral Counseling

LeRoy Aden

As a manifestation of Christian ministry, pastoral counseling is concerned basically with the moral and religious self-affirmation of the troubled individual.[1] Experiential evidence tends to indicate that this concern is often served by psychotherapy as it deals with the individual's personal and interpersonal difficulties. While this fact is explained in part by the wholistic nature of man, I also believe that the particular approach of the therapist can be and often is a decisive factor. I am thinking especially of the therapeutic approach of Carl Rogers, for his approach seems to me to be particularly relevant to the religious concerns of pastoral counseling. More specifically, it is my contention that *Rogers' therapeutic ingredients of empathic understanding, unconditional positive regard, and congruence tend to actualize certain organismic attitudes which can be of decisive importance in the individual's spiritual life.*

This contention contains at least two notions that deserve explicit elaboration. First, it asserts that each of Rogers' three ingredients tends to actualize a particular organismic attitude: empathic understanding tends to actualize increased awareness; unconditional positive regard, unconditional acceptance; and congruence, unconditional trust. In actuality, of course, the attitudes and outcomes are an indivisible whole, but my analysis, if correct, helps to lift up and clarify the implicit value and potential significance of Rogerian counseling for the ultimate concern of pastoral counseling. Since Rogers as a psychologist never develops the latent religious end points of his three ingredients, the formulations that follow emerge out of and attempt to conceptualize my own experiential observations as a Rogerian-oriented pastoral counselor.

Second, the contention deals with the ideal outcome of Rogers' therapeutic approach, not with what is actually achieved in any particular case. Consequently, our discussion revolves around the organismic changes which begin to emerge as counseling approaches the point of being maximally successful and tries to show how they can be of crucial significance in man's perception of and response to God. The term unconditional, then, must be understood in a qualitative, and not a quantitative, sense.

With this introduction we can give individual attention to Rogers' therapeutic ingredients and to their maximal organismic consequences.

I. Empathic Understanding

According to Rogers, one of the essential conditions of a healing relationship is empathic understanding. By empathic understanding Rogers means a sensitive attentiveness to the inner world of the client or, more specifically, a genuine and accurate attempt on the part of the therapist to grasp and communicate the moment-to-moment feelings and experiences of the client as the client himself sees and feels them. "It is a sensing of the client's inner world of private personal meanings 'as if' it were the therapist's own, but without ever losing the 'as if' quality." [2]

Empathic understanding is a direct antidote to man's basic malady. As Rogers sees it, man does not affirm himself unqualifiably. Instead he becomes immersed in a process of selective self-affirmation in which he owns or disowns particular segments of himself according to whether or not they are in accord with his self-concept. Experiences that are discordant are either denied or distorted, that is, either excluded completely from awareness or symbolized in a disguised and inaccurate way. In either case the individual becomes a divided and disrupted being, living on the surface of himself to the extent that he is estranged from the deeper dimensions of his existence. Rogers calls this duplicity, this state of inner disruption, an incongruence between the self and organismic experiencing.

Empathic understanding addresses itself to this radical self-alienation. As a serious attempt to grasp the contemporary experience of the client, it counters his tendency to deny or distort and facilitates the self-exploration of his inner world of feelings and meanings. Or as Rogers says, it seems "crucially important in making it possible for a person to get close to himself, to experience his most inward feelings, to maintain contact with his inner self-experiences, thus allowing for the recognition and resolution of incongruences."[3] Clearly, then, the chief consequence of empathic understanding is to reverse the individual's defensive stance toward life, making him more open to the panoramic totality of his organismic experience and thus making his perceptual relation to self and the world more adequate and realistic. He becomes more fully aware of his own inner reality, his feelings, attitudes, and desires, and at the same time he becomes more accurately aware of the reality that exists outside himself. In a word, he "comes to *be*—in awareness—what he *is*—in experience."[4]

Increased awareness can be of decisive importance in the individual's relationship with God because it tends to deepen both his perception and his valuing. On a perceptual level it represents an organismic plunge into the depths of oneself, a plunge in which the individual may gain a deeply existential knowledge of his predicament. In the early stages of counseling, the individual tends to have a shallow and rigid understanding of his plight. He denies or distorts the most undesirable aspects of his condition so that he tends to feel that his plight—and therefore his rescue—is connected with the doing or the not doing of particular acts. With increased awareness comes the realization that his estrangement and guilt are pervasive qualities having to do with the whole interior of his life.

In optimal counseling, especially in optimal pastoral counseling, the individual's recognition of this situation may approach what is called theologically an awareness of sin, even though the individual himself may not attach that label to it. In other words, he begins to experience what he has only sensed before—that his alienation is not simply an alienation from self and others, that in fact he is estranged from the ultimate and underlying structures of life, from that Reality or Power which is able to give real joy and final meaning to his existence. An individual of the Christian faith will of course use less neutral terms and will describe his plight as a self-centered separation from God or as a lack of real faith in Christ. Beyond the specific terms, however, is the more important fact that this kind of organismic self-awareness is a crucial factor in the individual's appropriation of God's grace. "Only one who has been awakened to the full seriousness of his own guilt, and his own inability to overcome it, is in a position to look for and to accept the only adequate remedy—namely, the saving power of God's love and forgiveness in Jesus Christ." [5]

Increased awareness may serve a second purpose on the perceptual level of man's spiritual life. It tends to make an individual's perception of and response to God more adequate and realistic. In the early stages of counseling, the individual tends to have a vague and faulty notion of God. He may even create God in his own self-image, primarily by denying or distorting those aspects of God which are inconsistent with his own self-structure. The most common distortion of God is to experience him as a punitive judge who requires full restitution for all Pharisaic sins, but even in less distorted perceptions the individual will tend to possess an inadequate notion of God's love and forgiveness. Increased awareness helps to correct this situation primarily because the individual begins to perceive in an extensional rather than an intensional way. That is, he begins to perceive that God as God is manifested in and through his own experience instead of fitting him into some preconceived notion or some abstract doctrine. In addition he becomes more open to the merciful dimension of God's being and begins to experience that mercy in terms of a more adequate and specific knowledge of his basic predicament.

Increased awareness is decisive in the individual's relationship with God in another and more basic way, for it has a salutary effect not only on what the individual perceives but also on what he values. Rogers gives psychological expression to this point when he says that man has two different valuing systems: the one, a function of his total being, evaluates experience in terms of whether or not it maintains and enhances his total life; the other, a function of his self-concept, is attuned to the individual's defensive need to gain a positive regard of self and others. As counseling increases and deepens the individual's openness to experience, the individual moves away from the parched desert of self-valuing and begins to return to the fertile plains of organismic valuing, that is, he moves away from a narrow and inadequate fulfillment toward a genuine and expansive fulfillment. Spiritually, this salutary movement means that God ceases to be a "strange law" who is imposed upon the self and becomes a gracious Power who is congruent with the individual's genuine and basic needs—the need for grace as pardon where the individual is estranged and guilty, the need for grace as power where he is under the mandate of his essential being. In other words, the individual is able to relate more fully to God, using his God-given gifts more appropriately while at the same time acknowledging his need for forgiveness more deeply.

II. Unconditional Positive Regard

The Rogerian fall into radical alienation through selective self-affirmation is a consequence of "a natural—and tragic—development in infancy." As the infant develops, he gradually comes to recognize a portion of his total being and functioning as "I" or "me." In a word, he comes to possess a self or a self-concept. Concomitantly, he develops what is called a "need for positive regard," that is, he must feel that his presence and existence make a positive difference in the world of the significant other, that he is respected, cherished, and loved. Consequently, he becomes attentive to the response of others and begins to evaluate his feelings and desires according to their negative or positive reaction. Gradually, according to Rogers, this whole process is internalized so that the individual takes on the values of the significant other and cannot regard himself positively unless his experience is in accord with these introjected values, these "conditions of worth."

As Rogers sees it, then, man does not love and respect himself unqualifiably. Instead he becomes immersed in a process of conditional self-regard in which he takes hold of his life and becomes dominated by the tendency to try to make himself acceptable according to the standards of his conditions of worth. For this reason, among others, Rogers maintains that one of the essential ingredients of a healing relationship is unconditional acceptance. "Acceptance" refers to a complex of attitudes on the part of the therapist, the attitudes of "warmth, caring, liking, interest, respect." More specifically, it means to prize and hold in valued esteem the other person as a unique and significant human being, above and beyond any external evaluations which one might place on his specific experiences. Thus unconditional acceptance means "a caring which is not possessive, which demands no personal gratification. It is an atmosphere which simply demonstrates 'I care'; not 'I care for you if you behave thus and so.' "[6] In short, it is a prizing with no conditions of worth attached to it, a fact that has prompted Rogers to describe it as unconditional positive regard.

In an efficacious relationship of unconditional acceptance the client gradually begins to take the same attitude toward himself. He begins "to feel a dawning respect for, acceptance of, and, finally, even a fondness for himself." More specifically, his conditions of worth tend to diminish, and he begins to manifest an organismic attitude of unconditional acceptance not only toward himself as a person of intrinsic worth but also toward life in general and other people in particular.

Unconditional acceptance can be of decisive importance in the individual's spiritual life because it tends to release the individual from the bondage of self-justification. An individual who lives by and measures himself against what Rogers calls conditions of worth is living a life in which he tries to make himself acceptable to self, others, and God. He is caught in an endless and futile process of taking matters into his own hands and attempting to be the source of his own acceptance. Counseling indicates that an individual's attempt at self-justification can manifest itself in at least two interrelated ways. On the one hand, it can manifest itself on an interpersonal level as an insatiable attempt to win the love and acceptance of significant others by living a life of ingratiating behavior. The individual does those things that fulfill the conditions of worth of others (God or fellowmen) and thereby hopes to receive some genuine measure of their positive regard. On the other hand, it can manifest itself on an intrapsychic level as a constant attempt to deny or distort those feelings and experiences that are inconsistent with the self-concept and with the conditions under which the individual can maintain an undiluted measure of positive self-regard. In either case the individual becomes ensnared in a tenacious bondage of self-justification.

Unconditional acceptance as a new attitude toward oneself breaks the tenacity of this bondage. By suspending the internal and counteracting the external need to measure up to conditions of worth, it puts acceptance on an entirely different basis. The individual begins to experience an acceptance that goes beyond the doing or the not doing of particular deeds, or more positively, he begins to see that his value and significance as a human being are prior to, and not based upon, what he has achieved or not achieved. He can begin to rejoice in his intrinsic and unique self-worth, and in his deepest moments of freedom from self-justification he can affirm himself unqualifiably not because he has made himself acceptable but because he knows that acceptance and being accepted transcend anything he can do or needs to do.

Unconditional acceptance as an organismic experience comes initially in the therapeutic relationship when the client realizes that the therapist's acceptance is not changed by the dark and intensely unacceptable crevices of his life. While the salutary significance of this experience cannot be denied, in optimal counseling, especially in optimal pastoral counseling, the individual realizes that the reality and meaning of the therapist's acceptance are not derived from or limited to his own person. In other words, the individual comes to feel in a deeply existential way that the therapist's unconditional acceptance says something about the basic nature of life itself, that it "witnesses to, and is grounded in, a larger structure of justification." [7] Implicitly and sometimes explicitly, this experience of acceptance approaches the Christian concept of forgiveness, even though the individual may not think of it in those terms. The individual comes to possess an organismic sense of being accepted by the ultimate and underlying structures of life in spite of the depth to which he is unacceptable when measured by legalistic norms. He may even come to possess an organismic sense of being acceptable, not because of his own intrinsic self-worth but because he is known and yet accepted and forgiven by *Christus pro nobis*.

III. Congruence

Empathic understanding without the warmth of unconditional acceptance can be a cold and ruthless instrument, while unconditional acceptance without the clear vision of empathic understanding can be a shallow and sentimental affair. Thus both ingredients are essential to any moment of Rogerian therapy, and yet by themselves they are not sufficient to constitute an efficacious therapeutic relationship. In fact, they can become very hollow and artificial unless they are rooted in and proceed from a third ingredient, namely the integrity and authenticity of the therapist. Rogers calls this third ingredient "congruence" and believes that it is "the most basic of the three conditions."

A mature therapeutic relationship, then, is not simply a certain stance the counselor takes toward the client, but it is also a certain stance the counselor takes toward himself and the deeper levels of his own organismic experiencing. It is a stance of openness and honesty, a willingness to tear down concealing facades in order to be a whole and more harmonious person. In a word, it is an accurate matching of experiencing and awareness, not in an absolute fashion but "in this particular moment of this immediate relationship with this specific person." [8]

Efficacious congruence educes in the client the feeling that the therapist is dependably real and trustworthy. In other words, genuineness, or unconditional authenticity, in the therapist tends to elicit confidence, or unconditional trust, in the client so that the latter is able to place his life unqualifiably in the hands of the therapist with the organismic assurance that the therapist *is* what he appears to *be*.

Unconditional trust is of decisive importance in the individual's spiritual life because it increases the depth to which he can give himself to others, especially to God.

Our previous discussion has made it clear that an individual in the early stages of counseling tends to move toward and be related to only a small portion of his total existence. He is estranged from himself and others by a wall of radical self-seclusion. An organismic move toward unconditional trust tends to break down this wall not only in the therapeutic relationship where trust is experienced initially but also in the individual's total relation to life and the world. Rogers emphasizes the interpersonal aspect when he maintains that the optimal person lives "with others in the maximum possible harmony." [9] In actuality, unconditional trust deepens and increases the individual's relationship to the totality of life, for it enhances his homonomous tendency to give himself to and to become an organic part of superordinate realities.

In optimal counseling, especially in optimal pastoral counseling, the individual's increased relatedness may approach what Christian theology calls faith. That is, the individual moves out of himself and is able to relate more fully and to give himself more completely to the ultimate and underlying structures of life, to that Reality which "sets the bounds and establishes the possibilities of our being." He is empowered by an organismic sense that he belongs to, and is in tune with, "the meaning of existence as it really is," [10] a meaning that transcends him infinitely at the same time that it fulfills him completely. In theological terms he is drawn out of himself and is empowered to trust in and to accept God's love and forgiveness as a pivotal fact in his life. In other words, the gratuitous and unconditional acceptance of God becomes an organismic truth in the individual's experience, enabling him to affirm himself unqualifiably in spite of the extent to which he is still an estranged and guilty person.

Conclusion

I have tried to show that the salutary effects of Rogers' therapeutic approach are not limited to the interpersonal and intrapsychic dimensions of an individual's life. As Rogerian counseling approaches the point of being maximally successful, it tends to become an effective instrument of spiritual transformation. More specifically, it tends to actualize three organismic attitudes which in optimal pastoral counseling are decisive events in the individual's perception of and relationship to God. Increased awareness, unconditional acceptance, and unconditional trust are essential aspects of man's subjective appropriation of God's gracious action. In this sense Rogers' therapeutic approach is relevant to the religious concerns of optimal pastoral counseling and can become an efficacious medium through which, though never the ultimate source by which, the individual is empowered to experience and accept God's gift of unconditional forgiveness.

Notes

1. For a detailed development of this conception of pastoral counseling, see my "Pastoral Counseling as Christian Perspective," *The Dialogue Between Theology and Psychology*, III, ed. Peter Homans (Chicago: University of Chicago Press, 1968), 163 ff.
2. Carl R. Rogers *et al.*, eds., *The Therapeutic Relationship and Its Impact: A Study of Psychotherapy with Schizophrenics* (Madison: University of Wisconsin Press, 1967), p. 104.
3. *Ibid.*, p. 105.
4. Carl R. Rogers, *On Becoming a Person: A Therapist's View of Psychotherapy* (Boston: Houghton Mifflin, 1961), p. 104.
5. David E. Roberts, *Psychotherapy and a Christian View of Man* (New York: Scribner's, 1950), p. 108.
6. Rogers, *On Becoming a Person*, p. 283.
7. Don S. Browning, *Atonement and Psychotherapy* (Philadelphia: Westminster Press, 1966), p. 178.
8. Carl R. Rogers, "A Theory of Therapy, Personality, and Interpersonal Relationships," *Psychology: A Study of a Science*, III, ed. Sigmund Koch (New York: McGraw-Hill, 1959), 215.
9. *Ibid.*, p. 235.
10. Daniel Day Williams, *The Minister and the Care of Souls* (New York: Harper, 1961), p. 66.

Motherly and Fatherly Modes of Pastoral Care

Robert E. Elliott

In the ongoing conversations between psychotherapy and pastoral care some of the loudest and most acrimonious debate has been stirred up by recent writings of O. H. Mowrer.[1] His sweeping attacks on psychoanalysis and on the "Babylonian captivity" of pastoral counseling to Freudian and Rogerian methods have disturbed and challenged a number of people, including this writer. His proposals dramatically upend much of what we have thought and done in the field of pastoral counseling, and to take them seriously would seem to require us to reverse the direction of much of our work in recent decades.

How seriously is he to be taken? I suggest: with considerable seriousness but with critical repair of the one-sidedness and imbalance of his position. What follows is the brief outline of a theory of pastoral care and counseling which attempts to provide something of that balance. It sets forth a model, drawn by analogy from observation of patterns of parent-child relationships, which I have found helpful in my own attempt to formulate what we can validly learn from Mowrer.

Let me begin with a report of an experience. A young man of twenty-four, married about a year, joined a newly formed counseling group. His main presenting complaints, offered in the first session, were depression and confusion about personal and professional goals. In the process of getting acquainted with the other group members and making himself and his own concerns for therapy known, he spoke of the fact that his wife's pregnancy had recently interrupted sexual relations and that he experienced this as a severe emotional deprivation. Because of his own unloving childhood family, he said he felt a special need for emotional closeness and reassurance from his wife and found this forced sexual separation very difficult to bear.

With the flat, discouraged tone of his voice and his defeated and depressed posture and bearing, it was tempting to see him as one who more than anything else needed some strong affirmation and loving support from the group. Members of the group initially tended to respond to him in this way, sympathetically inviting him to talk more about his feelings, which seemed mostly to be blurred and confused.

After an interval the leader suggested a new tack: perhaps, he said, the group ought to invite him to talk more about his living than about his feeling, about the day-by-day structure and pattern of his life, and the leader added that he had come to believe that troubled feelings often follow troubling behavior. The man was able to respond to this invitation by disclosing that for some years he had been taking small things from stores without paying for them. He had acquired enough psychological sophistication to connect this behavior with emotional deprivation and his need for signs of love. But his attitude toward these acts as he reported them was less one of defensive justification than of a kind of helpless confusion: "I know it's wrong, but I don't feel guilty about it."

The leader suggested that maybe he had come to the stage where his feelings had become a very unreliable guide to behavior and that while his conscience did not function clearly enough to check his stealing or to produce clear feelings of guilt about it, it apparently was making itself known in painful and indirect fashion in his symptoms of depression and distress. To find a guide for repairing his life the leader suggested he would have to look to some other resource than "feelings." After some further conversation about this pattern of theft, the leader somewhat startled him and the other members of the group by giving him an assignment. Before the next meeting he was to have undertaken to repay the store owners or managers for these recent thefts and was to report back the following week his successful completion of this assignment as a condition of his good standing in the group. The unexpected character of this approach from the leader caught the whole group somewhat by surprise, but they and he quickly responded to it in a positive way as a signal of seriousness and concern for the man and for his life. At the next meeting he reported that he had carried out the assignment and already had begun to show signs of recovery from his depression and of the emergence of more positive self-feelings.

One further dramatic episode occurred, having to do with some money he had misappropriated from his employer in order to buy his wife a cherished Christmas gift. This painful matter was disclosed first to one of the members of the group and then to the group itself. Working it through involved helping him to make a clean breast of the matter to his wife and then in consultation with her, working out steps to rectify and repair the situation with the employer. Through these stages and over several weeks there came a dramatic growth in this man's obvious self-confidence and capacity for responsible living.

Note that while he presented initially to the group an appeal for love in the form of a kind of dependent support he was met instead by the offer of suggestions for tangible actions through which he could undertake to recover and repair his badly damaged self-esteem. In terms to be described later in this essay, he asked for a kind of mothering care but was offered in its place a kind of fathering care.

It is also pretty clear that this case rather neatly fits Mowrer's guilt theory of personality disturbance. I assume the reader's familiarity with at least the outline of his thesis: that most psychopathology stems from some form of real guilt, by which Mowrer means two things: (1) some tangible acts of misbehavior, deeds done in violation of one's conscience, of the standards one has accepted as valid for his life, and (2) the concealment of such misbehavior from the significant others in one's world in order to avoid the pain of disapproval, punishment, or rejection. When this sequence is repeated often enough, it forms a pattern of duplicitous behavior resulting in one form or another of emotional trouble. As Mowrer sees it, most symptoms should be read as disguised and distorted conscience signals registering a genuine though often well-concealed moral conflict in the person's past and present life.

From this view of the nature of emotional troubles it follows that a program of treatment or repair will undertake to reverse the process. The hiddenness or concealment is repaired by acts of confession, by the honest disclosure of oneself to others and ultimately to the significant others in one's life. This step is followed by amendment of life, by alteration of the devious behavior and the undertaking of tangible reconstructive steps toward the repair of injuries done to others and to one's own self-respect.

This viewpoint has obviously far-reaching and dramatic implications for both psychotherapy and pastoral care. But the question remains, How true is it? Granted that it seems to be pertinent and illuminative of many situations, as for example that of the young man discussed previously, still one has to ask how generalizable it is, how adequate to the interpretation and treatment of all psychopathological problems.

I would like to explore here a tentative answer to that question. In formulating it I am especially indebted to some clues that appear in the writings of William Glasser and of Erich Fromm.[2] In his recent book *Reality Therapy*, Glasser holds that human beings have two basic needs beyond the biological level. One is the need to be close to at least one other person, the need to love and be loved. The other is the need to feel worthwhile to oneself and to others, the need for self-respect or self-esteem. Much of Glasser's book focuses on the second of these, but I would like to reflect for a moment on the relation between the two of them, which we may call *love* and *respect*, as the two fundamental human needs. These are obviously closely related but have interesting and important differences. For example, love in its essence has to be a *gift*, something freely given and received, neither earnable nor commandable. But respect, on the other hand, precisely *does* have to be earned. It belongs to the realm of effort and achievement and is earned or forfeited by what one does.

All of us need both love and respect, but it is interesting to reflect on the possible ways in which these needs can miscarry. Perhaps if a person has been forced to try to earn love, his life will be marked by a kind of chronic anxious insecurity. On the other hand, if a person has been illicitly given respect without having earned it through the disciplines of effort and achievement, he may well be in another kind of serious emotional trouble through his inability to know how to gain appropriate respect and esteem from others and from himself, or through the inner knowledge that he has achieved respect illicitly or deceitfully.

This polarity of love and respect corresponds in an interesting way to Erich Fromm's discussion, especially in the *Art of Loving*, of the relation between what he calls motherly and fatherly love. Maternal love in principle is pure, unearned gift, bestowed prodigally on the newborn infant prior to anything he can or needs to do to evoke it. The mother loves all her children equally simply because they are hers. Nothing they can do will finally extinguish that love or place them beyond its reach. It is simple gift, unearned, unearnable, unforfeitable. It is the initial form of love we all encounter in entering the relational world, and it presumably forms the basis of all feelings of at-homeness in the world.

Fromm is careful to state that he lifts up these categories of motherly and fatherly love as abstract images or ideal types. Actual mothers and fathers always embody some combination of both forms, but it can be revealing to abstract the essential principles that lie behind them.

Beginning within the sphere of the mother's love, the child in time begins to grow as well into the realm of the father's love. This form of love, in contrast to that of the mother, is in principle conditional and qualified and has to be earned or evoked. The father loves best that child who most nearly fulfills his expectations and hopes or demands. The father's realm is that of achievement, goals, values, purposes, and the son learns how to gain the father's respect and esteem and thus how to gain his own for himself. The father's love, being earnable, can also be lost of forfeited, but by the same token it can then be regained. If the mother's love is lost, nothing can be done to reevoke it. The child is simply helpless before that tragic circumstance.

Fromm goes on to note that in growing up we form a conscience on both fatherly and motherly models, which in effect is to take up the task of being both father and mother to ourselves. What he means by the motherly conscience is that rooted source of self-affirmation and care for ourselves which like the mother's love sustains us through thick and thin with a kind of deep and inextinguishable love for ourselves no matter what. On the other hand, the fatherly conscience is that capacity for objective self-appraisal which judges us in relation to our own standards for our behavior and measures us in relation to what we expect of ourselves. It metes out praise and blame, chastisement and reward, warning and encouragement. Indeed it performs in principle the function a loving father exercises in relation to a child he is trying to guide in his growth toward responsible adulthood.

Now if this kind of theoretical construct makes sense, I believe we can borrow it as a frame for appropriating in a more balanced way some of Mowrer's significance for us in pastoral care and for gaining a perspective on some of the currents and crosscurrents in the psychotherapeutic world.

Would it be allowable to say that both Freudian psychology and Reformation theology offer rescue to men whose predicament is seen as the result of "overfathering"? In Freud's case the oppressive father is the Victorian *paterfamilias* with his castrating authority, whom the son struggles vainly to relate to or to escape. In Luther's case the problem is that of the awesome, implacable, heavenly Father, whom he struggles to relate to and to please by means of penitential disciplines but who remains forever unapproachable.

In both cases the form of remedy is the provision of a kind of motherly affirmation and acceptance which undercuts and displaces the moral oppression and demands of the father. For Luther this is the discovery of what could be called the motherly side of God's nature, that is, his utterly gracious, unqualified love for his children, unmerited and unearned, indeed, unearnable. This free grace, preceding any act on the part of those on whom it is bestowed, is seen by Luther as the heart of the gospel itself, which sets men free, "justified by faith alone," to live before God in service and love to the brother.

At the risk of some oversimplification, one can point to a parallel in the emergence of modern psychotherapies, especially the nondirective therapies, in their emphasis upon the nonjudgmental, permissive, accepting stance of the therapist with the patient. Such attitudes and methods resemble in a number of ways what we have called the motherly form of care, in which acceptance, "unconditional positive regard," and the like are offered as a form of repair for the person who is assumed to have been wounded in the struggle with the father and his internalized representative, the self-punitive conscience.

I do not see how one can deny the truth and power of these images and of the programs, both theological and psychological, that have incorporated them in their own periods in the history of the West. The power of this form of good news to liberate men and to set them free to live has been testified in too many ways to be brushed aside as easily as Mowrer tends to do. However, there are many reasons to think that the situation to which these words were meaningfully addressed has altered profoundly and that it is no longer precisely our situation. As Erikson[3] suggests, a therapy for one man or one age may become itself the sickness of another. To be more specific, there are many reasons to think that the representative problems of our day have much more to do with "underfathering" than with "overfathering." Much evidence suggests that the predominant family problem in our time is not the tyranny of the father but his absence or weakness. Many studies draw attention to the developmental problems of children raised in families where fathers are absent or ineffective, where the task is that of finding or shaping some meaningful structure for one's life in the midst of role confusion and decayed relationship.[4]

Religiously, the problem in our time seems to be less that of dealing with the fearsome God than of finding or living without the absent One. Where the question was once, "How can I be saved from God's wrath?" the question has more often become "Is he alive?" The death-of-God theologians simply lift up the fact that the predominant religious experience in our time seems to be the experience of the absence of God and the absence of the attendant moral and metaphysical structures by which men have oriented their lives in the past.

To men in such a situation the proclamation of the gospel as pure acceptance or unearned grace may have a rather hollow ring. The implication that there is nothing needful except to receive by faith this gift of relation to God, that there is nothing which either can or need be done to affect one's relation to him, may be an invitation to despair. Correspondingly, the therapeutic stance which continues to offer a kind of nonjudgmental, permissive acceptance to persons who are in trouble because of moral confusion or the breakdown of responsible structure in their lives, may simply be compounding the problem itself. I am suggesting that care for such persons may need to be seen and exercised more in what we have called the fatherly mode, through helping to clarify the elements of personal structure and guiding the troubled person in the process of finding or reestablishing valid self-respect.

To come back to Mowrer, finally, he certainly can be seen as a trenchant critic of all "mothering" psychotherapies and pastoral theologies, and much of his value to us lies in the sharp and penetrating way he exposes some of these issues. Nevertheless, I am not as persuaded as Mowrer that mothering care is always irrelevant or inappropriate to the needs of particular persons or that the mothering contribution to the healing and enlivening of persons can be simply ignored. In this sense I believe that Glasser's program offers in principle a more balanced theoretical model, with his identification of both love and respect as irreducible human needs and in his incorporation of both these in his therapeutic method.

In summary, all men in all times need both love and respect. Perhaps some men in all times and most men at certain times can be seen to be in trouble in the sphere of what we have called overfathering. In other times, including I believe our own, the representative human problems are better understood as a consequence of underfathering, although these are oversimplified categories, to be sure. Theologically this thesis suggests that we need to recover procedures and images in the life of the church that can disclose and convey the fatherly side of God's love as well as his motherly side, perhaps in a rediscovery and reworking of the real dialectic of law and gospel, of judgment and mercy, in the Christian life. In pastoral practice it means working seriously at inventing and recovering structures for the process of confession and the restructuring of life in forms of disciplined community. And specifically it means recovering for Protestantism a positive and constructive meaning for *penance*, as reparative and reconstructive work.

Notes

1. O. H. Mowrer, *The Crisis in Psychiatry and Religion* (Princeton: Van Nostrand, 1961); *The New Group Therapy* (Van Nostrand, 1964).
2. William Glasser, *Reality Therapy* (New York: Harper, 1965); Erich Fromm, *The Art of Loving* (Harper, 1956).
3. Erik Erikson, *Young Man Luther* (New York: W. W. Norton, 1957).
4. Wolfgang Lederer, "Dragons, Delinquents and Destiny," *Psychology Issues*, IV (1964).

The Implications of Pastoral Theology for the Campus Ministry

Clyde J. Steckel

To discuss the implications of pastoral theology for the campus ministry, one must specify what kind of campus ministry is under consideration. The brief history of the campus ministry is one of changing forms and structures, fluid roles and tasks. If it is assumed that the campus ministry is essentially a chaplaincy, parallel to military or institutional chaplaincies, then the implications of pastoral theology will be similarly parallel. If, on the other hand, it is assumed that the campus ministry is an agency for social change, specifically for change in higher education, then the implications of pastoral theology may seem neither direct nor parallel to the implications for the parish ministry or institutional chaplaincies.

There are many kinds of campus ministries, of course, some of which are specifically called chaplaincies. There are chaplains of church-related, private, and even public universities and chaplains appointed and sent to university campuses by church bodies. Whatever these chaplains do in fact, it is generally assumed that their tasks are pastoral, ministering to and with persons of the Christian community who happen to work and reside in a specialized institution where the normal ministries of the parish church and clergyman are less likely to have the efficacy they are presumed to have in the regular communities of work and residence. Behind these assumptions, of course, lie all the postulates of the established church, with the notion that all accredited persons are baptized and confirmed believers, normally gathered into and served by parish churches, but with some exceptions for persons in universities, military service, hospitals, and prisons.

The fact of the matter, however, is that even where the campus ministers are called chaplains and are understood by their employers or constituents to be ministering to the community of faith, increasingly the campus ministries are emerging as one important element of a variety of new ministries which have in common a concern to recognize the demonic and dehumanizing elements in the society in which they exist, to confront these elements with the challenge of radical reform and reconstruction, and to work to create a new and different society in which human justice and love can be more fully actualized. The specialized urban ministries of the churches have been in the forefront of this change. Some of the very specialized ministries within leisure communities, night ministries, young adult ministries, and ministries to political processes are in the same direction. And more and more the campus ministries are addressing themselves to the issues which arouse anguish, anger, and moral passion in the young—issues of peace and war, race, poverty and affluence, and above all, issues related to higher education—what is the role of universities in modern society, how does the curriculum fit or unfit one to be a productive and compassionate person, how can universities be rescued from their enslavement to the business-industrial-military-government complex?

As the campus ministries increasingly align themselves with persons and groups who are trying to understand and do something about these issues, the style and stance of the campus ministries move away from traditional chaplaincies and in the direction of other agencies and movements which are working for social change.

There is no absolute dichotomy, of course, between campus ministries understood as chaplaincies and those understood as agencies of social change. There are still people inside and outside the community of faith who look to that community and its leaders for assistance of all kinds. There are still tasks of caring, of giving compassion and support, tasks which have changed little in their basic shape from those performed by the earliest Christian community.

But there is an important difference of emphasis which must not be overlooked. If one assumes that the basic quality of the society and the church are, on the whole, positive or at least benign, then the task of caring for those in need becomes centered on those acts which will help them share more fully in society and church. If, on the other hand, one assumes that there are important qualitative elements of evil, elements which are destructive and dehumanizing, it becomes necessary to move on a broad front to challenge and change these elements. Otherwise, the care for persons in need can never be truly rehabilitative and humanizing. They will always be thrust back into destructive social situations, perhaps no worse but certainly no better.

And it is more than a matter of declaring that there must be a division of labor in the ministry of the church, some to engage in prophetic challenge and some to engage in acts of care and compassion. Care and compassion become cheapened and degraded in a social situation which cries out for protest and resistance.

I

If the campus ministries are moving in the directions outlined above, then not only are the implications of pastoral theology to be seen in a fresh light, but also the whole character of pastoral theology is changed. There can be no clearly held assumptions about the organization of a stable church in a stable society, no clearly defined tasks of the officials of such an organization, and no clear delineation of certain tasks which can be traditionally understood as pastoral care and counseling, around which are developed a body of general principles which have come to be known as pastoral theology.

What I will propose, then, in the following discussion, is a possible outline of some new basic principles for pastoral theology, based on the assumption that the campus ministry is properly becoming a specialized ministry aimed specifically at understanding and participating in reform and change in higher education in our society.

A. The first principle is that the campus ministry is a corporate ministry, the ministry of a community of persons. While this is an obvious characteristic of the church, it is sometimes rather blithely assumed that the campus ministry is an individualistic exercise performed by some far-out young cleric who associates freely with a variety of persons and causes, lending some slight credibility to the notion that the church still cares for and is concerned with all sorts of people. But even where such a man does yeoman service, he usually requires some visible means of support, and most of the time this is a parish or bishop or board which represents a more conventional Christendom. Too often the consequence of such an arrangement is a less than fully corporate sense of the ministry of such a man.

By the corporate character of the campus Christian community I mean the necessary reality of students, professors, administrators, and other concerned persons, as well as campus clergy, who understand their existence as a community of ministry in higher education, who have a significant degree of actual responsibility for the conduct of the ministry in their own place, however much their financial resources are received through church bureaucratic structures, and who gather regularly both to do business and to do their main business, which is to pray, break bread, and be confronted by the living Word.

But this corporate character of the campus Christian community has an additional important dimension which is the reality of the whole body of persons whose lives are caught up in the enterprise of higher education in that place, and especially those persons with a vision of a better university and better life. It is this larger corporate reality which gives the campus Christian community its allies. Often the ministry to be performed is best shaped and exercised by those whose ideology or convictional framework is clearly other than that of the Christian community but whose goals of justice and love are clearly in keeping with the aims of Christ's people.

Now if pastoral theology is an ordered understanding of ministering acts, of deeds and words which give shape to justice and love, then both these corporate realities must be taken fully into account when trying to understand the implications of pastoral theology for the campus ministry. Pastoral theology, in other words, cannot belong to or refer to only those within the confessedly Christian community, even though the language in which pastoral theology is shaped will necessarily be problematic for the person or group standing outside the Christian convictional framework.

There is, of course, the risk that this duality of the corporate community can be dissolved to one side or the other. The tradition of Christian pietism which is separate from worldly concerns is not unknown on the university campus. But the risk on the other side is probably more sharply pointed today. In a society and in a specific community like the university where all the symbols and words of the Christian heritage are fraught with so many difficulties of use and misuse, it is tempting to let the theologians or the pietists have their word games and plunge vigorously into direct action alongside those who seem less encumbered and less defensive, more ready to and perhaps more skillful at moving out to take direct action which promises to have consequence. Now if one is speaking here about a matter of emphasis or a matter of learning how to recognize one's allies and to work with them without quibbling about fundamental ideology, then surely the campus ministries, and the whole church, need to be considerably more free from preoccupation with refurbishing the heritage or making ideological converts. But when all that is admitted, it is still the responsibility of some, perhaps for now it will be a small group within the larger body, to give careful and patient attention to the dialogue between the activities of an agency for social change and the traditions of the Christian community. At times the dialogue may seem escapist or irrelevant. It will certainly be difficult. But the dialogue cannot be neglected or suspended. Any theology of ministering which advocates a total absorption of the Christian body within a purely secularly defined cause of justice and love cannot be sustained. It is too messianic, too eschatological. The Christian tradition is best kept alive by being lived out, of course, but until that promised day has come when all shall love their neighbor, Christ's imperfect people must keep alive his memory and his teaching.

B. Within such a corporate community in higher education—those who minister openly in Christ's name and those who minister in his spirit but without his name—a variety of acts of ministry can be identified, all of which constitute the material for a pastoral theology appropriate to the new situation of the church and its society.

1. The most important of these acts of ministry, of course, are those directed to challenging and reforming the structures of society, specifically higher education. Such acts can no longer be classified as social action because, as has been increasingly recognized, to care for people is to care about all the ways in which social systems shape and determine the lives of people. But there are many ways to challenge and reform a social system, and a new discipline of pastoral theology in this framework will be concerned for the means employed so that destructive and dehumanizing methods will not produce as much evil as that in the system being challenged. This does not mean, of course, that one can adopt with any kind of finality methods which are totally educative and peaceful. A pastoral theology informed by the modern social sciences will be sensitive to dimensions of subtle or open psychological violence which are proclaimed to be nonviolent. The Christian community will strive to engage in acts of challenge and reform which wreak the least possible violence and destruction upon persons in the evil system, seeking to be faithful to its mandate to love all people. But such a pastoral theology cannot ignore the painful questions of relative degrees of violence and dehumanization, and the church cannot blindly pursue a so-called nonviolent

approach when to do so gives tacit approval and support to a system which thrives on violence and terror. On these painful decisions, of course, the church has tended in its history to become fully clear and aroused only very slowly and often at such a late time in the social process that its mobilized resources can do little. This is not to say that every new revolution should have speedy church sanction and participation, for revolutionary movements can be as demonic as forces of reaction. But the church cannot avoid facing the possibility of making such an alignment when entrenched evil can no longer be tolerated.

2. A second group of acts of ministry in such a dual campus Christian community comprises all those direct deeds of care and compassion for persons in situations of immediate need. These needs are of several sorts. Persons engaged in a social change ministry are on the one hand often prone to excessive self-righteousness and pride and can be maddeningly intolerant of the ideas and the weaknesses of other people in such a movement. Care and compassion in this situation involves a direct and honest confrontation of such persons, in love, with the requirement for greater tolerance and humility. Persons engaged in such a ministry, and often the same persons who can appear so self-righteous, are frequently subject to extreme personal anxieties not unlike the cultural shock experienced by those who move from one society to another. They are reacting against an identity given by the culture and given by their immediate family, and they are searching, sometimes desperately, for a new and solid identity. In their own way they are experiencing the late-adolescence identity crisis of which much has been written. But unlike so many of their peers and predecessors, these young people are not easily persuaded that a few conversations with the chaplain will materially aid the discovery of their new identity. The new style is to find identity through engagement, involvement. The ministering community must therefore not simply provide desk counselors but provide channels for involvement,

more mature comrades in direct action, in which and out of which the pastoral counseling situation arises.

Some of the people attracted to social change ministries are desperate, lonely, severely disturbed persons, but often brilliant and clever. A ministry of compassion to them involves accepting them in the enterprise, using the gifts which they can contribute, but also seeing that they receive the professional attention which they may require.

Another group of persons who need and should receive acts of ministry like those described above are those in allied groups not holding a Christian convictional framework. While the acts of ministry may be the same, the meaning may be of another sort. It may be a test, a test of good faith, of respect. It may be, in effect, a question addressed to the church and church people, addressed in both suspicion and hope: Do you really care, about me, about the cause? Or are you in this game for other reasons, to clean up the church's image or to make fresh converts? Do I have to confess Jesus to get the bowl of soup? It is depressing and illuminating to discover how much basic distrust comes to the surface in such situations. What must be done in these instances, of course, is to minister to need without giving back hurt for hurt and without at the same time giving out effusive disclaimers of any devious purpose, which only tend to keep the suspicion alive.

A final group of persons in need is comprised of all those in or around institutions of higher education who are victims of the university or society and who do not fall neatly into the manifold slots of professional services. There are many such—the runaway, the dropout, the freak-out, the pregnant girl who wants an abortion, the scared girl who wants the pill, the boy who does not want to be trained to kill but cannot put his feelings into terms his draft board can understand and accept, the potential professorial dropout—their number is legion, and often they are too fiercely proud to work through official channels even if the channels exist.

The community of ministry clearly has a responsibility to all such persons in need. While I suggested earlier that such a ministry cannot be the primary business of a social change agency, much more such work can be done without laying aside the tasks of social challenge and reform. Indeed, from such experience comes fresh conviction about need for reform in the system.

And most of the acts of ministry to be performed for such persons are just that, actions, not words. There is little disposition nowadays to turn to the Christian community, and especially to the clergyman, for leisurely conversation, however much the clergyman would like to remain in the more secure role of counselor. Counseling occurs, but within the context of deeds of concern and compassion which testify to his sharing the hurt and anger.

In this regard one must ask what is the place, in such an understanding of the ministering community in higher education, of the kind of pastoral counseling which has flowered in the modern pastoral theology and clinical training movements, informed by the methods of therapeutic psychology. I suppose that my only answer can be that the new situation has created the need for a new kind of clinical training, a variety of examined experience which the traditional forms of training and education have not yet envisaged. Persons in such a movement and society are neither so sick as those in the mental hospitals nor so complacent and culturally settled as those in the suburban parish. And part of the new situation is a respect for deeds with an accompanying suspicion of words—and whatever else happens in counseling, words are an important medium of communication. I must conclude, therefore, that we are not only attempting to come at the principles of a new pastoral theology, but we are also searching for new forms of clinical training appropriate to a new situation in church and society.

C. One of the ways in which the contemporary field of pastoral theology has given creative leadership is its continuing dialogue with the sciences of man, especially with therapeutic psychology. One of the characteristics of the ministry in higher education is its involvement of persons from many academic disciplines, and a word is in order on the implications of the dialogue developed in pastoral theology for such a ministry.

As the dialogue has developed in pastoral theology, emphasis has been placed upon the ways in which the modern sciences of man illumine and give specific substance to some of the classical Christian doctrines of man and the human community. While such dialogue has been indispensable for the renewed vigor of pastoral theology, it is difficult to demonstrate an equally important effect in therapeutic psychology. And when one considers that in many university psychology departments today therapeutic psychology has at best an orphan relationship, necessary for the training of clinicians but hardly on the level with a more rigorously disciplined scientific psychology, then the potentialities for a dialogue on the university campus like that pursued in pastoral theology become even more remote and peripheral. For dialogue to be genuinely productive, both parties must believe that matters of genuine moment are at stake and that the welfare of both parties demands that the dialogue proceed. Furthermore, there is in academic quarters a sophisticated suspicion of the real motives of church people in seeking dialogue, analogous to the suspicion noted earlier.

If we approach the question of dialogue from within the movement for university reform, however, then new possibilities emerge which do not simply reproduce the productive dialogue within modern pastoral theology but which instead open up a variety of new possibilities. For one of the aspects of university reform receiving a great deal of attention is the question of the wholeness of man and the place of the several academic disciplines in that wholeness. This question is being put in a new way when compared with the ambitious programs of general studies pioneered some decades ago at Columbia and Chicago.

This issue can be put in several ways. What is the social responsibility of the scholar for the use of his knowledge? How can the validity of specialization and narrow concentration be maintained without losing the breadth and vitality which ought to characterize the undergraduate introduction to an academic discipline? How can students already badly scarred by their previous educational experience come alive to the joy and freedom of learning in the present system of classified and graded instruction? Is there a way to reorganize much of the undergraduate curriculum around key problems and issues which confront the individual and society? These questions are being raised and pondered by many professors in many disciplines, especially those not trapped in narrow professionalism. And a great deal of interdisciplinary dialogue is already taking place around these questions. When persons from the Christian community in higher education bring a demonstrated competence and vigor to this dialogue, they are usually welcomed, and their stake in the outcome, while perhaps not understood theologically, is nonetheless recognized as valid.

While this kind of interdisciplinary dialogue is not so specialized nor so formally academic as that pioneered in modern pastoral theology, it promises, I think, to become fully as important in helping the university to recover part of its mission and in helping the church to recover part of its involvement in the formation of a fuller humanity.

II

In this essay I have argued that the campus ministry is increasingly becoming a specialized ministry of social change in higher education and that the forms of corporate life appropriate to this function require a new way of understanding pastoral theology and the ministering acts which have traditionally formed the substance of pastoral theology.

Three basic principles from pastoral theology have been presented and affirmed: (1) pastoral theology involves the ministering acts of the entire community of faith; (2) pastoral theology relates to all the acts of care or compassion for people in need; and (3) pastoral theology must be developed in dialogue with relevant academic disciplines.

But while I have maintained the validity of these three principles for the campus ministry, I have also suggested that the shift in the campus ministry from chaplaincy to social change requires that the substance of these three principles be significantly changed. (1) The definition of the faithful community must be broadened to include all those persons and groups allied for change and reform, so long as it is recognized that some persons must continue to understand and revise the Christian substance. (2) The meaning of acts of care or compassion must be expanded to include efforts to reform destructive social systems while not neglecting to care for the victims of these systems. Thus the old, facile division of labor in the churches between the social action people and the pastoral care people will no longer work. And (3) new models for the dialogue with the academic disciplines must be developed, models which will be less specialized in content than the psychotherapy–pastoral counseling model but more inclusive of many academic disciplines and more clear about the base of common concern upon which the dialogue proceeds.

And I have further suggested that if the changes in the social situation and forms of the church evident in the campus ministry are indicative of the changes occurring elsewhere in society and the church, then a new pastoral theology will be required, developed perhaps along such lines as those briefly sketched above.

The Counseling of College Students

William R. Rogers

It's a long and dusty road,
It's a hot and a heavy load,
And the folks I meet ain't always kind.
Some are bad and some are good,
Some have done the best they could,
Some have tried to ease my troublin' mind,
And I can't help but wonder where I'm bound,
where I'm bound,
Can't help but wonder where I'm bound.[1]

Amid the restless, driving quest of college students for a comfortable life-style and a meaningful grasp of a world, it is at times hard to differentiate the crises of pathological proportions from the fluid and at times tumultuous discords of the normal development of individual identity. Seen most broadly, the development of college students demands a constructive and flexible stance on the part of the counselor, a stance more concerned with understanding the present inner world of each student in all his chaos and possibility than it is with diagnosing and labeling particular pathologies as such. Eventually, of course, thoughtful developmental and pathological analyses must be integrated with phenomenological sensitivities and these in turn related to the most effective counseling principles. Hence in spite of a recogni-

By Tom Paxton.

tion of the fundamental necessity of an individualized understanding of particular students in counseling, the attempt of this essay will be to generate some broader analysis of the problems of college students at varying levels of intensity and distortion. In the course of this analysis I will indicate the implications that emerge both for operational principles in counseling and for a theological understanding of the dynamics under discussion.

This procedure is an effort at a constructive formulation of the problems involved in counseling college students rather than an overview of current practices and writing in the field. Such an overview might be obtained by looking at some recent compendia of discussions and research in the field such as *Counseling on the Liberal Arts Campus*.[2]

The following analysis will be undertaken under three general categories: (1) identity diffusion and centeredness, (2) emptiness and meaning, (3) nihilism and morality. Although intentionally nondiscrete, these categories deal with related psychological, theological, and ethical dilemmas in the development of college students.

I. Identity Diffusion and Centeredness

What turns me on? Am I really helpless about the war and the draft? What is my education relevant to? Whom do I really love? What kinds of responsibility, guilt, and identification do I feel toward my parents? Are the political and social structures worth working in, or is revolution the only way to social change? Aren't the immediate highs of sex and drugs enough? Damn this aching loneliness.

Probably more has been written about the problem of identity in late adolescence than about any other feature relevant to student growth. While some of this writing has had its own identity problems, Erik Erikson has done a great deal toward clarifying its meaning in his recent book *Identity: Youth and Crisis*.[3] Erikson deals with the process of identity formation not only as a quest for what is consistent, guiding, and central in the self-conception of an individual but also in a relational sense involving the individual appropriation of feedback from other important persons and the concomitant evaluation of this feedback. He states this in a somewhat complex way, as follows:

> Identity formation employs a process of simultaneous reflection and observation, a process taking place on all levels of mental functioning, by which the individual judges himself in the light of what he perceives to be the way in which others judge him in comparison to themselves and to a typology significant to them; while he judges their way of judging him in the light of how he perceives himself in comparison to them and to types that have become relevant to him.[4]

This involves an inner and an outer process: an inner process of self-awareness and historical consciousness and an outer process of receptivity and evaluation of responses from peers, professors, parents, the media, etc.

Such analysis has theoretical relevance not only to a dialogue between psychoanalysis and social psychology, as Erikson intends, but also to the inner and outer poles with which Jung deals in discussions of the persona and the soul, one looking outward and the other looking inward. The analysis is close to the discussion of centeredness in the third volume of Tillich's *Systematic Theology*, where he deals with the first crucial aspect of life processes as the movement outward from a centered self toward participation with others and then a return to one's own center. " 'Total centeredness' is the situation of having, face to face with one's self, a world to which one, at the same time, belongs as a part. . . . Therefore, the self-integration of the person as a person occurs in a community, within which the continuous mutual encounter of centered self with centered self is possible and actual." [5] Finally, though, "there can be no other uniting center than the ultimate concern of the mind." [6] The student in his quest for self-identity is clearly engaged in this inner and outer movement and seeking—often out of the boredom of immediacy—a genuinely centered focus of life, however incompletely this may be actualized.

I mention these theological considerations for both clinical and theoretical reasons. Theoretically, it is clear that the concept of centeredness carries a great deal of psychological and theological cargo while remaining a relatively neutral term. It comprehends the problem of identity formation in relation to interaction with the environment. Here we merge on the clinical usefulness of this conception, for it is usually at the point connecting self-understanding (taken too often as self-centeredness in the introspective egoistic sense) with receptivity to persons and agencies outside himself (taken too often as dangerous, enveloping, and binding) that the college student bogs down in his quest for centeredness.

Two contrasting problems are outstanding for the student in this regard. One is that he may become highly introspective, withdrawing into the inner confines of his own mind and seeking through privatistic symbolism some guiding images—but in the process becoming more and more lonely, cut off, fatigued, and despairing of authentic possibilities of either self-discovery or growth in personal relationships. This distortion may be unwittingly reinforced by counselors who passively encourage only the exploration of intrapsychic feelings in one-to-one relationships. Certainly the importance of group feedback and broader interpersonal controntation is implied in the theoretical comments above. The possibility of confronting a mature adult who has a significant stance about which he can communicate openly and sensitively, as well as confronting peers working through similar problems, may be of special importance to students experiencing depression, alienation, and withdrawal.

One must, of course, safeguard against the danger that such confrontations might manipulate the confused student into adopting only externally obligating patterns. However, I have become convinced that the best safeguard is not the concealment of a counselor's self-identity or his perspective on the student but rather an open and transparent sharing of this perspective. What is most open in a relationship may be less manipulative than what is subtly concealed but hence unconsciously binding.

An alternative problem that emerges is that students may become absorbed in the outer dimension of the process of identity formation. It may be that their inner world has no consistency other than blind allegiance to external conformity. There is apathetic resignation to the systematic demands of our technological society which outlines in advance occupational, political, military, and economic systems that easily engulf the life and the future of the college student. Capitulation to such environmental structures could be just as disastrous as escape into the internal caverns of the self. In each case genuine centeredness calls for sensitive interplay between self-examination and realistic appraisal of the realities of our social and political life. The wise counselor should be able to detect the overgeneralizing tendencies of the student in one direction or the other and enable him to develop both these inner and outer apperceptions.

As the counselor takes responsibility for the identity problems of students, he must also concern himself with structures beyond personal student relationships. There are environmental factors which either facilitate or hamper the student's development of centeredness. For instance, it is rather shocking that many outstanding colleges and universities tend to exaggerate unduly the anxiety connected with student development by subtly reinforcing anxiety. The rewards of esteem from one's peers and concern and respect from the faculty are given when a student is anxious about his work, struggling over his problems, depressed, overworked, or caught up in the complexity and ambiguity of his identity struggle. Somehow, colleges think this is more profound and existential and may judge those who are on top of their work as superficial, those who are more relaxed as uninvolved, facile, or incomplete in their observation, reading, or psychic life. Recognizing such distortions, the counselor should give encouragement to institutional patterns which support more healthy alternation between work and relaxation in learning and are attentive to optimal anxiety levels in the development of personal centeredness.

II. Emptiness and Meaning

A second major problem area for students is a recurring and frightening sense of personal and intellectual emptiness. In spite of periods of felt competence, there emerge feelings of restlessness and helplessness in the face of seemingly unconquerable problems of either intellectual magnitude within academic disciplines or in relation to the massive complexities of world tensions and the overwhelming burdens of the credit economy which enslaves the adult world. Sometimes the emptiness results from competitive but boring educational programs which dally in tired ways on what Whitehead calls "inert ideas." For others the emptiness emerges after a period of rebellion and rejection of previously held religious ideals, but after the fury and frustrations in battling this through with one's parents, a quiet stagnation may set in while one flounders with the fear that nothing worthy of commitment can be discovered to replace the old ideological securities of childhood.

It is clear that such an experience of emptiness is closely related to the problem of centeredness. At heart the experience of emptiness is the feeling of the loss of a center, an experience which Ronald Laing has termed "imposion," the bursting inward which is experienced as a shattering of those symbols and meanings which held life together and the fear of loss of control in the resulting chaos. The reintegration of a meaningful sense of self and world is both a psychological and theological concern and is characterized by a quest for the discovery of meaning and depth.

It is an ironic truth that some students who have even pursued an invigorating course of intellectual development also experience a profound sense of emptiness near the culmination of their quest. There are powerful cultural and intellectual forces which drive contemporary students to despair. The possibility of a rationalistic model integrating life as it did the enlightenment has been lost in a recognition of the irrational forces both of unconscious psychic life and of conscious international power complexes. The possibility of an economic model integrating life around increases in the standard of living seems burdened with injustice and hypocrisy, especially to affluent students. With Feuerbach and Freud the possibility of a religious model was also attacked. The psychological reduction of religious sentiments to unconscious wish-fulfillment, obsession, the return of the repressed, repetition compulsion of childhood patterns, or most especially a defensive illusion allowing man to mitigate the real suffering in life through the pretense of eternal security—all this has been deeply undermining.

Students are left as Rieff's "psychological man" or Esslin's "absurd man." Psychological man is resigned to accept hardship and ambiguity in life, seeking at best some sort of stoic independence, above all cautious against any evasiveness which might protect him from the desolation, brokenness, and painfulness of life.[7] There may be intellectual attempts to transcend psychological man through forms of humanism, self-actualization, or even sensuality, but some students see even these as defensive securities. Sensuality and an ethic of brutal honesty have only the most flimsy chance of protecting students from ultimate disillusionment; instead they reinforce a sense of absurdity. Students may confirm Esslin's dramatic conclusion: "For the dignity of man lies in his ability to face reality in all its senselessness, to accept it freely, without fear, without illusions, and to laugh at it."[8] But even dignity through absurdity cannot be sustained because of its own absurdity, and it is precisely this predicament that leads one in the writhing intellectual quests of our times to despair and feelings of emptiness.

Pertinent to the analysis of both Rieff and Esslin is an awareness of the absence of a communal and consensually valid "symbolic" or meaning within our culture. Men have taken up the quest autonomously and sought instead private symbols and meanings, frequently without avail. This is precisely the paralysis of many college students in that their suspicion of anything communal or "establishment" leads to a frantic attempt to find and do one's own thing, to say it the way it is (as I feel it). In the loneliness of idiosyncratic quests the analysis of identity formation again becomes relevant. There needs to be a reaching out beyond individuation toward participation, a rediscovery that meaning emerges most vividly within a significant group to which one belongs. In theological terms there needs to be a rediscovery of the sense of the communal, purposive participation of man as a people called and given a future. It must be the responsibility of the college to recognize this covert longing for a meaningful communal participation, a longing which student subcultures meet for only a brief period and which can lead potentially to a reawakened relevance of the church.

Feelings of loneliness, emptiness, and absurdity may lead to other student problems, such as self-destructive participation in drug experiences (sometimes a form of quest for community also), suicidal attempts, and the widest range of sexual abuses. Boredom with inert ideas or the fear that even the most respected ideas in our time lead to absurdity may drive one to seek, instead, the brilliance of experience generated within his own "expanded" mind. Whatever the authentic qualities of the drug experience, it is clear that for many it is a trap which leads down the tunnel to further despair about lack of intellectual productivity and desperate clutching at evasive "now" possibilities for relationships with persons, even though, ironically, it may have been the felt dissatisfaction with such relationships that initiated the drug usage. There is frequently a new identity problem, however, for students pulling back from drugs through the discovery of new personal or intellectual excitements. When one's life becomes so involved with friends related to the drug group, withdrawal means misunderstanding, a new kind of isolation, and a very difficult transition period, requiring an exceedingly sensitive, understanding, and reliable counselor for a period of time.

Sexual activity may also become empty insofar as the exploitive dimensions of sexual power-seeking or self-confirmation generate little real satisfaction. Permissive behavior sexually also ends in a kind of ennui that feels more futile than the loneliness which may have led to it, particularly if it means that one more route toward the potential discovery of relationships may have been cut off.

Suicide, ironically, is viewed by some students as the one possibility for a meaningful, self-controlled act in the face of overriding contingencies in our society and a behavioristic view of the determination of life so complete that one despairs of any other free act. The irony of an attempt to affirm life, freedom, and the possibility of a meaningful act in the destruction of life and hence of the potentiality of any further act is of course more apparent in detached analysis than in a desperate student's experience. Again, of course, the attentiveness, concern, and availability of a counselor are most crucial, as is his awareness that the underlying despair may run deeper than failure in academic achievement or in dating and personal relationships and may well drive to the heart of despair about the possibilities of meaning. But therein also is the potential for the discovery of meaning.

This implies that emptiness may well provide the prelude to the most hopeful development toward meaning. It entails what has been called "positive disintegration," recognizing that disintegration may occur as part of the process of the development of an ideology and hence a deeper sense of identity. This is close to a point which I have argued elsewhere,[9] namely that the full experiencing of one's inner chaos may also be a necessary experience in the process of successful therapy. In the clinical setting it may be that only after one has experienced the fearful intensity of internal conflicts and deep anxieties about helplessness, loss of control, and disintegration that he can begin to move with some surety toward reconstruction on a genuinely secure basis for ego strength.

It may in fact be difficult for counselors to allow students to live through a deeply anxiety-provoking crisis of sexual identification, fear of failure, or its concommitant fear of success and the attendant responsibility, or especially those anxieties connected with feelings of utter helplessness in relation to education or to the entire society and life itself. To be available to students in the depths of such anxious and fearful periods, however, may be of the utmost help. To avoid the temptation to short-circuiting such crises, triggered frequently by our own insecurity as counselors, may be one of the most reassuring and encouraging aspects of counseling.[10]

A few words may be in order at this point about the challenges and potentialities of behavioral approaches to counseling with students. As any observer of current psychological literature is aware, the strongest thrust in clinical practice today is in the direction of behavioral techniques, particularly systematic desensitization, aversive therapy, and other approaches based on behavioristic-oriented learning theories. Any counselor serious about working with college students should be aware of these techniques because of their demonstrable effectiveness and value in treating problems in relation to authority, to examination anxiety, to sexual phobias, etc. A challenge might be made by such behaviorists as J. Wolpe, A. A. Lazarus, and H. J. Eysenck, against the viability of a counselor's being attentive to periods of inner chaos and disintegration in working with students. It might be argued that such attentiveness would give positive reinforcement to the elaboration and extension of periods of felt emptiness, depression, and meaninglessness, and hence prolong the problem rather than help toward resolution and growth. But while such a danger must be kept in mind (and is indeed close to the psychoanalytic observation about development of neurotic dependency in transference), a more precise behavioristic observation might be that the possibilities for exploring the disturbing experiences of emptiness or conflict under the relaxed and accepting conditions of the counseling relationship would tend to juxtapose an experience of reduced anxiety with content previously highly anxiety-laden and thereby tend to extinguish much of the anxiety response. A similar observation regarding behavior therapy is that in spite of its usefulness in treating phobias and behavior disorders, the approach proves relatively unsuccessful in working with complex identity problems of college students. The construction of a meaningful orientation to oneself and one's world is an intricate and obviously more time-consuming process than the treatment of specific behavior disorders.

The movement through emptiness toward meaning has theological significance in that it involves what Tillich has called "radical faith." The feeling of emptiness and despair at the loss of meaning in life may open the possibility for a new sense of being grasped by the power of Being itself. As Tillich puts it, "As long as this despair is an act of life it is positive in its negativity."[11] It may lead to radical faith in that the student experiences the power to go on—a power which is unfathomed and hence is a faith without content save that in his own experience Being has overcome his dread of Nonbeing. Though not necessarily articulated, the hidden content of this radical faith may well be expressed as the God-above-God, the ultimate power which is the source of the courage to be: the initial, solid experience upon which new movement may be made in the affirmation of meaning that will be both durable and significant to students.

On the part of the counselor such a recognition of ontological power and healing should confirm one's trust in resources for growth and maturation which transcend the particularities of an individual counselor's skill or the variations of the therapeutic relationship. It also calls for a stance of receptivity, attentiveness, and patience, which permits even the bleakest of student experiences to be understood and accepted. It anticipates that the eventual movement of the counseling relationship will be in the direction of more constructive considerations of positive meaning in the self-identification of the student and his environmental and ontological context.

III. Nihilism and Morality

> Things fall apart; the centre cannot hold;
> Mere anarchy is loosed upon the world,
> The blood-dimmed tide is loosed, and everywhere
> The ceremony of innocence is drowned;
> The best lack all conviction, while the worst
> Are full of passionate intensity.[12]

Related to the earlier comments about emptiness and absurdity is the tendency of many students to move from their apprehension about the general state of social and political affairs to a type of nihilistic denial of any possibility of right or good in action, coupled with the attractiveness of existentialist concern, which champions spontaneity, sensuality, and immediate gratification in the present moment. This tendency toward nihilism has tempted many in the direction of Leary's beckoning, "Turn on, tune in, and drop out." The dismay about the world captured in Yeats's lines can and does lead some to the kind of despondency which generates only frustration and feelings of helplessness, at times pushing toward crippling pathological dimensions.

Unfortunately, however, the tendency of many observers when dealing with college students is to assume that such nihilism is broadly pervasive and is apparently confirmed by the anarchistic tendency of a new-Left political concern, an apparent breakdown in sexual morality and in conventional standards of dress, cleanliness, and hair styles. Fearful of institutional or personal criticism, we may find it easy to overgeneralize or rebuke such protests.

We must be extremely careful, however, to differentiate, as Kenneth Kenniston has done, between the protesting student who finds various forms of activism in which to express his dissent and the truly alienated student who will have little part in any social or political activity whatsoever.[13] Frequently the most conspicuously nonconforming student, the one who creates the most harassment for the institution and may most readily seek the services of a college counselor, may well be striving, however pathetically, with however much frustration, for some real possibilities for social change. The student who has really dropped out most likely leaves the institution and seeks his own community in the drug scene or elsewhere, and even though he may eventually return to the halls of academe and perhaps seek the services of a counselor, for the time being he is quite unwilling to seek any form of help from someone even faintly tinted with the establishment.

Furthermore, I am increasingly convinced that what appears on the surface as an amoral, nihilistic defiance of social and sexual codes may well be, under the surface, an attempt at self-purification and a deeply moral criticism of the hypocritical practices within the culture at large. What could be more telling than a dirty, bearded, and unkempt student raising ire and fear on the part of a neatly dressed, upstanding citizen, thus betraying fury against such emotional and deep-seated commitment to values of cleanliness and conventionality in the face of the agony of flagrant but subtle abuses against human dignity in the job practices, housing restrictions, and marital insensitivities in that "upright, well-kept community"? In subtle ways students seem to be attempting to call our adult world to its moral senses, even though we would like to think the adult world is trying to call youth to its moral senses. We denounce violence but blunder into a Bay of Pigs and Vietnam. We report deaths in the fighting in Southeast Asia as though they were baseball box scores. We cannot understand adolescent striving for short-range goals and inability to work for deferred gratification, yet we pollute the air and streams and disgorge our land of natural resources in the pursuit of our own short-range goals. What justice, they ask, for a student to get twenty years in prison for smoking marihuana while James Hoffa gets out in eighteen months? There is, I would argue, a rejection of hypocrisy in older sexual morality, a rejection of racial prejudice, a rejection of economic exploitation, and a rejection of violence in the settling of interpersonal and international disputes, ranging within the idealistic consciences of masses of students whom we might superficially condemn as immoral.

In the light of such an analysis the task of the college counselor must be seen as far more than a challenging and redirecting of the moral sensibilities of students. There are, I would suggest, enormous moral resources within the students themselves to which the counselor should be deeply sensitive. There is frequently a need for channeling these sensibilities, helping the student work out some consistent integrity in his own apprehension of these values, as well as some clarity in his vision of how they may be actualized. Indeed, the responsibility of the counselor may extend into the arena of political and cultural participation in the effort to clear the way for constructive activity on the part of these young men and women.

In taking this position, we may have to recognize that the new moral vision may take a shape different from the one with which we are familiar from the past. James Green of Antioch suggests one course this new vision may take.

> The moral vision that is emerging insists upon human well-being as the central moral category and requires that each law or authority justify itself through the contribution it makes to this end. It rejects the subordination of emotional, aesthetic, and sensory experience to the rational faculties, and holds that human well-being requires the cultivation of intelligence and the sensibilities, a greater capacity for rich erotic experience, heightened sensory awareness, and a cultivated aesthetic sensibility. It denies that nonaffective modes of human intercourse, mediated by decency of manners, constitute an acceptable pattern of human relations. Such modes of association, it holds, explain our tolerance of suffering and the exercise of power for merely selfish ends. Men must learn, we are being told, to develop a network of affective relationships that go beyond decency to genuine involvement in the well-being of others.[14]

The emergence of such a morality is deeply concerned with the fullness of actualization of our total being: cognitive, moral, physical, and aesthetic. It moves us in a direction that is, I believe, both theologically and psychologically profound. We are faced with a breakthrough, a new color of life, that may be redemptive in its vision of what is good both for the individual and for our culture. It may challenge the deceptions and social illusions that Freud and his followers have cautioned us against and put us in view of reality as it is. We are called to attend to that which breaks in upon us with its own power, not simply to what we want to believe or what has been convenient for us to believe in the past.

I would suggest that we are discovering a new theology of hope and revelation. God does break in upon history, and the structure and processes of Being make their own demands upon us. There are genuine moral demands to actualize life in concurrence with its created intention. This drives us to the heart of the matter in counseling college students. Through the experience of breakdown and recovery in personal or communal growth, it is evident that genuine discovery and change involve awareness that new reality has been discovered, that one has been sustained through times of fearful emptiness, that new possibilities for good have been discovered even amid the most nihilistic rejection of any structure of personal or social value.

Unless the counseling relationship with students drives to the level of such discovery and reveals for the student as well as for the counselor new potentialities for genuine life and relationship, the counselor has evaded his task. Simple advice-giving, study hints, testing and diagnosis, behavior modification—none of these may touch on the spiritual pilgrimage in which students are engaged as they move toward a morally and ideologically viable sense of their own centeredness. Only serious, attentive, sensitive, and open conversation about these more fundamental struggles of the student may be worthy of the more theologically and psychologically informed counseling encounter. Starting with whatever is presenting a problem, the counseling relation can and should move to levels of the disturbing but releasing discovery of life with a centered and meaningful identity that may not be what was expected and may not be completely finalized but may offer the undeniable assurance that the creative and healing power of life is a present reality.

"Surely some revelation is at hand." [15]

Notes

1. Tom Paxton, *Ramblin' Boy and Other Songs* (New York: Oak Publications, 1965), p. 54.
2. Joseph Heston and Willard B. Frick, eds., *Counseling on the Liberal Arts Campus* (Yellow Springs, Ohio: Antioch Press, 1968).
3. Erik Erikson, *Identity: Youth and Crisis* (New York: W. W. Norton, 1968).
4. *Ibid.*, p. 22.
5. Paul Tillich, *Systematic Theology*, III (Chicago: University of Chicago Press, 1963), pp. 38, 40-41.
6. Paul Tillich, *The Dynamics of Faith* (New York: Harper, 1958), p. 151.
7. See Philip Rieff, *Freud: The Mind of the Moralist* (Garden City, N.Y.: Doubleday, 1961), and *The Triumph of Therapeutic* (New York: Harper, 1966).
8. Martin Esslin, "Theatre of the Absurd," *On Contemporary Literature*, ed. R. Kostelanetz (New York: Avon Books, 1964), pp. 204-21.

9. William Rogers, "Order and Chaos in Psychopathology and Ontology," *The Dialogue Between Theology and Psychology*, III, ed. Peter Homans (Chicago: University of Chicago Press, 1968).
10. A further confirmation of the positive value of the experience of emptiness and disintegration can be found in recent developments in the black community in America. Erikson has pointed out that acceptance of negative identity by American Negro writers in their affirmation of the "inaudibility," "invisibility," "namelessness," "facelessness,"—"a void of faceless faces, of soundless voices lying outside history," as Ralph Ellison states it—has been crucial to the resurgence of communal identity and self-respect of the black community of America. "Acknowledging the depths of nothingness can contribute to something akin to a collective recovery." (Erikson, *Identity: Youth and Crisis*, p. 25.) This also leads us back to the individuation-participation polarity relevant to the earlier discussion and suggests that part of the discovery of communal meaning on the part of college students may emerge through such negative identity which some may mistakenly deplore as self-pity and overprotestations of technocratic subservience in a massive social and educational establishment.
11. Paul Tillich, *The Courage to Be* (New Haven: Yale University Press, 1952), pp. 175-76.
12. W. B. Yeats, "The Second Coming."
13. Kenneth Kenniston, "The Sources of Student Dissent," *Journal of Social Issues*, July, 1967, pp. 108-37.
14. James L. Green, "The New Student Morality," *Antioch Notes*, March, 1968.
15. Yeats, "The Second Coming."

Implications of Pastoral Theology for Intraprofessional Relationships

Kenneth R. Mitchell

Most discussions of pastoral work must assume for the sake of clarity that the largest and most important proportion of a minister's working relationships is with a congregation and its members. Neither new forms of ministry nor criticism of the notions of congregation and parish can entirely lead us away from the concept of a group of people who require the minister's help, his leadership, his skills, or his human understanding. The people with whom a minister works, as we meet them in most of the literature of pastoral care and pastoral theology, are seldom if ever his peers or his superiors.

Contrary to these necessary conventions in pastoral care writing, the people with whom a minister works are frequently other ministers. A future issue of *Pastoral Psychology* may some day carry a pointed editorial by Seward Hiltner entitled "How to Counsel Your Bishop," thus earning the accolade from a number of ministers. To date, however, articles about the pastoral care of bishops or of other pastors are rare. Wayne Oates compiled a book about the minister's mental health a few years ago; running throughout that book is an unspoken assumption that for the most part the pastoral care of pastors will not be done by pastors.[1]

In fact, an essay on the implications of pastoral theology for intraprofessional relationships would be limited if the dominating viewpoint lay entirely in the shepherding perspective. The organizing perspective is more attractive as a master perspective. In mentioning the organizing perspective, I am adhering carefully to Hiltner's warning that organizing "ought to mean . . . 'making into an organ,' the processes by which the organs (interconnected parts) are formed, maintained, and act, and therefore the processes by which a body is formed, maintained, and acts."[2] In this perspective, I think, we are somewhat freer than in the shepherding perspective to examine relationships within the ministry.

An organ is a collection of tissues which has a particularized function within a body. It is interconnected with the rest of the body, has its own special processes of formation and maintenance, and performs for the whole body a necessary function. We do no injustice to pastors to use the notion of an organ as a metaphor for the pastor since the pastor does work in connection with the other parts of the body of Christ, does have a particularized function, and does have his own processes of formation and maintenance.

In this essay we need to turn away from specific attention to the minister as carer and giver to look more closely at him as colleague and recipient. We shall be concerned with the processes by which the minister is formed, maintained, and acts, and with the ways in which he is interconnected with other ministers. What implications does pastoral theology have for an understanding of these connections and processes?

I. The Development of a Literature

We usually think of pastoral theology as a body of content. We do better, of course, when we remember that theology is something one does, a process. In that case, where is pastoral theology done? Leaving aside the very broad answer that it is done everywhere, we recognize that pastoral theology is largely done in two contexts: theological seminaries and clinical training centers. Pastoral theology is also done with perception and precision in some parishes, but with the exception of a few pastors the parish minister seldom sees to it that the theology he works out in the parish is transmitted beyond very local limits.

In fact, transmitting the theology we have been working out in any context has proved to be a problem. We have had to build a body of literature, much of it indigenous to the field, some of it borrowed. A very large part of that literature has come from the seminaries. Writers whose home base is a theological seminary are often rooted in speculative habits; they have often had to be pushed by a few perceptive teachers to ground their theologizing in concrete, living material. Those of us whose basic commitment is to clinical education have had a problem equally great; we have had to be pushed to write at all.

This problem has had its divisive effects. Seward Hiltner, whom I had in mind as one of the "few perceptive teachers" concerned for living material, is still accused of being too committed to the cognitive aspects of pastoral care and counseling. Similarly, many an article received by the editorial committees of the professional journals from clinical training centers betrays an enthusiasm untouched by discipline. Unfortunately some of these get printed.

Yet we have clearly *begun* to develop a literature which reflects both theological discipline and attention to the details of pastoral work. If we have not yet built a bridge between speculation and practice, at least there exist models. Students in theological seminaries are being taught to reflect theologically, ethically, and psychologically on pastoral counseling processes. Similar moves are taking place in clinical training centers, although these are somewhat limited by the traditional suspicion of intellectualizing which has long marked the clinical training movement. A patiently and painfully developed model is beginning to find use.

Here I see the first implication of pastoral theology for dealing with intraprofessional relationships. Our understanding of the issues involved in relationships between ministers is elementary. We are still at the stage of hints and helps. The development of pastoral theology implies that in order to move beyond the hints-and-helps stage it will be necessary for us to learn to look at concrete material in context and to do so with theological and psychological eyes.

Such a look at the history of the literature also reveals that pastoral theologians have had to learn what theological questions to ask. Theology does not spring full-blown out of a case study; it is the product of struggle and development. We have every reason to expect that learning to think theologically about case material will take us through the same painful growth process that has marked the development of pastoral theology. We have every reason to expect to have to learn how to ask theological questions of our material, though the way is not unlighted.

II. Examples of Case Material

There are basically four kinds of intraprofessional relationships, though one of these is specialized enough to require separate treatment. First, there are authority relationships within the ministry, such as the relationship of an assistant pastor to a senior pastor or that of a pastor to a bishop. Second, there are peer relationships as such between men who are not related to each other within a particular structure of authority. Third, there are relationships across denominational lines, which may turn out to be peer relationships in many cases but which have special features of their own. Fourth, there are educational relationships which take us into the specialized fields of theological education and continuing education.

I would like to offer the reader three vignettes, each of which illustrates one of the three relationships (continuing education excluded) and the kinds of problems which may arise in each.

An Authority Relationship

What follows is an account of a true situation. To protect the persons involved, I have taken the liberty of changing names, titles, and locations; other than that, the account appears below as the man himself wrote it. We shall call him the Bishop of Tillamook; Tillamook is a diocese of the Clatsop District of the United Evangelical Church, and the district is in turn presided over by a senior bishop. (For those with some knowledge of geography, let it be said that the actual locale of this story is *not* Oregon.)

One of the typical situations which a bishop faces is the one in which a church is divided in its support of the pastor. The case I have in mind found the church almost evenly divided on that subject, half of the people very much in favor of him and wanting him to continue as pastor of that church, and the other half very much opposed to him and wanting him to move on.

The situation was made more difficult by the unique personality of the pastor. He had the knack of winning almost worshipful devotion from those who liked him, but he would brook no opposition, and those who differed with him on any matters of church policy were given to understand that their judgment was poor and their character questionable.

Two members of the Minister's Advisory Committee called on me and gave me their grievances against the pastor, suggesting that it was time for a change. Soon after that I called on the pastor and his wife and told them that I had had some visitors and that the visitors had requested that I initiate a new call for the pastor. I avoided telling him who the visitors were or what specific things they had said. Neither he nor his wife took my visit very kindly, but their coldness to me was nothing to what happened the next Sunday. He went into the pulpit at that time and proceeded to skin his critics alive, suggesting that he knew who his critics were and what they were telling the bishop. This made it very hard for me to assure the people who had visited me that I had not violated their confidence. I finally managed to do it, however, as time went on.

Other members of the committee visited me and assured me it would be a mistake to start the call-and-transfer procedure at present, so, after consulting with Senior Bishop Jackson, I agreed not to start it. This went on for two years, and finally the situation became so divided that the future of the church was at stake. People of worth in the congregation began to take their membership elsewhere, and many anguished appeals were made to find a call for the pastor. At the same time influential people in the church told me he was the best preacher they had ever had and that he must remain. As I visited with him and his wife this time he turned his personal invective on me. Among other things, he said: "You used to be a pretty good guy, but now you have become like all those other bishops (and he named some he had dealt with); you are just a hard-boiled organization man."

I met with the Minister's Advisory Committee and found them

divided evenly just like the congregation. One man who favored the pastor said: "How can our pastor do the unkind things others report, when he is so kind and gentle to me and my family?" That was the big unanswered question in the whole matter. We seemed to have Dr. Jekyll and Mr. Hyde on our hands.

The upshot of it all was that this pastor was removed from the church he was serving, and he refused to take another pastorate.

This is the kind of situation that makes a bishop pray for wisdom and patience.

Though it will of course distort the picture somewhat, let us set aside the question of the bishop's relationships to the congregation, looking at his relationship with the minister. What is the bishop telling us about this specific relationship and the authority relationships of which it is but one? At first it appears that the bishop took immediate action; he responded to the signs of trouble. But he does not tell us what his intent was, and that is an early sign of difficulty. As we read further, the impression grows that the bishop did not know whether he intended to be a *pastor pastorum* or an administrator. In any case, he is effectively neither one, although the final action is an administrative one.

One way to look at such a problem theologically, as I have suggested elsewhere,[3] is in the light of the problem of grace and law. The bishop's approach makes us wonder if he equated grace with passivity or if he saw the use of law as a last resort. A judgment in the light of the limited data would be premature. But if the bishop did think this way, there is a theological mistake underlying his judgment. The mistake lies in conceiving of grace as absolutely antithetical to law, so that to use one's legal authority either precludes or contaminates the use of pastoral authority or even pastoral concern. Grace can and does operate within the context of legal structures; the bishop could have moved much more firmly, still exercising the pastoral concern he hoped to use. With a clearer understanding of the problem of grace and law as a point of departure, and perhaps with more precise data, a more extended analysis is possible.

Another means of analysis is available through the literature on management and the executive function. Pastoral theology has made extensive use of the psychological literature; in just such a way can ecclesiastical theology make use of the literature on management. Suppose the bishop had been familiar with Peter Drucker's contention that there are three basic misconceptions that trouble personnel administration: (1) that people do not want to work; (2) that a specialist, and not an ordinary manager, is the person to deal with problems with workers; and (3) that personnel administration is a fire-fighting or trouble-shooting procedure rather than a matter of careful planning and reliance on positive strengths.[4] If the bishop had been warned by this kind of advice from studies of management, he would have been at work with the congregation and the pastor much earlier and more constructively.

In authority relationships between ministers we have not been accustomed either to look at cognate disciplines or to examine situations with a theological framework in mind. The point of the abbreviated suggestions above is that pastoral theology has learned to do both things and that this has direct implications for the understanding of how ministers are formed, maintained, and act. I have tried to show, in the illustration above, where such a method could begin.

It should be pointed out that such a method transcends, to a large extent, the problems raised by the specific differences in polity between churches. The man we have called the Bishop of Tillamook could just as well have been a district superintendent in The United Methodist Church or the chairman of a Ministerial Relations Committee in the United Presbyterian system. With very few allowances for polity differences, the underlying dynamics of the problem are the same.

Peer Relationships

The following vignette is again a description of a real event by a participant. The material is an excerpt from a letter written by a minister to a former seminary classmate. Only a portion of the letter is reproduced; as before, some disguise has been applied.

The leader was Bill Berdon, one of the other pastors in presbytery. I guess Bill had been at one of those T-group or sensitivity training doojiggers at Spirit Lake. Anyhow, he'd convinced the council that everybody should take part in a T-group here in presbytery. I think they're planning to do one at senior high camp next summer, too. Well, they got sixteen of us together, pastors of churches in the presbytery. Everybody probably had *some* idea of what was coming off, but nobody really knew what to expect. So we began wondering aloud how we were going to begin, until Emil Greque said he was pretty bored. *That* was how we began. . . .

I didn't mean to give a blow-by-blow. What I wanted to tell you was that Jim Fress—you remember him?—came apart at the seams. Jim was always a stiff, reserved sort of guy. Hard to get to know, and standoffish, but a hardworking pastor. Well, in the name of honesty and fellowship, the group ripped into him: called him proud and snobbish, got from him a story of his adolescence which was pretty harsh and brutal, and forced out of him a confession how much he'd always hated his father. Afterwards, under a little more group pressure, Jim said it had been a real catharsis for him.

Yesterday, Jim dropped by to see me and said that in the three weeks since that sensitivity training experience, he hadn't been able to preach, had had a hell of a time with his Session, trying to tell them how unworthy and inadequate he was, and he'd just generally gone to pot. I asked him if he'd called Bill Berdon, and he said he had. Bill just told him to "hang in there, buddy," and he'd wound up thanking Bill for helping him see what an ass he'd always been.

What the hell is it that passes for honesty and fellowship, Joe? We're learning to scrape each other raw and calling it real relationship. And now presbytery wants to do it at summer camp! Meanwhile, Jim's been torn apart, and since I'm Mr. Chairman for presbytery, it's going to be my job to get help for him. He needs a psychiatrist.

Three observations can be made about peer relationships in the ministry, all three of which are in one way or another reflected in the letter excerpt above. First, there is an undifferentiated quality about peer relationships in the ministry; they tend to be vague, with little purpose agreed upon save perhaps the general ideal of "fellowship." Second, intraprofessional relationships within the ministry are frequently marked with considerable social distance, as though sometimes the minister is in too competitive a position to entrust his feelings to his peers. Third, intraprofessional relationships among peers sometimes achieve a crisis orientation in which we pay attention to one another only when a crucial moment supervenes.

Sensitivity training or other similar experiences constitute an attempt to respond to these problems in peer relationships. With roots in group dynamics and education for group leadership, sensitivity training has taken on a therapy-like appearance. The thesis seems to be that if psychological defenses are dropped, social distance will be closed, relationships will take on an intensely personal aspect, and we will pay attention to each other without waiting for a crisis to call our attention to one another.

At the same time, the letter excerpt reminds us of two major complaints leveled at sensitivity training.[5] The first complaint is that leadership tends to be inexperienced or irresponsible, or both, so that follow-up is problematic or nonexistent. The second complaint is that sensitivity training is grossly mistaken in its assumption that all defenses are bad and that the dropping of psychological defenses is an unalloyed good.

It is clear that sensitivity training for ministers is one way of trying to answer the question: How can the minister be maintained? The question refers not only to the maintenance of personal emotional health but also to the maintenance of the minister as an effective functioning organ in the whole body of the church. But the criticism says that, far from maintaining the minister, sensitivity training may just as easily destroy him or reduce his effectiveness. What implications does pastoral theology have for an examination of such a maintenance process?

One theme in pastoral theology which calls itself to our attention is the persistent challenge to various forms of imperialism. Whenever any discipline or perspective claims to be the touchstone by which other disciplines or methods must be measured, pastoral theology labels such a claim as probably imperialistic, raising serious doubts about its validity. Pastoral theology has itself gone through periods when it was tempted to turn romance into premature commitment without precise examination. There have been voices within pastoral theology at one time or another suggesting that everyone needs time in an orgone box, or that everyone needs (and can use) psychoanalysis, or that client-centered therapy is *the* method. Each time, however, a more rational voice has called for more careful examination lest a particular attitude or method imperialize its claims upon us.

This implies that we need to ask of any method which aims at altering relationships within the ministry whether enthusiasm has led to an exaggeration of claims. Sensitivity training is such a method; so is content-oriented continuing education; so is clinical pastoral education. We are reminded that we must ask whether a particular minister can make use of the kind of experience we have to offer. Some teachers and trainers have been learning to ask such a question very carefully—to wonder, for example, with a minister applying for training just what it is he hopes to derive from training. An examination of the future can be proposed, an invitation to the applicant to think together about how this experience is expected to contribute to his work as a minister or his professional relationships five years hence. All such questions are designed less to "accept" or "reject" candidates for a particular experience than to ask the leader or trainer whether the experience he wants to offer can genuinely be part of the maintenance of the minister.

Another theme which pastoral theology has raised is the question of definition of relationships: Does my functioning as pastor to another minister alter the rest of my relationship to him? This question of course also sends us back to the problem of authority relationships. It has a history, for in the canon law of the Roman Catholic Church priests who are religious superiors are forbidden to require the confessions of those who are directly responsible to them in the chain of authority. Whether there is a prior authority relationship or not, the hearing of a confession sacramentally, therapeutically, or in a sensitivity group alters the relationship between those who hear and those who confess.

This does not mean that ministries to one another should not be undertaken; it does mean that when they are undertaken, the relationship undergoes a change. It is necessary to make a careful decision with these implications in mind. In the vignette with which this section began Bill Berdon apparently tried to revert to his previous peer relationship with Jim Fress after he had led Jim to the expectation that a new relationship had begun and would be acted upon. Bill, apparently inexperienced, had moved to a pastoral relationship with Jim and had thought that he could immediately move right back out of it into an ordinary, though perhaps supportive, social relationship without going through the careful process of termination. Pastoral relationships are neither easily formed nor easily abandoned; to form them or to abandon them requires a process which has been noted, though not fully explored, in pastoral theology. Understanding intra-professional relationships requires that we pay particular attention to this process and that we explore it in more detail.

Relationships Across Denominational Lines

Relationships across denominational lines are a particularly complex form of relationships among ministers. In interdenominational relationships peerhood is challenged, its existence is rendered dubious, by our inability to accept one another's credentials. Moreover, both our differences and our similarities can become the source of subtle difficulties.

The vignette which follows, written in essay style, is derived from the notes of a supervisor in a clinical pastoral education setting. Disguise has been applied, but in addition the essential style of the writing has been altered.

The Group Concerns meeting was very lively today. After fourteen weeks of training together the men in the group are pretty deeply involved with one another. Today this involvement was shown when Eric [a Roman Catholic priest] mentioned that Christmas was coming soon and that this group felt more like a fellowship of Christians to him than the Flavians [his own religious order]. He wondered out loud if there was some way of worshiping together. The four Presbyterians in the group—Mac, Joe, Phil, and Sam—were immediately enthusiastic. So was Abe, our one Baptist. All five of them immediately began making plans for the service. In the midst of all this Warren [a Missouri Synod Lutheran] asked: "Were you guys thinking of Communion?" A little confusion, but then they said sure, why not. Warren pointed out that if it involved Communion, he couldn't take part. Some of the guys were annoyed but made it seem that it was too bad Warren's *church* felt that way. Warren picked them up on it, saying that it was not just his church but that *he* felt that way, too. By this time Eric seemed pretty confused. Here he was breaking out of the RC mold (he said) and ready to really get ecumenical in a meaningful way, and it wouldn't be the same if everybody didn't take part. No, Warren said, they should all go right ahead, and he'd be there but not take Communion. I [the supervisor] asked them why they wanted to do all this, and they seemed a little bit surprised I should ask. All fall I had been urging them to see beyond surface differences, and here they were doing just that, and here I was raising questions. I pointed out that just last week there had been some pretty hot questions dividing the group, and they'd been mad at each other, and now here was a proposal for group worship. I wondered what it meant. Sam insisted that it meant they were making real progress. They went ahead with the plans.

Later the supervisor records that the group had discussed their earlier proposal for a joint worship service and wondered how and why they had let it get away. But the group never sought again to engage in joint worship.

On the surface it might seem that the group had almost reached a high point of understanding and cooperation, spoiled only by the recalcitrance of the confessionally oriented Lutheran minister among them. The supervisor's response may seem puzzling. But in fact he remained aware of something the rest had overlooked, i.e., that the proposal was impulsive; and he was suspicious of such impulsive gestures. He was aware that the group had within it a great deal of anger, which was just beginning to be usefully expressed. He was aware that all of the others knew, whether they admitted it or not, that Warren would not be able to take part.

He was aware that Eric was in a period of hostile rebellion against his church and his order. The enthusiasm of Eric served to cover his rebellious feelings. The "forgetting" of Warren's limitations served to mask the group's moves to isolate Warren. The impulsive coming together of the group around a proposal for joint worship served as a denial of their angry feelings toward one another. The entire sequence was perhaps a scheme on the part of the group to manage their guilt while acting upon it. The hostile motivations could be denied; how could anything so obviously full of affection as an ecumenical worship service be hostile at its root? Yet without engaging in a direct interpretation and only asking a few uncomfortable questions, the supervisor reminded the men in the group of their varying attitudes toward one another.

To understand the intraprofessional relationships involved in the vignette is a problem in ecclesiastical theology. It raises questions of nourishing the growth of the men involved as Christians and as ministers. It raises questions of relating different Christian groups and their representatives to one another. It raises questions of protecting ministerial functions as well as churchly belief.

Some of the factors in the problem can be identified in familiar terms. If the church is thought of as the body of Christ, that body is marred and broken by the inability to celebrate the gospel together. For the others to regard Warren as only a wet blanket would be a theological mistake. Yet we recognize that Warren's position, a confessional position, springs from an intensely Protestant understanding of the church and that this understanding has been absolutized at many points in Protestant history. The tradition of Roman Catholic Eric, which he seemed to be studiously ignoring, has a quite different doctrine of the church, a doctrine which has also been absolutized. Eric, eager to work at relating his ministry to that of his Protestant colleagues, may have been discounting what his tradition has tried to protect, identifying much of that process as overprotection.

There is another set of factors in the problem not quite so conspicuous. Theological positions about worship were being used by these clergymen to mask their personal difficulties with one another in the group. But what they were doing was also a form of theological construction involving a doctrine of the church. They proposed to form an *ecclesiola,* a "churchlet" which would have its foundation in their current experience of one another. Just as their proposal disregarded or discounted some aspects of their respective traditions, so also it disregarded or discounted some important aspects of their relationships to one another. Their churchlet would have a rich but vague doctrine of the Holy Spirit; it would have a gravely deficient doctrine of sin precisely because it would be built upon the disregard of their own difficulties in accepting one another and working with their anger toward one another.

Notice that there is a two-way movement in the fragment above. Theological ideas cast a light on what was going on; that is movement in one direction. In the other direction a psychologically informed understanding of what was going on casts light on the theology involved in the proposal. In another excerpt the supervisor's notes make it clear that Eric was frequently in an elated mood. Elation, it is suggested in psychological literature, is a frequent mask for underlying anger and depression. A worship experience, a churchlet gathered in response to such elation, would then have within it the possibility of hidden difficulties based on anger and depression. The worship and the group as a worshiping group could both be significantly distorted. This in turn casts a new light on what Newbigin has called Pentecostal understandings of the church. As soon as we contemplate the possibility of working together as ministers, we are working in the realm of ecclesiastical theology, and we are working with some nascent doctrine of the church.

The implications of pastoral theology for this process are at least twofold. First, it has been pastoral theology which has suggested that beneath the proposals and the problems there lie personal dynamic considerations which must be considered if an adequate understanding of the relationship can ever be reached. Second, pastoral theology has consistently seen its methodology as a two-way street, previous theological formulations casting light on experience and experience, rightly understood, informing new theological construction.

III. Ecclesiastical Theology and Pastoral Theology

Intraprofessional relationships are relationships between human beings and so are subject to psychological understandings. The temptation in preparing this essay was to connect intraprofessional relationships to pastoral theology by means of the humanity of the minister, suggesting that ministers present a particular psychological picture. Instead I have chosen to look at the minister as an active part, an organ of the body which is the church. Doing so places the discussion in the organizing perspective and gives us access to the work of the minister with other ministers, which is relatively unexplored territory. The methodology of ecclesiastical theology is not yet established. Such a methodology will be more adequate if we can adapt the methods of pastoral theology and if we can learn lessons from the history of that discipline.

In the vignette involving the Bishop of Tillamook it may be important for us—and for the bishop—to gain some understanding of the motivations and problems of the parish pastor. But it is also important for the bishop to understand his own identity as a man with certain powers, to understand that these powers give rise to expectations in pastors, congregations, and bishops. The obvious contribution of pastoral theology moves us toward a pastoral understanding of the men involved. A less obvious but very important implication is that in understanding authority relationships we must make use of what theology has had to say about authority, power, and law, and their relationship to pastoral activity.

Peer relationships in the ministry are even more inchoate than authority relationships. They are handled on a variety of levels, all of which seem designed to manage the social distance and the loneliness of ministers. The vignette paid attention to one way of handling such problems. There is a reminder that more is at stake here than pastoral care of pastors, i.e., the maintenance of the minister as an effective functioning part of the church. Pastoral theology has repeatedly suggested that the *formation and termination* of special relationships which go beyond simple social relationships are crucial processes which are ignored at peril. Since we are handling many aspects of peer relationships by special methods, this warning carries over into the organizing perspective.

The search for working relationships across denominational lines is influenced by personal factors which are best known through pastoral theology. But this search is also a form of theologizing, and the theology we develop as we engage in the search must be the kind of two-way process for which pastoral theology has shown the way.

A few of the implications of pastoral theology for intraprofessional relationships have to do with content. Much more vital, however, are the implications about method. Attention to these implications is of primary importance for those of us who are seeking to understand how to form an ecclesiastical theology which will enable us to study how ministers are formed, maintained, and act.

Notes

1. Wayne E. Oates, *The Minister's Own Mental Health* (New York: Channel Press, 1961).
2. Seward Hiltner, *Preface to Pastoral Theology* (Nashville: Abingdon Press, 1958), p. 198.
3. Kenneth R. Mitchell, *Psychological and Theological Relationships in the Multiple Staff Ministry* (Philadelphia: Westminster Press, 1966), pp. 229 ff.
4. Peter F. Drucker, *The Practice of Management* (New York: Harper, 1954), pp. 276-77. Drucker's better known work, *The Effective Executive* (New York: Harper, 1967), is equally stimulating but is not so systematic a treatment of management problems.
5. "Sensitivity training" is actually a phrase denoting a certain method of group experience and group discussion. I use it here, however, to denote the whole family of techniques which use this method and a variety of others.

Preface for a Pastoral Theology of Ministry to the Dying

Thomas W. Klink

One of the striking phenomena of our days is the resurgent interest in the dying person. This concern for a proper thanatology and thanaturgy is evident even in the work of hard-nosed practitioners of the soft sciences of medicine, psychiatry, and sociology.[1]

Whatever else may be indicated, the growing corpus of reports and studies reveals that dying, like so many other activities in our culture, has been operationally rationalized. The care of the dying is increasingly the task of specially designated institutions and persons.

I. Statistics of Mortality and Other Facts Concerning Death, 1961

In the year 1961: 1,702,000 persons died; 1,037,000 persons died in hospitals or institutions; 665,000 persons died outside a hospital or institution. Only 474,000 persons who died outside a hospital or institution had had no hospital or institutional experience within the last year of life. Almost half of this group were persons whose cause of death was heart disease.[2]

Such cold statistics make it clear that modern care of the dying is preeminently the task of the short-stay medical and surgical hospital, augmented by institutions for the aged. It is now almost impossible to die at home! This means that the terminal processes of life are moving into a complicated and highly specialized institution where many forces, many persons, and many different professions are organized into social systems of interrelated work activities. Dying has become the work focus of an interprofessional "team" operation in a complex institution separated from the ordinary pre-morbid environment of the dying patient. It is as a participant in such a team operation that the modern ministry to the dying takes place. Once, the care of the dying could be subsumed under the religious categories of sacramental ministry, preparation in faith, and *diakonia* (simple, humane, compassionate care). The modern revolution in the care of the dying has made the terminal process of life more fully a technical rather than religious matter. To this process the technical methods of research, experiment, skill, specially designed tools and equipment, and programmed invention, are becoming applicable. If pastors are to be faithful both to their historic roles and their modern identity, they shall have to be more energetic in defining the functional goals of ministry, observing results, identifying unique places (as parish pastors and institutional chaplains) in a complex system, and reporting on work for the benefit of other ministers and colleagues in service for the dying. A contemporary redaction of the classic pastoral theology for ministry to the dying is necessary.

II. Four Perspectives on the Dying Patient

The encounters of the clergyman and the dying patient may be understood from four interconnected but distinctive perspectives, which are revealed in the following description.

The dying patient is one who has been ascribed a *radically new social status* on the basis of certain expectations concerning *physiological processes* within which a certain range of predictable *psychological adaptations* can be expected and which may evoke needs for a distinctive *religious ministry.* The primary perspective is the change in social status which is ascribed to the dying patient by those who are important to him or crucial to his hospital environment. The dying patient has entered upon a *career*[3] which is bounded on the one hand by a terminal prognosis and on the other by death or occasionally by the socially deviant action of unexpected recovery. (A career is a process by which a person passes from one status through a series of intermediate statuses to a terminal status. Other career processes have been designated by use of the word passage.[4])

Such generally applicable sociological concepts give expression to the basic Christian conviction that death is not a singular event but an event in a history to which the familiar theological categories of the creation, as well as the fall and the gospel, are relevant. The ministry to the dying is less a special ministry more a regular ministry in special circumstances.

III. The Central Task of the Ministry to the Dying

The first and central task of the ministry to the dying is to aid them to maintain continuity with the past in a setting of change where many forces tend to effect a radical disjunction. Many of these disjunctive forces are peculiar to the modern hospital. The claims of this central task are relevant to each of the four central perspectives on the dying patient: social, physiological, psychological, and religious.

The Affirmation of Identity in Institutional Admission. The Christian church may take pride for its part in the beginnings of special care institutions like the hospital. However, the original impetus for the church's role in hospital-founding was charitable or compassionate, not technical. The church opened its doors to persons who were afflicted and offered them the opportunity to affirm their religious identity by bringing their distresses to such-and-such an institution. To enter a hospital was an affirmation of identity; only secondarily was it a search for competent technical assistance.

Implications of admission today are radically different. Referral to a hospital, whatever the name over the door or on the chapel hymnal, is referral for some measure of secular competence. Such expertise is secured at the price of entering an institution which has its own distinctive character and tends to take away from patients their life-sustaining extramural identities, giving them new designations in keeping with their demands upon the technical care system of the hospital. This fact is true of all patients, but it becomes of critical significance for the dying patient who, in addition to his own identity, must take on the onerous task of assuming a sharply new identity as a specifically mortal man.

The Role of Denial in Dying. One of the most massive and effective constructs of human society and personality is that which denies human mortality. We are all going to die! Mortality is a quality of human life. Yet although we concede intellectual assent to the general proposition, we are socially and conventionally supported in our denial of the specific personal application of the general proposition. Having given up the phrases of conventional piety ("If I should die before I wake . . ."), we lack even such reminders of mortality.

We have disconnected the general proposition concerning human mortality from its personal application by an adverbial omission. In a legislative metaphor, we "strike the enacting clause" by omitting the adverb for "when." This is such a useful trick! It makes it possible, for example, for a man writing about dying to type away on a manuscript with cigarette in mouth and a package labeled, "Caution: Cigarette smoking may be hazardous to your health," lying longside the machine. The structure of denial is a sturdy edifice! Masserman has called this one of the (creat)*ur*(e) defenses of mankind.[5]

Immense personal and social profit from denial sustains such a widespread enterprise. Disconnection of the general fact of mortality from the specific prospect of personal death is a highly productive act in the social and psychological economy of the human race. Five "gains" can be cited:

1. The appropriate and fundamental human anxiety about mortality is time-bound to an indefinite future time.
2. The relative equality of demand and responsibility, imposed by a society on all its members, is maintained without complicated exceptions.
3. The denial of death and the segregation of those who are not susceptible of such denial maintains general social discipline

for as many as possible, for as long as possible, in as many situations as possible.

4. Maintenance of investment of personal energy in ordinary tasks and relationships is supported by denial of death.
5. The favored self-image of the hospital and its personnel—as a place where people go to "get better"—is maintained by the denial of death as long as possible.

The hospital, like any institution which supports such denial, shares in the profits derived. On occasion, however, and with increasing frequency, the hospital is appointed to the radically different function of disrupting the denials and connecting the general proposition of mortality to a specific individual. The hospital launches a few persons on the career of dying, a novel work status calling for varying outputs of behavior in a strangely novel role.[6]

IV. The Social Perspective on Dying in a Hospital

The entry event to the career of dying is a social event. On the basis of general technical knowledge someone makes, more or less accurately and more or less explicitly, a temporal connection between the acknowledged general proposition of mortality and personal death. This act ascribes to the terminal patient a new status, a new identity, and implies expectations of new behavior over some newly defined period of time. This ascription of new status may be accomplished by a variety of persons and actions within a variety of interactional systems. It may be accomplished by a hematologist consultant, reading the early and obscure indices of a malignant leukemia and communicating his expectations to the physician in charge. It may be accomplished by a surgeon, discovering an inoperable metastasis of a cancer, deferring prognosis to the patient, but communicating the new status in an informal aside to the chaplain. The new status may be ascribed and communicated to the family and validated by a revealing change in visiting regulations. A cardiologist can report on a morbid prognosis by changing the orders for nursing care with or without communication to the patient or family except for careful outlining of the regimen "most likely to help this very serious heart condition." The new status may be ascribed by a forthright and detailed report to the patient, indicating the malign process and outlining the expected course of the disease plus any palliative or management prospects. The new status, especially in the case of those without apparent capacity to understand or with young children, may be communicated to one or more members of the responsible family, leaving with that person the choice of further dissemination of the information. And so on.

These various combinations of possibility in communicating the new status of the dying patient are intended to make clear what Glaser and Strauss have called "awareness contexts." They make it clear that the simple platform question, "Should the dying patient be told?" is only a platform issue. Reality is far more complex: What shall the dying patient be told when, by whom, in what detail, and who else shall be told under what restrictions of repetition and within what projection of time and details about the course of illness? Glaser and Strauss conclude that the best care of the dying—and the best utilization of family and other personnel—creates the least discrepancy of "awareness context" between all those involved. They observe that no matter what the formal policies of the hospital or physician in charge, there is an observable set of informal actions which serve to reduce discrepancy, effect a greater mutuality of awareness, and create a new system of cues and expectations for all involved.

However the communication of new status is achieved, whatever the voice which carries the message, despite the physiological content of the information, the first effect of the message is social: in radical disjunction from the previous pattern of denial and in interruption of previous identity or present hope, the terminal patient is given a new status. In hospitals, as might be expected from so rationalized a social system, this ascriptive process is often highly ritualized.

Initial Impact of Ascription of Dying Status. Rarely does the communication of a terminal prognosis create promptly and easily a whole new set of adaptive and appropriate relations. There is the stubborn and well-reinforced pattern of denial—in the patient and in the others around him. Furthermore, the stubbornly empirical character of medical practice means that the prognosis tends to be initially conditional, statistical, or just humble. Ample room is left for hope, denial, doubt, change. Encouragement may be given—unintentionally perhaps—for the patient to seek another doctor or hospital or even to find a place where "they have had good results" with his disease. Such conditional projections of the diagnosis may be reinforced by an undercurrent of magical religious expectations, and miraculous divine intervention may be the focus of defense against the new status and its demanding schedule of work.

The primary impact of the ascription of new status is the experience of change and the prospect of new work, illustrated in the following statement of a state hospital patient following an exploratory surgery which had revealed an inoperable malignancy. His words are illustrative of the situation for many other, psychologically more defended patients:

Patient: I feel like I'm a new man with a big work to do and I don't have to be crazy anymore; I'm finished with that. I've got to die and I'll have to work hard to get that done. Maybe you can help me.

The patient says in his own way exactly what a newly moved housewife might say about her status: "I've just moved into this new house. There are all kinds of changes for us and lots of work too. I haven't even met my new neighbors. I'm not sure where to start or even where to find reliable help." Less forthright—but more familiar to most of us—is the reaction of a nonpsychotic but terminally ill patient:

Patient: Look at those damned flowers and cards. I feel as though everything had changed. There are people sending me cards and flowers who wouldn't have given me the time of day, last week.

Pastor: It hits you just like an unexpected transfer would hit a man on a new job. Everybody expects something from you, and they all look different from this new spot.

Patient: That's sort of it. (*Almost playfully in tone.*) It's even hard to be sure who I am any longer when everybody acts so differently all of a sudden.

The Task of Maintaining Continuity. The first working task for the dying patient is to establish and maintain some sense of continuity with his past in his new and disjunctive status. The central strategy of the ministry is to aid the patient to resist the excommunicating and estranging effects of his new status and new milieu. This strategy is accomplished by (1) symbolic continuities with the past such as are represented by the sacrament of Communion and visiting by a representative of the extramural community of faith, (2) by conversational methods in which the patient is aided to reintegrate his self-understanding in the light of his past and in the face of his present, and (3) by methods, both conversational and administrative, which aid the patient to clarify for himself and with significant others the probable events and stresses of his anticipated career as a dying patient.[7]

V. The Physiological Perspective on the Dying Patient

The physiological perspective on the dying patient, however central for others, is not the primary concern of the pastor. We need, however, some point of view for assimilating the multiple evidences of physiological change. The physiological aspects of terminal illness also constitute a disjunctive force threatening the carefully established continuities of the self. Every adult person has had some considerable previous experience in meeting disruptive physiological changes. The paradigmatic event is puberty—another radical transformation of the physical self, fraught with complex psychological significance, associated with a sharply different social status, and calling for major effort to assimilate. Formally, not factually, dying is like puberty and adolescence.

The formal equivalence of puberty and dying suggests that

the person has had previous experiences which may permit him to cope on the basis of previously learned adaptive methods. Any experience in which the patient has successfully mastered radical change is a noteworthy asset in coping with death: occupational change, social revolution, emigration and settlement, traumatic injury and recovery, previous hospitalization for himself or serious illness in others.

The central strategy for ministry regarding physiological change is to use the pastoral relationship to aid the patient to assimilate without estrangement from self or others the physiological changes which accompany the course of illness. The central tactic is *conversation concerning the body*, the casual day-to-day report of pain and relief, strength and weakness, function and incapacity, plus the emotionally lively *celebration of the enduring person in a changing body*. Indications of the experience of alteration in physical state are important. The lively assimilation of change—as contrasted with the stoic endurance of new conditions—is the heart of the process.[8] Such assimilation and celebration most often emerge from an alert awareness to physical metaphors.

Pastor: Good-morning, Mr. Z.

Patient: Hello. (*Weakly.*) I'm not much good today. That pain in my shoulder has been worse.

Pastor: Like always, good days and bad, but today, especially bad in the shoulder.

Patient: Yeh, it's not easy.

Pastor: Darkness and light, strength and weakness?

Patient: It was worse last night, early morning.

Pastor: Still rough but better than then. Busy work and rest. It's all happened before, and by God's grace you have been his child, Charles, through all the changes. . . .

We give thee thanks, O God, wearily, that thou hast made us creatures of flesh wherein we have known joy and relief as we have known weariness even pain. Help us to trust thy creation even as we trust thee. Amen.

This conversation reveals how physiological change presents itself to the pastor—as the experience of singular pain and change which can be related to previous experiences of altered bodily state or may continue to distress as a disturbingly novel event. With a few patients we can shorthand the conversational process if they have been excellently trained in the highly symbolic and abstract words or sacraments of religious celebration. For most patients, however, there is no short-cutting the search for the metaphor of bodily and present event in which the enduring and living Word can be preached.

The Pastor and the Practical Theological Problem of Pain. The central Christian attitude about the reality of pain was made clear in the third century in the bitter debates over the heresy of Docetism. The credal "suffered under Pontius Pilate" makes clear that there is an ineradicable distinction between denial of the reality of pain and Christian hope and comfort in the midst of pain.

However clear the doctrine, the pastor discovers denial and hope confusingly intertwined, one of the psychological results of dying. The experience of pain tends to narrow the span and range of attention: "I was hurting so bad I couldn't think of anything else." Attention is narrowed and focused on the pain; the alarm signals of pain become all-demanding. Yet for the terminally ill patient there are very few actions within his power to respond to the alarm of pain and relieve the distress. In this situation the pastor can function to support any evidences in the patient of his discrimination in attention to pain. His words or actions do not attempt to deny or minimize the pain; it is one of the facts of life into which our Lord also was born. But the pastor communicates a faith that the pain is to be attended to as *one* of the facts of life, not its supreme reality. He supports the patient's marginal mastery of pain by supporting his attention to the fuller panorama of experience in his present situation in the concrete language which the pain-burdened can hear.

VI. The Psychological Perspective on Dying

The anxiety associated with dying is precipitated by physiological signals of danger, by the anxiety of disorientation (confusion), by the demand for object disengagement, by the threatened return of long-repressed psychological materials, and by the necessity to cope with critical adaptive problems in the novel setting of a hospital where long-distance controls, minimum feedback, and dependence upon strangers are the necessitated style. Each of these elements is significant in the preface to a pastoral theology for ministry to the dying patient.

Let me illustrate my point by a wild fantasy. Imagine yourself in a dreamlike urgent state, seated in the backseat of a strange, high-powered, rental car, maneuvering down an unfamiliar road toward a dimly conceived destination where you must disengage yourself from the vehicle. You control by the use of a pair of strings tied to the wheel; one of them looks strangely like a bell cord, but response to pushing the button is often delayed. There are also flexible poles for accelerator and brake. Some of the scenes along the road remind you of pleasant places in the past; some scenes are reminiscent of past trouble. You cannot decide whether to pause or to accelerate. As in all dreams, strange things happen. Your passage down the road is marked from time to time by the arrival and departure of various persons—nurses, doctors, family, friends, clergymen—they come and go while you stay. You give them messages, and promptly or with delay they report that they have done well. At other times they reveal that they have done ineptly the errand you commissioned. Finally, while still moving at top speed, a traffic policeman pulls alongside and asks you for your name and license and inquires, "Do you know what you're doing?"

This anxious fantasy is a parable in grossest caricature of the central situation of anxieties for the dying patient: the anxiety of strangeness and disorientation, the anxiety associated with dependence upon others who perform with varying degrees of proficiency, the anxiety of reminiscences—the return of forgotten or repressed memories, the anxiety of danger and inadequate controls, and the anxious pressure to disengage oneself from an attractive but time-limited possession of a vehicle. This is a parable in caricature, composed specifically to highlight the multiple sources of anxiety for the dying patient.[9]

VII. The Spiritual Perspective on the Dying Patient

The spiritual perspective on the dying patient is summary and reiteration in faithful terms of the experiences of the Word-made-flesh in living history. Erik Erikson's eight stages of man end in the stage which he describes as the tension between "ego integrity and despair."

> Only in him who in some way has taken care of things and people and has adapted himself to the triumphs and disappointments adherent to being, the originator of others or the generator of products and ideas—only in him may gradually ripen the fruit of these seven stages. I know no better word for it than ego integrity. Lacking a clear definition, I shall point to a few constituents of this state of mind. It is the ego's accrued assurance of its proclivity for order and meaning. It is a post-narcissistic love of the human ego—not of the self—as an experience which conveys some world order and spiritual sense, no matter how dearly paid for. It is the acceptance of one's one and only life cycle as something that had to be and that, by necessity, permitted of no substitutions: it thus means a new, a different love of one's parents. It is a comradeship with the ordering ways of distant times and different pursuits, as expressed in the simple products and sayings of such times and pursuits. Although aware of the relativity of all the various life styles which have given meaning to human striving, the professor of integrity is ready to defend the dignity of his own life style. . . . For he knows that an individual life is the accidental coincidence of but one life cycle with but one segment of history; and that for him all human integrity stands or falls with the one style of integrity of which he partakes. The style of integrity developed by his culture or civilization thus becomes the "patrimony of his soul," the seal of his moral paternity of himself. . . . In such final consolidation, death loses its sting.

The lack or loss of this accrued ego integration is signified by fear of death: the one and only life cycle is not accepted as the ultimate of life. Despair expresses the feeling that the time is now short, too short for the attempt to start another life and to try out alternate roads to integrity. Disgust hides despair, if often only in the form of "a thousand little disgusts." . . .

Webster's Dictionary is kind enough to help us complete this outline in a circular fashion. Trust (the first of our ego values) is here defined as "the assured reliance on another's integrity," the last of our values. I suspect that Webster had business in mind rather than babies, credit rather than faith. But the formulation stands. And it seems possible to further paraphrase the relation of adult integrity and infantile trust by saying that healthy children will not fear life if their elders have integrity enough not to fear death.[10]

Notes

1. Herman Feifel, *The Meaning of Death* (New York: McGraw-Hill, 1959); Adriaan Verwoerdt, *Communication with the Fatally Ill* (Springfield, Ill.: Charles C. Thomas, 1966); Sigmund Freud, "Thoughts for the Time on War and Death," *Complete Psychological Works*, Vol. XIV (London: Hogarth Press, 1957); Kurt Eissler, *The Psychiatrist and the Dying Patient* (New York: International Universities Press, 1955); D. McK. Rioch, "The Psychophysiology of Death," *The Physiology of Emotions* (Springfield, Ill.: Charles C. Thomas, 1961), p. 181; A. D. Weisman and T. P. Hackett, "Predilection to Death and Dying as Psychiatric Problems," *Psychosomatic Medicine*, XXIII (1961), 232; "On Death and Dying," *Chicago Theological Seminary Register* (special issue), December, 1966; Robert Fulton, ed., *Death and Identity* (New York: Wiley, 1965); Barney G. Glaser and Anselm L. Strauss, *Awareness of Dying* (Chicago: Aldine, 1965); *Time for Dying* (Aldine, 1968).
2. "Hospitalization in the Last Year of Life," *Vital and Health Statistics*, September, 1965, pp. 14-15, 18, 30.
3. See Everett Hughes, *Men and Their Work* (New York: The Free Press, 1958); Fred Davis, *Passage Through Crisis* (Indianapolis: Bobbs-Merrill, 1963); Arnold Gennepp, *Rites of Passage* (Chicago: University of Chicago Press, 1960).
4. Erving Goffman, "The Moral Career of a Mental Patient," *Psychiatry*, May, 1959, p. 123; Thomas W. Klink, "The Career of Preparation for the Ministry," *Journal of Pastoral Care*, Winter, 1964, p. 200.
5. Jules H. Masserman, "Faith and Delusion in Psychotherapy," *American Journal of Psychiatry*, CX (1953), 324.
6. Glaser and Strauss, *Awareness of Dying* and *Time for Dying;* also Renee Fox, *Experiment Perilous* (New York: The Free Press, 1959).
7. Fred Davis, "Definitions of Time and Recovery in Paralytic Polio Convalescence," *American Journal of Sociology*, March, 1956, pp. 582-87; "Uncertainty in Medical Prognosis," *American Journal of Sociology*, July, 1960, pp. 41-47;

also A. N. Exton-Smith, "Terminal Illness in the Aged," *Lancet*, August 5, 1961, pp. 305-8; B. G. Glaser and A. Strauss, "Temporal Aspects of Dying as a Nonscheduled Status Passage," *American Journal of Sociology*, June, 1965; Austin Jones, P. M. Bentler, and Georgia Petry, "The Reduction of Uncertainty Concerning Future Pain," *Journal of Abnormal Psychology*, LXXI, 87-94; Julius Roth, *Timetables: Structuring the Passage of Time in Hospitals and Other Careers* (Indianapolis: Bobbs-Merrill, 1963).

8. R. G. Barker *et al.*, *Adjustment to Physical Handicap and Illness* (New York: Social Science Research Council, 1953); D. A. Hamburg and D. Z. Lebowit, "Coping Behavior Under Extreme Stress," *Archives of General Psychiatry*, V, 423; D. A. Hamburg, *Psychological Adaptive Processes in Life-threatening Injuries* (Washington: National Research Council, 1953); V. A. Rosen, "Role of Denial in Acute Post-operative Affective Reactions Following Removal of Body Parts," *Psychosomatic Medicine*, XII, 356-61; H. Shands, "An Outline of the Process of Recovery from Severe Trauma," *A.M.A. Archives of Neurology and Psychology*, LXXIII, 403-9; J. C. Zinker and S. L. Fink, "The Possibility of Psychological Growth in a Dying Person," *Journal of General Psychology*, April, 1966, pp. 185-200; Thomas W. Klink, "The Pastor and the Crisis of Involution," *Journal of Pastoral Care*, XIII, 24-30.
9. Elaine Cummings and William E. Henry, *Growing Old: Process of Disengagement* (New York: Basic Books, 1961); E. Cummings, "Disengagement, an Approach," *Sociometry*, XXIII, 23-35.
10. Erik Erikson, *Childhood and Society* (New York: W. W. Norton, 1950), pp. 268-69.

The North Woods Revisited: New Developments in Guiding

Frank M. Bockus

"Seated at the typewriter in a shack at the middle of the island, surrounded by spruce and fir and pine trees and with a distant view of the water"—thus wrote Seward Hiltner in describing the setting in which his *Preface to Pastoral Theology* was written. No doubt richly inspired as he looked out on the view of MacMahan Island, Maine, he spun a vivid analogy between a guide to the North Woods and one to the spiritual life:

> Assume that we contemplate a trip through the North Woods and want a guide. From this guide we shall expect certain things: familiarity with the terrain, with dangers peculiar to the region, with the kinds of animals that may be hunted and the conditions pertinent to each, and the like. On other matters we rightly expect him to know more than we do.
>
> About other things, however, our knowledge is greater than that of the guide, and we rightly expect him to pay attention to us at these points. Even though one animal is plentiful and easy to find, we may have good reason for wishing to seek another that is more elusive. We may have an allergy to the material contained in the kind of sleeping bag the guide recommends, and we shall expect him as a result to take second choice. However superior may be the guide's general knowledge of trips like this through this general terrain with such people, there are crucial points to which the guide's general knowledge is not relevant unless it is supplemented by specific knowledge of us, our goals and our idiosyncrasies. In order to be a guide, he does not have to coerce us, or ignore us, or override us.[1]

In elaborating his analogy Hiltner points out that the spiritual guide too must achieve a delicate balance between his general knowledge and his parishioner's inner needs. Basically, guiding is eductive, for it presupposes a person's deeply felt need and receptivity to help and draws forth his actual or potential internal resources. Reliance upon external means such as coercion or persuasion is rejected. Furthermore, as Hiltner conceives it, guiding pursues the welfare of the individual or the small group and is thus distinguished from efforts to preserve the interests of the wider community.

Any truly reliable guide, including one in matters spiritual, needs an occasional refresher course to keep his general knowledge up to date. And in that spirit of continuing education, with which Hiltner assuredly concurs, we shall here examine some recent developments in guiding and their implications for churches and clergymen. *I believe that the neighborhood congregation, through a ministry of guidance in family relations and child development, is uniquely situated to contribute to the development of mental health.* Specifically, we shall consider (1) the importance of an open style of family relationships in mental health development and the prevention of illness and (2) a model of guiding suited to churches and clergymen through which this more open way of life can be taught.

I. Mental Health: An Open Pattern of Adapting

The most common denominator of human development is change. During the cycle of life persons pass through a series of critical stages and transitional episodes. As Erik Erikson puts it:

> The healthy child, if halfway properly guided, merely obeys and on the whole can be trusted to obey inner laws of development, namely those laws which in his prenatal period had formed one organ after another and which now create a succession of potentialities for significant interaction with those around him.[2]

Beyond the larger stages in the life cycle and within them there are other, briefer crises. Such critical incidents can take many different forms. Some are primarily events that are biologically determined, such as birth, puberty, pregnancy, or old age. Other acute episodes are more socially or culturally defined. These are transitional moments in the life history, such as going to school for the first time, to college, to military service, or to one's first job. Quite often these critical incidents cluster around some important loss in the individual's life such as the death of a loved one or the end of a long-cherished but unattained goal.[3]

Obviously such crises upset an individual's normal life balance. Facing novel situations with demands for which old patterns are untested, an individual may easily and normally become confused and unsure of himself. During such an episode he may feel anxious and disorganized. This state is a normal response to a disquieting situation. His usual mode of living in upheaval, a person is faced with challenges to which he must respond, and his response can be either maturing or weakening.

In growing up, people appear to learn different ways of adapting to life's critical moments. Generally speaking, persons—or groups, such as the family—who cope with these occasions most creatively seem to face them openly for what they are. They persist in grappling with their problems by openly confronting the frustration and confusion that go with them. Furthermore, they are not ashamed to express their feelings and to share their anxiety and distress with family members and friends. They are not reluctant to seek help. In fact, they often ask others to help them clarify the crisis and to provide guidance.

For persons who take this approach the critical episode, in retrospect, seems temporary and understandable. They feel a sense of mastery and satisfaction in resolving the crisis. Moreover, having learned the resources to draw upon in one moment of crisis, a person acquires a style for approaching later times of disjuncture. In one sense successful adapting is cumulative. However, we should hasten to add that a given crisis, under certain circumstances, may tend to overthrow the resources of anyone.

But other people seem to learn another course for meeting life and its changes. Theirs is a more closed mode of adapting. Crises are denied in a number of ways. Gritting his teeth, the individual staunchly tries to make old patterns fit new situations. Feelings of anxiety and confusion are repressed, or at least they are left undisclosed. Perplexed and disorganized, the individual tries to live as if he were not so. Cut off from himself, he also becomes withdrawn from others. They cannot help.

This latter route seems destined toward a sense of isolation and loneliness. Furthermore, the individual may feel that he alone suffers from such uncertainties and doubt, and thus he begins to feel different from others around him. He comes to feel generally that others are more adequate in life than he. A heightened image of others is set alongside a diminished sense of self.[4]

Inherent in these existential moments in the life history are profound questions of ethics and morality. Such critical episodes demand value judgments and commitments. Often they require binding choices about life's meaning and purpose. Moreover, many of the issues implicit in these transitional stages are frightfully ambiguous. They are the perplexities of man living in the modern world—the meaning of suffering and death; morality upheavals in a culture of change; conflicts between technology and human sensibilities, war and peace, racial and class justice—the list could go forward at length. All profoundly moral concerns, they lift before contemporary man some of the most ancient dilemmas of human existence.

The hothouse atmosphere in which many if not most of these developmental crises are faced is the primary setting of the family. There in the often tacit but emotionally tinged assumptions and expectations of family relationships, personality is shaped. Incidents taken by themselves seem relatively insignificant, but their cumulative impact is potent.

Once ambiguous questions are raised in family relationships, together with the disquieting and ambivalent emotions they arouse, several things can happen and often do. Family members become completely cut off from one another, quit listening, or subtly try to coerce one another into feeling differently. Unsure of their own beliefs and convictions about some of these issues, they attempt to dodge the conflict. Talking too knowingly or self-confidently, not talking at all, or insisting that one's own views be adopted are often good clues to doubts and anxieties about the matter at hand. Particularly do these concealing mechanisms become operative at times when adults seek to protect younger children from exposure to some of life's harsher realities, such as death, suffering, or violence.

In recent years one family therapist and educator has explored in depth the problem of parental vulnerability, as he refers to it. He has discovered that quite often parents cannot talk with their children about some deeply personal matter of life, some experience about which they themselves are perplexed or squeamish. Troubled by such problems when they arise in parent-child relationships, they pretend greater certainty than they truly possess, or in the name of sheltering the child from pain, they avoid the issue. In actuality, of course, they are protecting themselves from the onrush of disturbing and disquieting ambiguity.

His investigations have disclosed further significant findings. Indirectly, parents who remain concealed teach their children a closed way of life. The unnerved and unperturbed parent tends to evoke feelings of uncertainty in the child. On the other hand, that parent who is able to remain transparent with his child, who can remain open and exploratory about problems of value and morality, tends to be reassuring. In learning that his parents face problems and feelings similar to his own, a child comes to regard his own experiences as normal and human. In short, that parent who openly faces critical episodes with frank expression of feeling and mutual openness tends to exert a humanizing effect on his child.[5]

It seems obvious, therefore, that the maximal learning moment in psychosocial development lies within these critical episodes. They are, generally speaking, common to all men. The conflict and the coping that accompany them are both normal and appropriate. During such times persons acquire the attitudes and mind-sets with which they face life and its changes. To put it briefly, it is during such moments that persons can learn the open approach to life so necessary in today's changing world.

II. Teaching Openness in the Neighborhood Congregation

In October of 1963 Congress enacted legislation which set our society on new directions in the field of mental health. "A bold new approach"—as President Kennedy described it in his message proposing the program—the new philosophy sought to end the practice of "putting them away," meaning the humiliating and debilitating process of removing persons from their families, jobs, and communities. The community mental health movement places stress on providing care for all people within the community and on doing so on a comprehensive basis. Rich and poor, young and old, transient or resident—all are best served by programs tailored to meet their needs as soon and as specifically as possible. By conserving an individual's resources, he can be helped back to his feet in the shortest period of time and with a minimum amount of loss.

One of the truly challenging opportunities afforded by the new community mental health program lies in the area of primary prevention. Here emphasis shifts from the alleviation of symptoms or the treatment of illness to the development of mental health in the community. Primary prevention is concerned with identifying and modifying those harmful factors within the community which influence large numbers of people toward illness.

But primary prevention in its most positive sense entails the construction of adequate human development systems in the community. It seeks to provide those resources which are necessary for healthful human growth. One social scientist puts it in this somewhat simplified but clarifying way:

1. There are identifiable critical stages that individuals must pass through.

2. At each stage there are critical inputs from the environment which the individual must receive if he is to pass through that stage successfully.
3. At each stage there are possibilities of either too much or too little of the critical input.
4. There are identifiable diagnostic symptoms that reveal that too-muchness or the too-littleness.[6]

We have already said in our earlier discussion that the psychosocial inputs so necessary to mental health development are provided primarily through interpersonal, emotionally charged family relationships. It follows therefore that the fundamental setting for primary prevention and mental health development lies within such critical incidents in family relationships. It is within this milieu that the normal crises of life are encountered. It is here too that the incipient or early stages of inappropriate emotional conflict often originate.

We can conclude that a basic model of primary prevention consists of providing support systems to families during normal critical episodes in life. Learning groups in such human development guidance can take many shapes, depending upon the particular developmental stage under exploration. Topics for consideration focus around the thoughts, feelings, values, and conflicts of people facing common human situations. Young couples to be married, newlyweds, or older partners who wish to strengthen their communication; parents with young children or parents with youth; youth facing the decisions of college, first job, marriage, military enlistment, and so forth—in each instance groups are focused around a common transitional episode to be examined together.

The neighborhood church, characterized to a considerable extent by its nearness to the residential sector of life, can play a major role in fashioning these human development environments. Simply from a spatial standpoint, the church geographically is often close to the family circle wherein mental health development occurs. Moreover, from a cultural viewpoint the church is intrinsically identified with human development values. Many of the sacraments of religion are clustered around life's critical moments, such as birth, marriage, and death. In addition, through its ministries of family life and child development the church possesses vast resources for human development guidance.

There will be many, no doubt, who will shy away from such proposals about the church's human development ministry. Some people believe, with some justification, that the church has bogged down with just such emphases in the past. Or they feel that when the church did undertake such endeavors it performed very badly and often did more harm than good. But these bygone deficiencies do not eliminate the lingering need for the church to strengthen its human development resources.

According to one national study of American mental health, 42 percent of those persons who seek outside help with their problems consult a clergyman first.[7] Most of the people seen by ministers in marriage or family counseling are not mentally ill. They are, in fact, quite normal by most man-in-the-street standards. But they often have come to believe that deeply felt anxieties and uncertainties are to be kept inside. In so doing they cut themselves off from deeper levels of human interaction and consequently come to feel lonely and isolated. In counseling, such persons begin to unlearn earlier patterns of living. By daring to share their uncertainties in a trusting relationship, by opening their confusing and disorienting feelings to others, they discover their common humanity. Life's perplexities do not go away. But in experiencing them they stop feeling so different and isolated. Here is the way one man expressed it during the final session of a church counseling group:

> As far as our group is concerned, it has helped me relax, if that's the way to describe it. For the past ten years I kept myself locked in a shell and felt that I was the only one unhappy, that nobody else was unhappy. I was not able to communicate and became a little cynical. After I came here and heard everyone else talking about his most

intimate problems, well, I was just able to relax as I never had before, and to communicate.

Or in the words of another participant in the same group:

Part of the problem is that when a person starts experiencing difficulties, he is inclined to feel deep inside that he is different and that everybody else is more adequate and happy, and able to work things out smoothly. He feels different and isolated, inadequate to cope. But here, in this sharing, I find that other people are just like me.

Professional psychosocial resources need no longer be confined to times of acute crises. In one sense the therapeutic benefit of counseling comes in unlearning a closed mode of life and in discovering an open one. I am proposing, to repeat, that such openness can be taught and that the teachable moment comes during the normal crises of life. In this human development model the clergyman steps across the thin line from counseling to guidance. This new educator will be equipped with the traditional skills of counseling, depth listening, and communicating. But he will need to apply these resources in group process with normal families.

Audio and video recordings, traditionally the tools of clinical and supervisory settings, become curriculum media in human development guidance. Quite often such emotionally laden material can quickly evoke empathic responses and provide common frames of reference for group members. One psychiatrist-turned-educator, together with a team of technicians from WGBH-FM in Boston, has produced a series of imaginative media for use in teaching the psychodynamics of family relationships. This *Chance to Grow* program, consisting of eleven high-fidelity records, was produced out of interviews with families facing normal though critical transitions in life. In one, for example, a son faces military enlistment. In another a young man copes with an adjustment to his first job. In yet another, parents and graduating high school seniors discuss their aspirations and expectations for forthcoming years of college.[8]

That media like these have burst into public visibility is indicative of reassuring shifts in our cultural outlook regarding mental health. Once we were more inclined than now to regard mental unrest as a sign of abnormality. We believed that crisis with its disorienting and unsettling character was grist for the clinical setting or the mental hospital. Today disquieting emotions can be expressed more openly. Such feelings are regarded as appropriate to the life situation at hand.

In these proposed human development learning groups there are some secondary advantages consistent with a primary prevention goal. Often in the community there are people who experience mild degrees of emotional conflict but who have no place to turn for help. Such people are not disturbed to a debilitating degree. They really do not need the help of a professional psychotherapist. At the same time, their unrest bears the seeds of more acute crisis. Human development groups can provide an outlet for such people. Such groups can provide the avenue through which these individuals can gain access to pastoral counseling or other means of help.

A further gain of such learning groups lies in cross-cultural confrontation between different families in the community. In our urban environment, fragmented as we are into levels of age, race, class, and culture, the church at its best could be the very kind of community toward which much of our present social planning is taking us. More often than not, groups from the gilded ghettos of suburbia and the grimy ghettos of the inner city have no way to bridge their differences. Yet they face similar needs within a common life cycle. Through the use of audio and video recordings in human development groups it is possible, for instance, to expose the suburban family with its attitudes and environment to those of its neighbor family in the ghetto—and vice versa.

In our pluralized and rapidly changing world man is developing a kind of experimental style of life. As cultural traditions, values, and mores give way, we have come to expect both change and crisis. We now regard change and conflict as normal ingredients of human existence. In such a world the character ideal of human development is the open self, one who has the capacity to cope creatively with change. In all probability, in tomorrow's world the mentally healthy individual will be he who is able to face change and crisis openly and confidently. For some of us this entails considerable unlearning, a breaking loose from a closed mode of living. For nearly all of us, it means learning a great deal anew.

Furthermore, such an open and experimental approach to life, I believe, is quite consistent with a biblical point of view. Biblical writers, above all else, looked on man's character as the clue to his religion, to his values and deepest loyalties. His beliefs and actions issue forth in the way he lives. A closed life style, so the biblical writer thought, is an indication of a person whose life is oriented around a false god. He has ceased to change, to meet life's novelty and possibilities. An open person who trusts in the one God, Yahweh, so he thought, seeks constantly to break out of closed attitudes and mind-sets in order to meet life freshly. Knowing that reality is both complex and everchanging, he tries to keep himself open to the disclosure of new life.

If we can increase our knowledge of human development, its critical stages, and the dynamics for coping with them and if we can create groups for teaching such openness, we shall be much better prepared for life in the culture of constant change.

Notes

1. Seward Hiltner, *Preface to Pastoral Theology* (Nashville: Abingdon Press, 1958), p. 145.
2. Erik Erikson, *Childhood and Society* (New York: W. W. Norton, 1950), pp. 62-63.
3. Gerald Caplan in A *Chance to Grow* (Boston: WGBH Educational Foundation, 1967), p. i.
4. *Ibid.*, p. ii. This is a succinct presentation of Caplan's "crisis theory" in psychodynamics.
5. Norman Paul in A *Chance to Grow*, p. iv. Portions of Dr. Paul's theory have been derived from conversations and workshops with him.

6. Harry Bredemeier, "Proposal for an Adequate Socialization Structure," *Urban America and the Planning of Mental Health Services* (New York: Group for the Advancement of Psychiatry, 1964), p. 450.
7. Joint Commission on Mental Illness and Health, *Action for Mental Health* (New York: Wiley, 1961), p. 103.
8. Information about the *Chance to Grow* program, the book of verbatim transcript, and the record album, may be obtained from WGBH, 125 Western Avenue, Boston, Massachusetts 02134.

The Master Hand: Psychological Notes on Pastoral Blessing

Paul W. Pruyser

Recently I had occasion to plunge into a library of books on pastoral care, pastoral counseling, pastoral psychology, psychology of religion, and practical theology, searching the indexes of well over one hundred volumes for the words "blessing" and "benediction." Most of the books were respectable in their field, and many were quite contemporary. They were heavily weighted toward Protestantism and toward America. Many had such index entries as "prayer," "forgiveness," and "acceptance." Some had "confession," and in one I spotted the rather ridiculous item "constipation." Strangely, one book had no entries under *B* at all, which misses out on that old standby, "Bible." Only two books had the words I was looking for. One of them turned out to be largely a collection of historical documents concerning the "pastoral arts"; the sources in which the words occurred were all from before the sixteenth century, and even so they were merely passing references.[1] The other one was a book by two Dutch authors on pastoral conversation,[2] containing a short section on the blessing, to which my own thoughts have been parallel for a number of years.

I also rediscovered an old truth, namely that some books have no indexes, and many books have very poor indexes. Thus my abortive journey into the literature could be seen as a foolish endeavor in the first place. Perhaps the ideas of blessing and benediction were tucked away somewhere in the text of a few of those books, but their authors had not bothered to give them a place of their own in the index. What scholar would rely on so poor a tool as an index! However, the more I think of this disappointing episode, the more I am impressed by its message. It must be that for most pastoral experts in the American Protestant mainstream, blessing and benediction are not imbued with life, are unworthy of recognition, and are of no purpose.

Prior to my library search I had become convinced of this on other grounds. Over the years, in attending worship services, I had gradually become accustomed to ministers' terminating their services with a rushed and hardly audible benediction, uttered on the way out from the back of the sanctuary where nobody could see them. And if the benediction was pronounced from the pulpit, audibly and visibly, the spectacle for the beholders was often little more than a slovenly gesture, consisting of only one arm, raised half-heartedly and only halfway up, against the force of gravity to which that poor limb would quickly succumb again.

Both experiences convey the truism that there has been a steady decay in Protestantism of once powerful and wholesome symbols, or what I have elsewhere described as the replacement of symbols by mere emblems.[3] In the case of blessing and benediction such decay is manifest in the gradual loss of meaningful and beautiful gestures also and, as I shall try to show, in the withholding from the congregation of a wonderful pastoral gift.

In my childhood, only less than half a century ago, blessing and benediction played a key role in my own and many of my fellowmen's religious awareness. In corporate worship the introductory phrases "Our help is in the name of the Lord" or "Grace be unto you, and peace" were accompanied by the gesture of one uplifted arm, slightly bent toward the congregation—one of the most ancient and almost completely self-explanatory cultic gestures. Sometimes both hands were used, spread out downward and with the palms turned invitingly to the congregation. At the end of the service came a more magnificent variant of the same gesture during the solemn and yet intensely benevolent pronouncement of the benediction: "The grace of the Lord Jesus Christ, the love of God, and the communion of the Holy Spirit, be with you all." The gesture consisted of the minister's raising both arms full length, upward and outward, again slightly bent toward the congregation. It is a beautiful, stirring gesture, reminiscent of the perennial themes of the psalmist who sang of the hen covering her chicks under her pinions, of angels being given charge over the faltering steps of mortal beings, of fresh oil being poured over a tired head, of a rod and a staff giving comfort. It is also the natural gesture for sending people forth and out into the world where work is to be done or back into their homes where peace may be had. Two hands raised upward and forward also suggest radiance and emanation; they give and communicate power to those who appreciate having part of it. Hands stretched out flat and raised up are reflecting surfaces which cast light on the children who dwell in darkness. Stretched outward, as in the beginning of an embrace, they convey the outpouring of love, anticipate the clasp to the heart, and portray the encompassing strength of providential support. And yet, since these are the gestures of just another human being, even when he is a priest or minister, the upward arms and hands also suggest the common human plight of perplexity and helplessness in the face of calamity and tragedy.

It is psychologically easy to move from the distant, visually perceptible gesture of the corporate benediction to its directly tactile root in the private and intimate blessing. One merely has to move backward to one's own, and probably mankind's, beginnings in which direct body contact, the sense of touch, and the delights of tactile messages had not yet succumbed to the more discerning clarity of the distant receptors of vision and hearing. The hands of grownups dangle naturally at the height of young children's heads, and in the parent-child situation a large number of messages are given through adults' hands touching children's heads, or by head-tapping accompanying adults' voices. Indeed, so ingrained is this childhood experience, and apparently so desirable, that on certain occasions later in life a grownup will kneel before another adult in order to recapture the old experience in ceremonies involving the laying-on of hands. Artists have dwelt on this experience; one of its most beautiful portrayals is Rembrandt's drawing (and a painting as well) of the return of the prodigal son to his father.

From the touch on the head in the private blessing to the visual-motor act of the corporate benediction one can move back and forth with rich associations. The handshake, given in greeting or in parting, is one of the most obvious links. Although this gesture is completely secularized, the words uttered while shaking hands are sometimes very close to its religious source: the Frenchman says *adieu,* the Spaniard *adios,* the Austrian *grüss Gott.* The English "good-bye" is linguistically derived from "God be with you." They are all well-wishings which dedicate the individual to the divine providence. Homecrafted by the available domestic talent, the signs on the wall say, "God bless our home." Consecrations continue in blessings rendered before family meals. From outstretched arms to the symbol of the cross is only a short step of the imagination, and millions of people indeed make miniature crosses, i.e., make the sign of the cross, while pronouncing blessings on their food. One of my own youthful associations to the gesture of the benediction occurred when I saw in the harbor section of the city a large billboard advertisement of a maritime establishment connecting the British and the Dutch coasts across the North Sea. It portrayed a broadfaced, smiling, utterly trustworthy and benevolent sea captain who embraced the edges of both coasts and the large sea within, with a few tiny ships on its surface, with his two outstretched arms. I was consciously aware at the time that this man was a marvelous image of God, perfectly inviting, strong and sustaining, with all-fatherly care. Many years later I saw the same image on a Rorschach card, with the same feelings and the same backlog of strings of associations.

If this were a more scholarly and ambitious paper, I should produce data from comparative religion and the history of religion in order to elucidate the origin and meaning of blessing and benediction. I should point to the Moslem *Bismillah* ritual, which as an introductory formula "in the name of Allah" marks the beginning of theologically significant actions, from slaughtering animals for sacrifice to the invocation which starts worship. It is also pronounced during sexual intercourse. I should point to the sacred meanings given to hands, and even in a more specific way to each finger of a hand; to the different meanings attached to right and left hands (*dexter* and *sinister* in Latin). I should point out that invocations do not only call upon the presence of the deity, or his assistance, and consecrate man's worshipful doings to him, but also declare by implication that all the sacred acts which are to follow are forms of divine revelation. And I should not forget to elucidate that blessings, in whatever form they are given, have their superstitious use. They may be approached as one does a charm: to make something safe, to ward off the evil eye, to guard against incubi and other satanic intrusions. And it may well be that such mechanical blessings as are heaped at the asking on harvests, homes, barns, and breeding bulls in many agragrian countries by an all-too-willing Catholic priesthood are one of the historical reasons why Protestants seem to have followed a policy of abstinence or great sobriety regarding blessings, words and gestures, and all.

But I have in this essay only a low-keyed ambition. My intention is no more (but also no less) than to ask whether this Protestant reaction may not have gone too far. I wonder whether pastors should not reconsider the appropriate use of the blessing in pas toral work and a more formal and splendid giving of the benediction in the liturgy. I am aware that in raising these questions I am guided only by a context of personal experiences and rather casual inquiries and impressions. I wish I could speak from hard data regarding the occurrence of any blessing in the practice of pastoral counseling, its frequency distribution in denominations and sects, how often clients ask for it and in what way they may signal such a desire, and what rules pastors have, if any, which guide their decisions to give blessings or omit them.

There is reason to think that reliable data on these points may be hard to get. Well-trained pastoral counselors, after having absorbed the psychological literature, may be unwilling to reveal any practices of blessing for fear that this may indicate psychological naïveté or an unresolved countertransference problem. The very well-trained are likely to point out the risks involved and the clinical reasons for *not* giving blessings during interviews. They may declare the laying-on of hands as *ipso facto* rather sectarian. Similarly, I am far from sure that clients, if sampled, would consciously declare their wishes for a blessing—it would sound so Romanish, so pietistic, so superstitious even! But such conscious objections to answering a poll do not cancel the strength or frequency of unconscious or preconscious longings for the act. Moreover, even if clients were aware of such a desire, would they have in Protestantism a language in which to ask for its gratification? Indeed, how does one ask for a pastoral blessing within a religious tradition that has no entries for it in pastoral handbooks and that has implicitly declared the practice defunct? Could a nervous giggle, a great hesitancy in parting at termination, or a tendency to drag the hour on beyond its formal end be interpreted as a nonverbal demand for a pastoral blessing?

If they have both psychological and theological sophistication, pastors responding to an opinion poll on the practice of blessing may even raise that old bugaboo: whether an act of blessing is to be seen as efficacious *ex opere operato* or as a sign or seal of divine promise, irrespective of the pastor's own personal disposition, or whether it is to be approached as a genuinely pastoral practice, even an expression of pastoral niceness at times. Different denominations may have different opinions about these issues, and within a denomination there may be different opinions about them among its pastors. What I wish to stress is not its sacerdotal but its pastoral use, not its sacramental status but its direct human relevance, not its function as a prescribed ritual but its possibility as a pastoral response to human need.

Further, it will have to be acknowledged that English-speaking people are prone to a peculiar subject-object confusion which stems from using the verb "to bless" in two entirely different senses. "To bless" means to perform an act whereby in the name of the deity a person or thing is consecrated or hallowed, but it is also used, by an odd role reversal, for the act of man praising God. The important underlying questions are: Who blesses whom? Who is the subject, and who is the object in an act of blessing? Who takes the initiative; who has the power to bless? French suffers from the same confusion with its word *bénir*. German and Dutch have two entirely different words for the two acts: *segnen* and *zegenen* are acts of God even if mediated by ordained men; *loben* and *loven* (like the Latin-derived verb "to laud") are the appropriate designations for acts of men paying tribute to their God.

It would also have to be recognized in any survey among pastors that the prevailing theological climate is not conducive to eliciting the proper rationale for the use of blessings in pastoral contacts. It is no accident that the decline of blessings and the decay in the performance of benedictions coincide with the erosion of a classical theological focus: the doctrine of providence. In its history this doctrine has carried a heavy baggage of metaphysical speculations regarding free will, divine foreknowledge, election, and differentiations between first and second causes, all of which have helped bring discredit to its status. But these unfortunate incrustations should not obscure its basic message, which is that the Creator is also the Reconciliator and that history is a purposive unfolding rather than "one damned thing after another." Belief in providence is belief in order and meaning—ultimately a belief in divine benevolence. In terms of the cultic gestures we are dealing with, belief in providence is trust in the divine hands and an awareness of the possibility of having contact with them.

Though I am not competent enough in historical theology to trace the course and reasons of the dwindling status of this theological theme, I wish to call special attention to one very obvious psychological reason for the disappearance of thoughts on providence. In our own technological century, described as the space age, man's increasing sense of competence and the feeling that he has come of age are prone to lead thought away from the idea of a divine Provider whom one needs to have on his side for success in his endeavors. Since concrete inspection of the celestial sphere by Sputnik astronauts did not disclose his presence there, the mere thought of a Provider has become ever more mythical. Or has it? It all depends on what one takes as the model for man's competence. While considerable competence has been demonstrated in his technology, of which space ventures are only one example, the quality of man's relations to man on earth is not such a glorious model of competence. Our interpersonal, international, and interracial conflicts continue in unabated vigor, and intrapsychic conflict is as rampant as ever. Indeed, these sad observations if honestly faced can quickly lead to the further scoffing of any thought of providence, for they may be taken to mean that the deity has not been on man's side in ordering human affairs. Nothing gets as easily projected as blame, and the poor gods have long been accustomed to being the recipients of both good father and bad father images.

In the practice of pastoral care and counseling one will thus meet many persons seeking help who because they may feel competent in some successful, limited project, will not give the slightest thought to any need of providential care. Indeed, the basic philosophy of much counseling, which is "to help the person help himself," seems itself to militate against the client's seriously learning to entertain such thoughts. The central conceptual role of the self in counseling theory and technique may further reinforce the importance of the competent *I* who must solve *his* problems, gain *his* insights, exert *his* will, improve *his* reality testing, register *his* feelings more accurately, and be more responsive to the feelings of *his* wife and children. And if *his* pastor helps him do all this in *his* church, what need is there for providence? I do not think the task of the pastoral counselor is finished when his client has merely become more skilled at handling his domestic turmoil, his social roles, or his bothersome symptoms.

The issue of providence will have to be met head on (no accidental metaphor!), or else there is little to distinguish pastoral care and counseling from the forms of assistance rendered by other helping professions. There must be clarity about basic premises. All pastoral care is providential care mediated. Poimenics presuppose providence. Shepherds tend flocks and guard straying lambs by guiding them to places where food can be had and dangers are minimal, but at all times they do so by embedding the sheep in the basic conditions of nature, i.e., in a transcendent arrangement of life and death. Shepherds also act ordinarily on behalf of the flock's owners—in a sense both shepherd and flock are engaged by a third party who makes the basic decisions. Shepherding involves, according to Hiltner, healing, guiding, and sustaining. All three involve an awareness of powers which transcend the two-party negotiations between the helper and the helped.

I am not advocating sermonettes on providence during counseling sessions, nor do I wish to urge pastors to engage in indiscriminate tactile stimulation by laying on hands or incessantly tapping the skulls of their clients. One could quickly lose some clients this way or be tapped back hard on one's own skull. I see little need for ritualistic phrases rattled off at the end of a trying hour instead of the customary handshake. But I do think there are many reasons why pastors might reconsider the thoughtful use of blessings in pastoral contacts with individuals and a more articulate use of the full gestures and words of the benediction in corporate services.

The first reason is doctrinal-pedagogical. If it is true, as I have intimated, that recognition of providence is at a low ebb among both theologians and laymen, the church stands in need of reeducating itself on such elementary theistic assertions as, "All that is exists for the divine purpose," and, "All things proceed from his fatherly hand" (in this image lies one theological rationale of hand symbolism). Rather than teach such propositions abstractly, would it not be better to stylize their logical implications in the acts of blessing and benediction so that people can raise questions about these acts if they are puzzled, which can then lead to discussion? Or else, if tacit acceptance is the response, would not this be proof that a need has indeed been met, that a Provider has been recognized, and that the pastoral initiative has been appreciated?

The second reason lies in helping pastors realize their professional identity. When worship leaders perform sloppily in their liturgical work, they are obviously not attributing a high professional value to this part of their activities. And when they perform badly in benedictions, the unspoken messages to the congregation are that: (1) benedictions are rather meaningless, (2) the pastor does not deem the people worthy of receiving them, (3) the pastor himself has long given up thoughts of providence, or (4) the pastor refuses to shoulder the shepherd's role. Perhaps more important than all these conjectures is that he does not seem to know enough about people and their needs or that he is so caught up in his own conflicts that he cannot respond to the needs of others. Although these deeper problems cannot be solved by attempting to give the liturgical benediction properly, movements and gestures are psychodynamically so important in life and are so closely interwoven with emotion that attempts at performing the proper motion are very likely to stimulate the corresponding emotion also. Giving the benediction is not only a meaningful act but like most liturgical words and motions also a beautiful act, and its proper aesthetic performance may give several side benefits to the pastor as well as convey a great gift to the congregation.

The same principles hold in pastoral care and counseling. In bedside visits to the sick and dying the pastor has several established practices from which he can choose. He can read scripture, he can utter a joint prayer, he can converse upliftingly or in consolation, he can remain mostly silent and yet be meaningfully present, and he can bless—with words and hands. If he does not know what to do, he can fall back on a short liturgy which his church provides. But if he utterly does not know what to do because of his and the patient's radical perplexity or despair, the most appropriate acts are to lay on hands (one or both), to touch the patient's head or hands with any or all fingers (for no one finger is particularly sacred), and to utter words of blessing. Most pastors know this and do it almost instinctively, i.e., not because they learned it in seminary or in clinical pastoral training, but because they know "in their bones" that tragic situations always call for some kind of touch, some kind of effortless self-giving, some direct, primitive, unreflected, spontaneous spilling over of affect into the motor system. Stylized or not, the crux of the matter is the empathy conveyed, and as *pastoral* empathy this also represents the divine empathy. I hope the reader will recognize that "divine empathy" is only a modern way of describing an aspect of providence, whereas our forebears focused on the divine power to arrange, steer, preside, or forecast in their concepts of providence.

In counseling and other forms of pastoral care the situation will call for deliberation and astute judgment, but while counseling, the pastor should not forget the lesson learned by the bedside or at the end of corporate worship. If a client is seriously conflict-ridden about his relation to the church, if he has deep doubts about the very premises of faith, if he has become suspicious of other people, if he is phobic, explosive, or "touchy," a blessing may be seen as irrelevant or intrusive, and body contact is not to be engaged in lightly. But it is still a possibility of which the pastor should be aware. It is still an option, and the client's omnipresent propensities to test out his counselor during any of the sessions may include the items: What will my minister do that is truly pastoral? What will he do that psychiatrists and social workers cannot do?

This is only a minimal possibility, to which pastoral counselors may want to be alert. I think there is a much greater possibility in the majority of cases that clients positively expect and deeply want their pastors to do something with them which is germane to the churchly context of the pastoral office. After all, when they chose to come to their pastor, they also selected not to go to other caretakers and helpers, for various reasons. But the attitudes with which people seek out their pastors do not only reflect their cold, cognitive awareness of the social roles which pastors play, with the implied expectancies of moves and countermoves, stylized dialogue, selected focus for discussion, and special language and metaphors chosen to fit the pastor-client situation. Some expectancies are also radical expectations based on vital needs. They may come for solace, not because the church is a comforting institution but because they are in dire despair. They may come to gain hope not because the church has always preached it but because without it they would be at road's end. They may come for warmth, not because the pastor is known as evangelical but because they feel frozen. And so they may like to be blessed, not because this is one of the possible rituals one puts up with in church but because they need providential support in their weakness, providential peace in their struggles, providential direction in their lostness, providential grace in their self-accusations. And so they may also wish, deep in their hearts, that someone will put a benevolent hand on their heads for just one moment—someone who not only may like to do such a thing but who is appointed to do so, someone who wields the master hand. Should persons with such needs be deprived of the great gift pastors—and only pastors—can bestow?

Moreover, if blessings and benedictions are expressions of providential care, there may be a point at which the pastor may do some testing instead of solely being sensitive to the ways in which he is tested by the client. To put the issue in a stark form: If the pastor offers to give the client a blessing, will the client accept it? Might he protest? Might he deny its relevance? More strongly, might he deny any need of it? Any of these reactions would seem to imply the rejection of a need for providential support, which is at bottom a denial of creatureliness. In other words, fussing over a blessing that is being offered gives a clinical clue to the dynamics of narcissism, just as refusal to accept the sacrament as a means of grace by depressed or obsessional patients is a form of their profound disturbance in object relations. Not to need grace, not to need others, not to accept love when it is tendered—these are radical theological and clinical problems. They signal grandiosity behind the mask of depression, extraordinary self-love beneath the wail of self-accusations, an inflated sense of competence behind a facade of bumbling and fumbling. In such cases one needs diagnostic perspicacity, and the offering of a blessing may be a useful pastoral-diagnostic tool.

Finally, it seems that many pastors are hard-pressed to seek something special that clearly demarcates their office and functions from those of other caretakers, healers, guides, and teachers. The so-called pastor's identity crisis is not an invention of sociologists and psychologists but a phenomenon first and foremost acknowledged by pastors themselves. I have little to offer in helping to solve this crisis. But I hear many pastors complain that while they have a good deal of knowledge and a good many skills, they do not feel proud of these because many other professionals have better or more useful knowledge, or the same knowledge more articulately, and similar skills bigger and better. They claim that their work does not have a cachet of its own. This claim is unjustified if these same pastors are the ones who refuse to raise their hands fully in the benediction, who never think of the role of the blessing in counseling, and who have no theology of providence. In these pitiful omissions they have themselves removed the special cachet which tradition, good theology, and good psychology have always given to pastoral activities. It is a dear price to pay for one's own secularization!

Notes

1. W. A. Clebsch and C. R. Jaekle, *Pastoral Care in Historical Perspective* (Englewood Cliffs, N. J.: Prentice-Hall, 1964).
2. Heije Faber and Ebel van der Schoot, *The Art of Pastoral Conversation* (Nash-

ville: Abingdon Press, 1965); see also my extensive review of this book in *Pastoral Psychology*, April, 1963, pp. 17-21.

3. Paul W. Pruyser, "Life and Death of a Symbol: A History of the Holy Ghost Concept and Its Emblems," *McCormick Quarterly* (special supplement on myth and modern man), January, 1965, pp. 5-22.

Biographical Sketches

LEROY ADEN is associate professor of pastoral theology at the Lutheran Theological Seminary at Philadelphia. He received his B.D. from Wartburg Theological Seminary, his M.A. and Ph.D. from the Divinity School of the University of Chicago. Previously he taught for six years at the University of Chicago Divinity School and served for two years as director of the Pastoral Counseling Center in Pittsburgh.

FRANK M. BOCKUS is executive director, Ecumenical Center for Religion and Health, South Texas Medical Center, and adjunct associate professor of human ecology, University of Texas Medical School at San Antonio. He received his A.B. from Southern Methodist University, his B.D. from Union Theological Seminary in New York, and his Ph.D. from the University of Chicago Divinity School. Previously he was associate professor of pastoral theology at the Institute of Religion in Houston and director, Department of Social Health, Methodist Board of Christian Social Concerns in Washington, D. C.

ROBERT H. BONTHIUS is director of the Internship for Clergymen in Urban Ministry, funded by the NIMH and administered through Case Western Reserve University, where he is an associate Professor in the Department of Psychology. He received his B.A. from Hope College, Holland, Michigan, his B.D. from San Francisco Theological Seminary, his MA. and Ph.D. from Columbia University. Previously he served as pastor of the Westminster Presbyterian Church of Portland, Oregon.

DON S. BROWNING is associate professor in religion and personality in the Divinity School of the University of Chicago. He received his B.A. from Central College in Fayette, Missouri, his B.D., M.A., and Ph.D. from the University of Chicago Divinity School. Previously he held several pastorates in Missouri and was minister to students at the University Church of the Disciples of Christ in Chicago.

LOWELL G. COLSTON is professor of pastoral care at Christian Theological Seminary in Indianapolis. He received his B.A. from Drake University, Des Moines, his B.D. from Union Theological Seminary in New York, and his Ph.D. from the University of Chicago Divinity School. Previously he held pastorates in Iowa and New York and was special minister of counseling at the Bryn Mawr Community Church of Chicago.

SIMON DONIGER was until January of 1969 editor of *Pastoral Psychology*, which position he had held from its inception. He received his B.S., M.A., and Ph.D. from New York University. Previously he was director of a child guidance agency in Newark, New Jersey, and taught in the graduate division of Hunter College, New York.

LELAND E. ELHARD is associate professor of pastoral theology at the Evangelical Lutheran Theological Seminary, Columbus, Ohio. He received his B.A. from Capital University, Columbus, his B.D. from Evangelical Lutheran Theological Seminary, his M.A. and Ph.D. from the University of Chicago Divinity School. Previously he was pastor of North Cape Lutheran Church of Franksville, Wisconsin.

ROBERT E. ELLIOTT is associate professor of pastoral theology, Perkins School of Theology, Southern Methodist University in Dallas. He received his B.A. from the University of Puget Sound, his B.D. from Yale Divinity School, and his Ph.D. from the University of Chicago Divinity School. Previously he was pastor of the Highline Methodist Church of Seattle, Washington.

JAMES G. EMERSON, JR., is general director of the Community Service Society of New York City. He received his B.A. from Stanford University, his B.D. from Princeton Theological Seminary, and his Ph.D. from the University of Chicago Divinity School. Previously he held pastorates in New York and New Jersey and was counselor on the staff of the Fourth Presbyterian Church of Chicago.

GRAEME M. GRIFFIN is professor of church and community at the Theological Hall, Ormond College, Parkville, Victoria, in Australia. He received his B.A. from Sydney University, together with a diploma in applied psychology from Sydney Technical College, his B.D. from Melbourne College of Divinity, and his Th.D. from Princeton Theological Seminary. Previously he was an industrial psychologist in personnel work with the Department of the Navy in Australia and for three years was chaplain to Ormond College and lecturer in pastoral theology in the Theological Hall.

DONALD A. GROSKREUTZ is an instructor in pastoral theology, Wartburg Theological Seminary. He received his B.A. from Wartburg College, his B.D. from Wartburg Theological Seminary, his M.A. and Ph.D. from the University of Chicago Divinity School. Previously he was pastor of St. John Lutheran Church, Morgan, Minnesota.

JOSEPH HAVENS is a clinical psychologist at the University of Massachusetts and is engaged in community mental health work in Holyoke, Massachusetts. He received his B.S. from Massachusetts Institute of Technology, his M.A. from the University of Southern California, and his Ph.D. from the University of Chicago Divinity School. Previously he was assistant professor of psychology, Wilmington College, Wilmington, Ohio, and college counselor and assistant professor of psychology, Carleton College, Northfield, Minnesota.

PAUL E. IRION is professor of pastoral theology in the Lancaster Theological Seminary in Pennsylvania. He received his A.B. from Elmhurst College, Illinois, his B.D. from Eden Theological Seminary, Webster Groves, Missouri, and his M.A. from the University of Chicago Divinity School. Previously he held pastorates in Illinois and was chaplain of the Evangelical Deaconess Hospital in St. Louis.

THOMAS W. KLINK is chaplain and director, Division of Religion and Psychiatry, Menninger Foundation, Topeka, Kansas. He received his A.B. from Pacific University, Forest Grove, Oregon, and his B.D. at Chicago Theological Seminary. Previously he held pastorates in Oregon and Iowa and was supervisor of clinical pastoral training at Topeka State Hospital and the Menninger Foundation.

JAMES N. LAPSLEY is associate professor of pastoral theology, Princeton Theological Seminary. He received his B.A. from Southwestern at Memphis, his B.D. from Union Theological Seminary in Virginia, and his Ph.D. from the University of Chicago Divinity School. Previously he was assistant minister of the Gentilly Presbyterian Church in New Orleans.

COVAL B. MACDONALD is associate professor of religious studies at Rice University. He received his B.A. from Gordon College, Boston, his B.D. from Fuller Theological Seminary, his S.T.M. from Harvard Divinity School, and his Ph.D. from the University of Chicago Divinity School. Previously he was pastor of the Trinity Presbyterian Church of Oak Lawn, Illinois, and assistant professor of pastoral theology at Princeton Theological Seminary.

LEIGHTON M. MCCUTCHEN is assistant professor of psychology and theology and counselor to students at the Hartford Seminary Foundation in Connecticut. He received his B.A. from Davidson College in North Carolina, his B.D. from Union Theological Seminary in Virginia, and his Ph.D. from the University of Chicago Divinity School. Previously he was assistant minister of the First United Presbyterian Church, Hammond, Indiana.

KENNETH R. MITCHELL is director for training, Division of Religion and Psychiatry, Department of Education, Menninger Foundation, Topeka, Kansas. He received his B.A. from Princeton University, his B.D. from Princeton Theological Seminary, and his Ph.D. from the University of Chicago Divinity School. Previously he was chaplain, Vanderbilt University Hospital, and assistant professor of pastoral theology and counseling at Vanderbilt Divinity School, as well as assistant professor of counseling, Division of Human Behavior, Department of Psychiatry, Vanderbilt Medical School.

GARDNER MURPHY is visiting professor of psychology, George Washington University, Washington, D. C. He received his Ph.D. from Columbia University and directed M.A. and Ph.D. research in social psychology and personality. Previously he was chairman of the Department of Psychology at City College, New York, and director of research at the Menninger Foundation, in addition to teaching at the Menninger School of Psychiatry and the Topeka Psychoanalytic Institute.

WILLIAM B. OGLESBY, JR. is professor of pastoral counseling at Union Theological Seminary in Virginia. He received his B.A. from Austin College in Texas, his B.D. and Th.M. from Union Theological Seminary in Virginia, and his Ph.D. from the University of Chicago Divinity School. Previously he held pastorates in Louisiana and Arkansas.

JOHN H. PATTON is director of pastoral counseling for the Georgia Association for Pastoral Care. He received his B.A. and B.D. from Emory University, Atlanta, and his Ph.D. from the University of Chicago Divinity School. Previously he held pastorates in Illinois and Georgia and was director of chaplaincy services, Emory University Affiliated Hospitals.

PAUL W. PRUYSER is director, Department of Education, Menninger Foundation. He was graduated from Amsterdam Avond Gymnasium in Holland and studied at the University of Amsterdam. He received his Ph.D. from Boston University. Previously he served as staff clinical psychologist at the National Veterans Epilepsy Center in Framingham and Boston, Massachusetts, and in various capacities at the Menninger Foundation in Topeka, Kansas.

WILLIAM R. ROGERS is associate professor of psychology and religion and associate dean of the college, Earlham College, Richmond, Indiana. He received his B.A. from Kalamazoo College, Michigan, his B.D. from Chicago Theological Seminary and his Ph.D. from the University of Chicago Divinity School. Previously he was research consultant, North Central College, and teaching fellow and counselor to students, Chicago Theological Seminary.

JAMES E. SPICER is minister of the First Congregational Church of Des Plaines, Illinois. He received his B.A. from Franklin College of Indiana, his B.D. from Colgate-Rochester Divinity School, Rochester, New York, and his Ph.D. from the University of Chicago Divinity School. Previously he held pastorates in New York and Tennessee and was director of field education and assistant professor of pastoral theology at Vanderbilt University Divinity School.

CLYDE J. STECKEL is campus minister at the University of Minnesota for the Commission on United Campus Christian Ministries and adjunct professor of Christian faith and human personality at the United Theological Seminary of the Twin Cities, Minnesota. He received his B.A. from Butler University, Indianapolis, his B.D. from Chicago Theological Seminary, and his M.A. and Ph.D. from the University of Chicago Divinity School. Previously he was Protestant chaplain, Illinois children's Hospital-School, and chaplain and assistant professor of religion, Illinois College, Jacksonville.

Biographical Sketches

DANIEL DAY WILLIAMS is professor of systematic theology, Union Theological Seminary in New York. He received his B.A. from the University of Denver, his M.A. from the University of Chicago, his B.D. from Chicago Theological Seminary, and his Ph.D. from Columbia University. Previously he was minister, First Congregational Church, Colorado Springs, and professor of Christian theology, Federated Theological Faculty, University of Chicago.

index

Index

Index

Index